You Owe Me That Chick

Nance —

I hope our journey
inspire's your life's journey!

John Smith

You Owe Me That Chick

Julianna's Inspiring Journey Through the World of Childhood Cancer

JoAnn Smith

TATE PUBLISHING
AND ENTERPRISES, LLC

You Owe Me That Chick
Copyright © 2014 by JoAnn Smith. All rights reserved.

No part of this publication may be reproduced, stored in a retrieval system or transmitted in any way by any means, electronic, mechanical, photocopy, recording or otherwise without the prior permission of the author except as provided by USA copyright law.

The opinions expressed by the author are not necessarily those of Tate Publishing, LLC.

This book is designed to provide accurate and authoritative information with regard to the subject matter covered. This information is given with the understanding that neither the author nor Tate Publishing, LLC is engaged in rendering legal, professional advice. Since the details of your situation are fact dependent, you should additionally seek the services of a competent professional.

Published by Tate Publishing & Enterprises, LLC
127 E. Trade Center Terrace | Mustang, Oklahoma 73064 USA
1.888.361.9473 | www.tatepublishing.com

Tate Publishing is committed to excellence in the publishing industry. The company reflects the philosophy established by the founders, based on Psalm 68:11,
"The Lord gave the word and great was the company of those who published it."

Book design copyright © 2014 by Tate Publishing, LLC. All rights reserved.
Cover design by Rtor Maghuyop
Interior design by Joana Quilantang

Published in the United States of America

ISBN: 978-1-63306-890-2
Health & Fitness / Diseases / Cancer
15.01.26

This book is dedicated to my amazing daughter Julianna who inspired many by her spirit and strong will in her fight against cancer.

Contents

Introduction... 9

1   Diagnosis.. 13

2   Pooh Bear Rules 17

3   There's No Place Like Home 51

4   You Owe Me That Chick... 67

5   We Are "Normal".. 85

6   The Infamous Kidney Stone 95

7   Not Coping.. 131

8   Our Village.. 155

9   Real Chicks.. 173

10   Lots to Share 195

11   Supersibs! And Flashes of Hope............................. 205

12   Happy Ninth Birthday 223

13   No Coincidences 237

14   Songs of Love.. 253

15   Vacation?.. 259

16   Chemo Cut.. 271

17   Lives Forever Changed in a Good Way.................... 281

18   One Thousand Cranes... 297

19   When Will This Craziness End............................... 321

20   It's a Mom Thing.. 327

21   Ronald McDonald House....................................... 349

22   One Year 353

Closing 365

Introduction

December 2007, my eight-year-old daughter Julianna, came down with a high fever with no other symptoms—no runny nose, no sore throat, no vomiting. I figured it was one of those crazy things kids get, and when the fever subsided after a few days, she went back to school as normal. A few weeks later, the same thing happened. This time, the fever lasted only two days, so again, we went back to our normal routine. On February 8, Julianna came down with another fever. This was now her third bout of fever with no other symptoms. It made no sense, and so I took her to the doctor, and they ran blood work. The next day, the doctor called and said her blood counts were low, and maybe it was neutropenia, or maybe it was just a virus. They couldn't really say anything conclusive, and they told us to have the blood work repeated in a week.

The following week, we went and had blood work drawn. A few days later, the doctor called and said Julianna's counts were still low, but the platelets had seemed to correct themselves. Previously, the doctor had mentioned neutropenia, but she said she spoke to the hematologist and he did not think this was the case. She said we would recheck again in three to four weeks.

Two weeks later, on February 27, I received a call from the school nurse. She said Julianna was in her office and said her hands hurt. The nurse had her soaking them in warm water.

I said, "Her hands hurt?"

The nurse said, "Yes, she said it happens all the time at home, and she puts them in front of the fire."

I said, "Is she cold?"

The nurse then apologized and said three kids had come in at once, and she hadn't even taken Julianna's temperature. She said she would take it while I was on the phone, and she asked me to hold. Ten seconds later, she came back on the phone and said Julianna's temperature was 103, and please could I come in and get her. I called the doctor before I left the house. She didn't call me back until 6:00 p.m. She said it was probably just bad luck and that now Julianna was probably coming down with something.

That same night at midnight, Julianna came and got me out of bed. She said her head hurt. I grabbed some medicine from the hallway closet, and we went back to her room. When I got close to her, I couldn't believe how warm her entire body was. I never felt a body burning up the way hers was. I took her temperature, and it registered at 104.3. I was completely beside myself with fear. I put cold compresses on her forehead and stayed with her. I wanted to take her to the emergency room, but I hated to make her go anywhere. I looked it up in my medical book, and it said a temperature of 105 warranted a trip to the ER, so I figured I would wait it out. She eventually fell asleep. At 5:00 a.m., she woke up in a complete sweat, and her temperature was 100.6. At 9:00 a.m., Julianna's temperature was back up to 102, so I made an appointment to see the doctor that afternoon. Once again, the exam showed no other symptoms, so they ran blood work again.

The next morning, I received a call from the doctor's office. They said something had happened, and they could not process the blood work and could we go to our local hospital right away and have it run again. I started to cry because I just knew deep down this was bad. I did come to learn later on that due to the results they saw, they actually needed to have the blood work run again to be sure it was correct.

By the time we returned home from the hospital, there was a message from Julianna's doctor saying that I should call back right away—it was urgent. When I called, she said Julianna's counts were low and her white blood cell count was even lower than the first time they had the blood work run. She said Julianna really had no immune system, and we would have to get to the hospital for intravenous antibiotics right away.

She then said matter-of-factly, "When you get to CHOP, enter through the ER. I have phoned ahead to let them know you are coming."

I said, "We are going to CHOP?"

She just answered, "Yes." She said we would probably be there two days so get our things together and try to get there quickly. This began our journey.

1

Diagnosis

On March 1, 2007, Julianna, was diagnosed with leukemia. She was eight years old at the time. The moment when the hematologist uttered those words will forever be ingrained in my mind. The picture of us all sitting around the conference room table is crystal clear. The pause the hematologist took after he gave us the diagnosis—knowing we would have a reaction. I immediately began to sob. My husband, Brian, wrapped his arms around me and rested his head on mine. The social worker wrote down the ensuing conversation for us, knowing that we would not be able to really listen to much else after hearing the words *leukemia* and *cancer* in reference to our child.

It was so hard to believe we had entered the world of childhood cancer. A world that I would say many times later, I really wished I did not know about and wished I was not part of. Even our social worker would say to me at times, "All parents say this is not a club they ever wanted to join."

While talking to a friend recently, she made the analogy that she thought our experience was like being hit by an enormous ocean wave. The wave hits you, and you are being thrown about by a force much too strong for you to fight, you are disoriented from the motion, your mind is racing and reeling, but you know you feel scared. Eventually, you are able to stand back up, and you get yourself back together, and get your wits about you. Then, another wave hits you. I loved this analogy because it really does describe our experience. If I were to take this analogy further, I would say that after even more time, you regain enough strength to come out of the water. Then you go rest in the warmth of the sun. Sometime after this brief rest, you are thinking clearly again, and you look at the ocean and once again appreciate its beauty.

Julianna's journey has very much been like this analogy. After the reeling and whirling subsided, the beauty and goodness of people who reached out to us was staggering. I have never in my lifetime been as inspired as I have been through this experience. Many friends and family members were also inspired by this journey.

In addition to Julianna, we have a son Jeffrey. I gave birth to Julianna on June 17, 1998. Jeffrey arrived to be with our family two and a half years later. We adopted him from Korea when he was just five months old. For as long as I remember, it has been in my heart to give a home to a child in need. Jeffrey was born in Seoul, Korea, on August 23, 2000. He is the sweetest younger brother to Julianna. At different times, before Julianna was diagnosed, if she was being punished for some reason, and I took away something as a punishment, Jeffrey would go and give her his. He could not stand for her to be punished. Having her be sick is hard on him, but because of his amazing love of her, he always wants her to have what she needs. He is totally understanding of the time and care she needs. When a situation arises where there needs to be a choice, he always wants Julianna to get what she needs or wants. She doesn't appreciate it now, but I hope someday, Julianna will realize that, without question, she has the best brother ever.

What follows is a personal account of our experience. Due to technology that is available today, we have what is called a CarePage. It is a website provided by Children's Hospital of Philadelphia (CHOP) that gives people going through an illness a vehicle to communicate with their friends and family. We were able to set up Julianna's CarePage from the very beginning of her journey. Not only was it a fabulous way to let everyone know how she was, it became very therapeutic for me as the Mom and primary caregiver. The truth is that from the beginning, it felt really good to share my pain with others. It helped me to feel that I wasn't so alone in this. What was also great about the CarePage was that people could write messages to Julianna. It was, and still is, a highlight of our day to read fun and encouraging messages from our friends and family.

This book is simply our journey, in raw form, as recorded in Julianna's CarePage. I also kept a personal journal during the beginning of this journey. While I had never kept a personal journal before, once Julianna was diagnosed, I became obsessive about journaling everything that happened every day. I guess it was my coping mechanism.

In the end, it turns out that being part of the world of the childhood cancer has truly been a blessing in our lives. My hope is just to share all the goodness that does still exist in this world—in people of all ages—and highlight some wonderful organizations that are serving children in amazing ways. If you feel inspired in some way at the end of this book and have gained a better appreciation of things that matter in your life, then this book has served the purpose I was hoping for.

2

Pooh Bear Rules

CarePage Post March 08, 2007, at 10:00 p.m. EST

I finally had a chance to sit down and figure out this web page for communicating updates about Julianna. Based on information I have received from people who have experience with this—it seems this will be the best way for us to communicate and share information regarding what we are calling "Julianna's Journey." Julianna's CarePage name is PoohBearRules.

CarePage Post March 08, 2007, at 10:13 p.m. EST

Hi all. First of all, I just wanted to send a *huge thank you* from our family to all of you who have reached out to us. Our support network is *truly unbelievable*. I have been feeling like I want to communicate with the outside world—and trying to do it by phone is very difficult since it is a bit of a whirlwind here every day.

So here is some "stuff" I just want to tell you all. It's just kind of random information and thoughts that I wanted to share...

Thank you to everyone who has us in their thoughts and prayers—the *only* explanation for the strength I am sustaining is the outpouring of prayers, love and support that I feel surrounded by. Thanks also for the cards, balloons, flowers, gifts, etc., etc. Julianna's room is extremely cheerful. It is equipped with a computer, Playstation 2, and a DVD player. Also, Brian was thinking the next person who asks what she needs, we would answer "a nice flat-screen plasma TV for when she comes home"—Ha! Ha!

Julianna has been a total trooper!! We are amazed at her. She has named her IV pole "Charlie" and we walk him wherever we go—which isn't very far because she is not allowed out of her room. She has also already corrected me when I referred to her PIC line as an IV. It is hard to use the words cancer and leukemia with her but we do because the docs use those words and they suggested we get her used to them. Everyone comments on her pretty smile and her silky pajamas. They say she is such a darling, sweetie, etc—all of those things you already all know about her. She started "school" here today with Miss Joan who will be coming to her room Monday-Friday at 11:15. Yeah—I get to leave the room for 45 minutes, although I am afraid to go anywhere because I don't think I will find my way back.

Please feel free to tease Brian about "passing out" on day 2 of our stay here and ripping the shower curtain right off the hooks.

Last night I got klunked in the head with a stuffed animal because Julianna needed to get up to go to the bathroom and I did not hear her calling me.

I am not allowed a hair dryer here. It's a good thing I have a "wash and go" haircut right now.

CarePage Post March 08, 2007, at 10:15 p.m. EST

Overall, Julianna's diagnosis is very positive and the doctors do not give statistics but have been using the words "very treatable." She has predominantly what they refer to as ALL (Acute Lymphoblastic Leukemia), although she did have some AML(Acute Myeloid Leukemia) cells. She did not have any leukemia cells in her spinal fluid yesterday and that was *big* news. We actually did not realize the seriousness of that test until after it was over—which I think was actually a good thing—especially since we got good news. I do not go near the Internet at this stage to investigate leukemia—I just talk to her docs. They did give us a book about childhood leukemia- again, I can't bear to open it.

This hospital and staff is *amazing*!!! I feel so confident every time we meet with her doc—which is every day. She is apparently one of the best oncologists here and she is married to one of the top oncologists. The nurses could not be any nicer and caring. Her resident doc is exchanging jokes with her everyday—so we are working on our joke collection. Feel free to send any good, short jokes you know.

One of Julianna's saddest moments—and there haven't been many—was when we had to discuss her hair falling out. It will start within 10-14 days and she will probably be completely bald in a month or so. Please pray for her about this. Her doc said most girls her age do get over this aspect pretty quickly and we pray this will be the case with her also.

I have decided that this journey is really taking on a life of opposites. There is definitely bad, bad, bad, but there is also so much good, good, good. One of the most amazing things are the generous donations that show up here. For example, a group makes these really colorful pillow cases for these kids to use because as their hair falls out it looks really awful and scary on the white hospital pillowcases. Yesterday, there were these really cool journals here for the kids with these great dog pictures on them.

I have one last prayer request. It will be so much easier on Julianna if she can swallow a lot of her medications in pill form. She has learned already how to do this quite well with the small pills, but is struggling with the bigger ones.

Love to all, JoAnn

A lot of the kids decorate the door to their rooms—this is Julianna's.

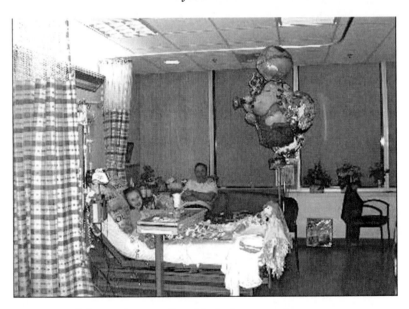

Jules resting comfortably in her very nice room.

CarePage Post March 09, 2007, at 04:50 p.m. EST

Friday—Day 4

Julianna's treatment plan, or "roadmap" as the docs here refer to it is detailed by day #—beginning with day 1 of treatment. That is how we have kind of been referring to the day—so I thought I would stick with it for these postings. Julianna got so see her very good friend, Cailyn, yesterday. I think it was really nice for both of them. For the past 2 nights Julianna has had some stomach discomfort. This has been hard—as with anyone it is never fun to feel bad. She did get unhooked from Charlie today, and if she continues to drink enough she can stay unhooked for a while. As much as Charlie has grown dear to us—we are happy to have a rest from being connected to him.

Julianna continues to love her prayer clock—for those that don't know—people from our church signed up for different hours of the day—there are one or more people praying for her round the clock. She made this big number clock out of paper and put the names of the people that are praying day and night. We look at it throughout the day and every night—we seem to be up 3 times a night, and without fail, she asks me who is praying for her. This has become very important to her.

We learned today that a friend of mine that I used to work with is friends with the parents of Julianna's friend from school. When I told Julianna the connection she started to sing "it's a small world…" Oh how I love these lighter moments of the day.

Today I had my sweat pants on backwards for a good part of the day. They are just plain black pants with a drawstring, but it was pretty funny when I realized it.

Julianna and I talked about maybe next weekend I could go home overnight and her Dad could stay with her. Although I said to her we would need to bring in some bricks to throw at him if she needed to get up in the middle of the night, because he would never wake up with just a stuffed animal being thrown at him like I am. This sent her in to hysterics.

Today Jeffrey visits—Julianna is not so thrilled—but *I can't wait.*

This is a very cheerful poster from Julianna's friend, and it is surrounded by the Prayer Clock Julianna made listing who is praying for her at each hour of the day.

CarePage Messages

From Anna

Anna March 9, 2007, at 6:19 a.m. EST

I will take this "journey" with you!

Much love always,
Anna (cousin)

Hi Jules!

Lynne March 09, 2007, at 08:40 a.m. EST

Hi there Jules,

Wow! Your very own web page. I love the name because everyone knows Pooh rules. We can't wait to see you, we hope it is soon. I think Charlie is a great name for your pole. I am thinking of making something to jazz it up a little. Any ideas? Chiffon? Butterflies? Just let me know. Well, some of us still have to work, so I better go for now, but I will check back again.

I Love You and am praying that you get better very soon.

Love,
Aunt Lynne

Greetings from Wendy and Family

Wendy March 09, 2007, at 08:47 a.m. EST

Hi Julianna, Brian, JoAnn and Jeffery—

Of course Pooh rules! But…I'm an Eeyore kind of girl myself. We are praying for all of you and there isn't a minute in the day that you're not all in our thoughts. We miss you and hope to see you soon.

Love—Wendy, Rick and Rusty
(church family)

Hey Julianna

Liz March 09, 2007, at 08:56 a.m. EST

It took me a few minutes to figure out how to reply back to you!! This is very cool, your very own webpage. We all miss you and can't wait to see you when you are feeling better. This message contains a huge hug and kisses from all of us!!!

Love Aunt Liz,
Uncle Andy, Jake, Tea and Nathan:)
(family friend)

Smile

Andy March 09, 2007, at 11:07 a.m. EST

Hi Julianna,

I heard about your web page and wanted to send you a note telling you that we've been thinking about you and praying for you all day every day.

You know—a lot of funny stuff goes on in a hospital if you look for it. I was hoping you could keep an eye out for some silly things and if they make you smile—send me a note and we can laugh about it together.

We love you,
Uncle Andy (family friend)

Looking forward to seeing you!!!

Amy March 09, 2007, at 12:36 p.m. EST

Hi to All of You,

I am getting ready to go to the wax museum and will be taping it for you to see. Allison will bring it to you on Saturday!!

Our Love and Prayers are with you,
Amy & Family (school friend)

Hi Julianna, Joann, Brian

Leslie March 09, 2007, at 01:29 p.m. EST

Love and Prayers and Strength and Happiness are coming from Tom, Nicole and I to *you* and your mom and dad! you will be fine because you are strong and you have *so* many people who care about you! You are an inspiration to us all!

Love Leslie
(family friend)

Hi Julianna

Monica March 09, 2007, at 01:34 p.m. EST

Hi Jules

Feel better soon so we can have a picnic!!!

Love Samantha and Dylan
(cousin)

Silly Joke #1

Laurelle March 09, 2007, at 01:57 p.m. EST

Hi Julianna, I thought you needed to smile so I have a Joke:

There are 2 brothers one is named; Shut-up and the other is; Trouble. One day Trouble gets lost at the store and Shut-up goes to the police to file a Missing Person's Report. The policeman asks; "What is your name?" He says; "Shut-up." The policeman asks; "What are you looking for? Trouble?" (Hehehehehehe!)
  Hope that at least made you smile! Feel better.

Laurelle
(cousin)

Thinking of you

David March 09, 2007, at 02:18 p.m. EST

Julianna,

I hope you're feeling better. Dylan is sending you a picture that he has been working on.

We love you, David, Cathy and Dylan.
(cousin)

Hello Julianna

Melissa March 09, 2007, at 03:02 p.m. EST

Hello Julianna, Jeffrey, Brian and JoAnn! This website page is so cool! Ms Pauline told us what was happening and we have been thinking about you all since then. Keep yourself busy and get well so we can see you.
  Hope you like this one…

At the doctor's office, a woman touched her right knee with her index finger and yelled. "Ow, that hurts!" Then she touched her left cheek, and again yelled, "Ouch! That hurts, too." Then she touched her right earlobe, "Ow, even *that* hurts," she cried. The doctor looked at her a moment and said, "You have a broken finger." Ha, Ha, Ha…we'll send more later.

Love, Matt, Melissa, Jessica
and Leanna (family friend)

Elephant Jokes

Simon March 09, 2007, at 03:15 p.m. EST

Hi Julianna… I don't know any Pooh Bear jokes (although I do have a little Pooh Bear on my desk next to my phone in the office), but I do know some Elephant jokes:

What cheers you up when you are sick? A Get Wellephant card.

What game do elephants like to play most? Squash

Why do elephants paint their toe-nails red? So they can hide in a strawberry patch.

Why do elephants hide in strawberry patches? So they can jump out and stomp on people

Why do elephants stomp on people? That's how they play squash!

Thinking about you and wishing you all well,
Love Simon & Pam (family friend)

6AM Prayer

Mary March 09, 2007, at 03:34 p.m. EST

Dear Julianna,

I told your Mom I will pray for you at 6AM every morning when my alarm goes off. I'll also say another prayer before I fall asleep. That will be a different time every night so I can't predict an exact time.

I felt sad when your Dad told me you were sick and had to spend time at CHOP. I know you are at the best children's hospital anywhere and will return to us at Buckingham after your treatments.

I am thinking of you often and sending you invisible hugs and lots of prayers.

Your School Nurse
(you would see me during vision screening)
and every Thursday and Friday.

Hi From Mrs. H. and Mrs. F.

Mrs. H March 09, 2007, at 04:31 p.m. EST

Hi Julianna,

We really miss your big smile and great attitude. Miss Joan just raves about you! We had the Wax Museum today. Congratulations…your board received many compliments. We hope you get to see the Wax Museum video soon. Please know that we think about you often and we miss hearing your great answers and reading your interesting writing. Take care!

Love, Mrs. F and Mrs. H
(school teacher)

Hi Friend & Charlie

Emily March 09, 2007, at 04:45 p.m. EST

Dear Jules, Missing you at school. Can't wait for you to come home so we can have a beauty party, with our foot spas and cucumber on our eyes (or sliding down our cheeks!!). Today I saw your triboard at the wax museum, it was cool!

Lots and Lots of LOVE
from Emily (school friend)xxxxxxxxxxxxxxxxxxxxxxxxxxxxxx
xxxxxxxxxxxxxxxxxxxxxxxxxxxxxxxxxxxxxxxxxxxxxxoooooooo
ooooooooooooooooooooooooooooooooooooooooooooooooo

Hi From Cousin Barbara

Barbara March 09, 2007, at 07:01 p.m. EST

Hi Jules,

I know Jennifer got to visit today, I wish I were her and could visit too. If there are any other types of games you would like, tell Jennifer when she come again and she will do her best to get them for you. I will be saying a prayer for you each night at eight o'clock.

Love and hugs, Barbara
(cousin)

Silly Joke #2 and #3

Laurelle March 09, 2007, at 07:55 p.m. EST

#2. If a chicken and a half can lay an egg and a half in a day and a half, how long does it take a grasshopper with a wooden leg to kick all the seeds out of a dill pickle???? #3. What do you call a sleeping bull? A Bulldozer!!!!
I warned you that they were silly!!! Hope they made you smile, anyway!!!

Love, Laurelle
(cousin)

CarePage Post March 10, 2007, at 06:38 p.m. EST

Saturday—Day 5

I didn't think I was going to write today because I am *sooooo tired*, but I can't sleep right now, and I can't figure out what else I want to do, so here I am… Julianna has been very tired the last 2 days—which is expected. And yesterday and today her jaw is a bit sore—a side effect from one of her medications—which will hopefully go away soon. Yesterday, she had to get a shot in each thigh. Two nurses came in so that they could do it together. My Mom and Jeffrey happened to be here when they did it, and Jeffrey hid behind Brian for fear that they might try and give him a shot too. The doc today said she most likely won't have to get any more shots for at least the next 30 days. Another one of the docs told me that they actually work very hard at not giving medications via needle at much as possible—this is a very good thing for all of us.

So yesterday Julianna wanted to watch a DVD—Anne of Green Gables that her Aunt Linda brought her. The DVD plays in the Playstation system. Somehow I figured out how to get to the movie to play, but later on when the nurses, etc came in we needed to pause the movie, and then figure out how to get back to the spot where she had seen to—all using the playstation controller. I could not figure it out to save my life and all I could think was "where's Jeffrey when I need him." I did eventually figure it out.

Yesterday, Julianna's cousin Jennifer came for a visit. Jennifer lives only 10 blocks from here and we decided it would be crazy for her *not* to come see us. Her and Jules played UNO and I got to leave the room and make a few phone calls. I am still not venturing far, but I may actually leave the building tomorrow—I will keep you posted.

Another special friend of Julianna's from school, Ally, got to visit her today. Julianna was so happy for the visit. We are taking a break from visitors tomorrow because Jules is pretty tired. We are trying to figure out the balance between having friends come— which makes her *soooo happy*, and keeping her rested.

I decided today that I will not drink another cup of coffee out of a styrofoam cup, and didn't Brian show up here today with a basket from my neighbor Pat that included her famous banana bread, some teas, and a real *coffee mug*.

I will end today's "post" with a prayer request. I was reading some of Julianna's medication paperwork last night because when she said her mouth hurt I knew I had seen that listed somewhere. I decided I should be familiar with the side effects so that I would know what to watch out for. As you might imagine, there are very serious side effects that could occur with each of her medications. Many of the serious ones are listed as rare which means 1-4%, but after reading through this I am feeling in need of prayer about this issue.

CarePage Messages

Hi!

Annie March 10, 2007, at 08:49 a.m. EST

Hi Jules. I miss you so much! Yesterday was the wax musem. A lot of people came. At recess when we play freeze tag it is not as fun when you are not here.
    Here's a silly joke what do you call a 1 eyed dinosaur?... a do- u -think -he- saw -us!
    Do you use magnets to decorate Charlie? I cannot wait to see you next week.

Annie
(school friend)

Hi Julianna

Rose Marie March 10, 2007, at 12:48 p.m. EST

First want to tell you some of Isabel's jokes. Knock knock, who's there? Banana. Knock knock, who's there? Banana. Knock knock, who's there? Orange you glad I didn't say banana!

Knock knock, who's there boo! Boo hoo?? You don't have to cry about it.

The second one has to be told to Grandpa, don't you think!!

We love you a bunch of bananas and oranges!!

Auntie Ro and Uncle Ed

We Loved Seeing You Today!

Amy March 10, 2007, at 04:22 p.m. EST

What a great visit we had today!! Thanks for inviting us!! We are already looking forward to our next visit!!

Love to All
Amy & Family (school friend)

Feel Better Soon:):):)

Melissa March 10, 2007, at 08:38 p.m. EST

Dear Julianna,

How are you feeling? When I dropped off your gift I saw a picture of you and your room! You were smiling and that made me happy! Each day since you were in the hospital I have been wearing the necklace that you gave me for my Birthday and I think about you *all* day long! I miss seeing you at lunch and playing with you at recess! I am keeping you in my prayers *every* night.

Love Melissa
(school friend)

Good Morning Sunshine

Lynne March 11, 2007, at 07:57 a.m. EDT

Hi there,

We just got back from church and I wanted to make sure you know that everyone in the whole parish of Assumption BVM is praying for you every day at every Mass! That is a whole lot of people! And our pastor, Father Devine (isn't that funny?) used to be the chaplain at CHOP. He said he has seen lots of little boys and girls who were sick like you get all better. So there you have it…you are getting better already!

Please tell your father we think he is funny asking for a flat screen tv for when you get home…and tell him Nice Try! We can't wait to come visit, even if it is just for a minute. I know you have been tired so it is better that you get rest right now. We will have plenty of time for visiting soon.

Cara and Mia say 'arf arf woof arf-arf-arf-arf' which is 'we love you Julianna' in maltese. I guess you have to come play with them when you get home. And, yes, you can bring Jeffrey too. Aunt Carolyn will make popcorn in your special bowls and we can watch a disney movie. maybe I will get Peter Pan, have you ever seen that one? 'I won't grow up' is one of my favorite songs.

I really need another lesson in finger knitting, you won't believe how tangled I managed to get my yarn. You make it look so easy, but it really isn't that easy to do without a teacher like you around.

One more thing before I go. Here is a joke to tell your nurses. Pooh and Piglet are hungry, so they look in a cupboard and find 10 jars of honey. Pooh says, "look Piglet,

10 jars of honey! that is 8 for each of us". Piglet scratches his head and says "how does that work out?" Pooh says, "I don't know, but I have already finished my 8!"

Take care, and we love you and are praying for you every day!

Love, Aunt Lynne and
Aunt Carolyn and Mia and Cara too

Silly Jokes #4 and #5

Laurelle March 11, 2007, at 08:11 a.m. EDT

#4 What did one strawberry sat to the other? "If you weren't so fresh we wouldn't be in this jam!"

#5 One day a snail went to buy a new Mercedes. He told the car salesman; "Before I pick up the car, I'd like you to paint the letter, S on the side of the door." The car salesman asked; "Why?" The snail answered, "Because when I drive down the street, I want everyone to say, 'Hey, look at that S Car Go!'"

Feel better soon!!!

Love, Laurelle
(cousin)

Hey Jules

Liz March 11, 2007, at 09:32 a.m. EDT

Just wanted to say "hi" and let you know we are thinking about you, (actually you're always in our thoughts and prayers!) We miss you and hope you feel better. Give your Mom a big hug from me!

Love you,
Aunt Liz (family friend)

Good Morning!

Amy March 11, 2007, at 10:12 a.m. EDT

Julianna, we just got back from church and you were in the congregation's prayers. Of course you are always in ours. Allison misses you already. We had a great visit. Keep drinking that water and get plenty of rest. We will visit again soon!,How we love to see that beautiful smile. Give our love to Mom.
 Love from our family.

Amy & Family
(school friend)

Hello Julianna and JoAnn

Beth March 11, 2007, at 07:49 p.m. EDT

We want to let you know that we are thinking about you and hope that your treatments go smoothly. We also hope that you are able to come home soon. I spoke with Andrea today and she told me about this web page. You all are in our thoughts and we hope for the best for you all.

Love, Beth, John, Hayley,
and Jenna (cousin)

Happy To See You!

Ravenna March 11, 2007, at 08:35 p.m. EDT

Thank you for the wonderful pictures!
 Sleep well, I hope you have a good day tomorrow.

Lots of love,
Ravenna (family friend)

CarePage Post March 12, 2007, at 01:19 p.m. EDT

Monday, Day 7

A lot has been going on, and Juianna has not been feeling great, so we have lots of prayer requests today:

For the last 3 nights, Julianna has had a belly ache. It is from the meds and her digestive system being a bit out of whack. She is eating well which is good, so please just pray for her various bodily functions to return to normal.

She developed hives/rash on Saturday night. This would have been considered a side effect from the shots she had on Friday—but only if it occurred within 30 minutes of receiving the shots. There were a few minutes of panic, because the nurses weren't sure what was going on, but it was just a rash and it began to disappear as fast as it came. At this point, the doctor said she doesn't know what caused it and if it doesn't happen again we are not going to worry about it. Please pray it doesn't happen again!

Yesterday, Julianna's nose started running and she developed a cough. Today is the same, her throat is red. They prefer not to give her medicine to treat the cold, so please pray that it will not get worse and will actually go away fast.

Tomorrow Julianna will be sedated—which she actually likes—and they will be doing a spinal tap and a bone marrow test again. She will also be receiving chemo into her spinal fluid and will be receiving her weekly IV push of chemo. Please pray for all this to go smoothly and again, please pray for no side effects.

Julianna is doing excellent swallowing her pills. We are so thankful for that.

I met a really nice Mom today who's daughter is further along into her illness. We discussed the hair thing because her daughter is a year younger than Julianna. She offered for Julianna to peek her head into her daughters room and "have a look." I mentioned it to Julianna and she game me quite a look—making it very clear that she was not interested in doing that. So please keep praying for her comfort level to increase regarding this issue.

I just told Julianna all the prayer requests I am making and asked her if she had any. Her response, "to go home soon."

CarePage Messages

Cool photos:-)

Linda March 12, 2007, at 07:18 a.m. EDT

Good morning Julianna! I just saw the photos from Cailyn's visit last week. You look wonderful:-) Your room is so bright and cheery and of course your smile lights it up. We are looking forward to coming down soon. I'll speak with your Mom and we'll decide when Cailyn can find her way back. I love, love, love your prayer clock! Please know that our family is also praying for you to be all better soon. We miss you! We'll look for some funny jokes to make you smile even more. What a great idea that was to start sending jokes along. See you soon. Love from our family.

PS A big bunch of hugs to your Mom & Dad and Jeffry from us too!

Linda
(school friend)

Mouth Sours—From Leslie

Leslie March 12, 2007, at 07:35 a.m. EDT

Joann/Brian/Julianna—my brother has had terrible mouth sores in relation to the chemo he is on. He was put on a trial drug that has done *wonders*!!!! Those mouth sores can be painful and are normal…you may want to ask the dr about medication…just a thought…Please call us and let us know how we can help!!!!

Les
(family friend)

From Basketball—Maggie's Mom

Suzy March 12, 2007, at 08:54 a.m. EDT

Dear Juliana, Coach Joe just told us yesterday after our last game about you! Everyone is pulling for you to get better fast! Tonight is our pizza party and Maggie and I are going to ask if anyone wants to pray with us for you. Maybe someone will come to know more about Jesus because of this! Is there anything you would like us to tell our basketball team? Our whole family is praying for you and we look forward to hearing how you are doing. Please tell your Mom I said a great big hello.

Love, Maggie's mom
(family friend)

Coconuts

Christine March 12, 2007, at 11:02 a.m. EDT

Julianna,

Abby, Nathan, Kevin & I are praying for you all of the time… you need to get your strength back up so you and Abby can do the Hawaiian hula (with the coconut bra tops!!!) again very soon… You and Abby were muchhhhh-hhhhhhhhhhhhhhhhhh better than your Dad and Kevin… they just couldn't pull it off like you two girls!
Thinking of you bunches and bunches…

Love, Christine, Kevin, Abby & Nathan
(family friend)

Olivia

Sue March 12, 2007, at 01:53 p.m. EDT

Hi Julianna,

How are you feeling today? How is the food in the hospital? We are praying for you every day. Can you play Webkinz with me? What is your user name? I am home sick from school today. I'm sorry your tummy is feeling sick. I miss you.

Love Olivia
(school friend)

Julianna

Cathy March 12, 2007, at 03:30 p.m. EDT

I have our group family picture in my office on my board so i everytime i look up i pray for you to get better...i will be back with some awesome jokes to make you smile...we love you very much and will continue to pray.

Biggest hugs and kisses
from Cathy,Dave and Dylan xoxo
(cousin)

Cooking class

Melissa March 12, 2007, at 06:00 p.m. EDT

Dear Jules,

Hey! Today I went to cooking class (happenings)! I wish that you could do it with me! Today we made banana bread and Irish Potatoes (it's a type of candy)! Maybe some time we can do Webkinz together. What's your user name? You can add me to your friends list! How many Webkinz do you have? Miss You Lots!

Your Friend,
Melissa (school friend)

Hey Jules

Jessica March 12, 2007, at 08:27 p.m. EDT

Hey Jules!

I miss you a whole lot! I wish I wasn't at school right now so I could come see you. I will be home the last weekend of March and you will definitely be my first visit. But because I can't come see you sooner I have a little something special that I am going to send your way, hopefully it will be there by the end of the week! I hope it will keep you lots of company since I can't. Though I may not be on your prayer clock, I am praying for you all the time, so you can just add "and Jess" to every hour. Tell your mom I said hi, even though she's probably the one reading this too you (Hi JoAnn!!). I am hoping to write to you everyday! Miss you tons!

Love you,
Jess (babysitter)

It's Me Again

Jessica March 12, 2007, at 08:35 p.m. EDT

Jules,

So after sending the last message, which I somehow sent twice, I was wondering where your mom would want me to send the package to. The house, or if I could send it right to you.

Love you,
Jess (babysitter)

Silly Joke #6

Laurelle March 12, 2007, at 08:50 p.m. EDT

One day this Piece of String went into a restaurant and tried to order a hamburger. The waitress looked at The String and said; "I'm sorry but we don't serve string, here." The Piece of String was very hungry and went outside. He scratched his head and then thought of a brilliant idea. He saw a couple walking by and asked them to tie his 2 ends together in a knot, which they did. Then he asked if they could pick him up and rub him against the sidewalk a few times. After they had finished, The Piece of String went back into the restaurant. The waitress said; "Hey, aren't you that same Piece of String that was in here a minute ago?" The String answered; "No, I'm a Frayed Knot."

Laurelle
(cousin)

Cailyn

Cailyn March 12, 2007, at 08:50 p.m. EDT

Dear Julianna,

Feel better!!!!! I hear you don't wear Charlie anymore but you have to drink lots of water! To let you know—Courtney and I went on your Webkinz to see how it was doing and its health was at 60 something but we did something on your Webkinz! First we got it a new room. Next we got lots of money but it is a surprise. But don`t worry, Courtney and I are taking good care of your Webkinz! Tomorrow is (P.S.S.A). Reading but we don't have any homework! Got to go on your Webkinz now. I hope your tummy feels better soon & I can get to see you again. I said my 8 o'clock prayers for you. I'll say more when I go to bed. See you soon I hope.

Your friend,
Cailyn (school friend)

Thinking of you

David March 13, 2007, at 09:03 a.m. EDT

Julianna,

I hope today is a better day for you.

Thinking about you, David, Dylan and Cathy
(cousin)

Poem for Jules

Monica March 13, 2007, at 09:23 a.m. EDT

Hi Jules

I heard you are having belly aches. I wish I had some jokes for you, but I don't. I was up last night thinking about you and I wrote a poem for you. Here goes...don't laugh... Julianna is so pretty, she makes me feel so witty, I'm going to send her a letter, because I want her to feel better!!!! Are you smiling???? I hope so!!!

We love you lots—Monica, Dave,
and everybody!!! (cousin)

Happy Tuesday!

Lynne March 13, 2007, at 09:42 a.m. EDT

Hi Julianna,

Just a little note to say Hello and let you know we are thinking of you. If I sent one every time you popped into my head, I would never get any work done! I hope your tummy feels better today.

Aunt Lynne & Aunt Carolyn

Tuesday

Linda March 13, 2007, at 11:50 a.m. EDT

Hi there!

It's almost lunch time and I wonder if you are all done with your procedures for today. Prayers are being said all over for you:-) I am looking forward to taking Cailyn back down for a visit with you. I know that you need to feel a bit better before that so I'll pray for that too. Cailyn was nervous today about the PSSA tests. The summary is what she is most worried about. I think that you girls have done so much learning this year that it will be a breeze! I must run out for a while to pick up some healthy snacks for school. Cailyn will write to you again tonight and let you know how today was. A big "Thank You" to Mom for keeping us all up to date on this page. We're thinking of you—all the time!!

Big strong cyber hugs to you from our family.

Linda
(school friend)

Hi Julianna!

Lois March 13, 2007, at 11:51 a.m. EDT

Julianna,

Here's a funny joke I heard in the lunchroom from one of the first graders—hope you like it! "What do you call a pair of banana peels?"

"Slippers!!" Ha Ha Ha!! I miss seeing your smiling face in Math class—my prayers and thoughts are with you and your family!

> Love, Lois
> (school friend)

Hope to see you soon

MomMom March 13, 2007, at 12:41 p.m. EDT

Dear Julianna and JoAnn,

Hope today is a good one… Poppi figured this out hooray..

> Love MomMom and Poppi

Hi Julianna & JoAnn

Susan March 13, 2007, at 02:28 p.m. EDT

I have been thinking and praying for you all! Julianna, I prayed for your belly ache and for the procedures to go well. I've been praying for your doctors and nurses too so they take good care of you.

JoAnn, You are in my thoughts constantly. I wish I could talk to you, but please know that my heart is with you! Thanks for keeping us posted on how everyone is doing.

> Love,
> Sue (church family)

Love From Us

Amy March 13, 2007, at 02:33 p.m. EDT

I hope that this note finds Julianna feeling better! Our prayers and love are coming your way!!! Allison had PSSA's today and was a little nervous. (Can you believe that Julianna?) We hope that you got the gerbera daisies today. They reminded us of Julianna's bright and beautiful smile(of course nothing could really be as bright or as beautiful as that smile). Allison will email you tonight.
    Love to all

Amy & Family
(school friend)

CarePage Post March 13, 2007, at 03:31 p.m. EDT

Tuesday—Day 8

I have *awesome* news!!!! Julianna's doc just came in with this mornings bone marrow results—and she is considered "in *remission.*" This is amazing news and the best possible news we could have hoped for. I never imagined it could happen so fast!! They are saying we are even going home today! which means I need to go order that u-haul to bring all of our stuff home. I have to go start packing up—thank you for all the love, and notes, and most of all prayer—because this is truly an answer to Julianna's prayer request from yesterday. We love you all!!!!! J & J

CarePage Messages

Checking Out!

Ravenna March 13, 2007, at 04:09 p.m. EDT

I am so thrilled by the great news! Remission!! This has made my day. I am so happy that you can go home.
 Lots of love to all of you!

Ravenna
(family friend)

Cailyn

Cailyn March 13, 2007, at 04:12 p.m. EDT

Dear Julianna,

I read the news you're going home today!!!! Yaaaaaaaayyyyyyyyyyy!!!! Hope I can visit you soon!!!! When you get home go on your webkinz—Courtney and I got you a large room for something!!!

Love your friend,
Cailyn Yaaaaaaaaaa Can't Wait.
(school friend)

Olivia

Olivia March 13, 2007, at 04:16 p.m. EDT

Julianna,

This is the best news ever!!! I am so happy for you!! I can't wait to see you!

Love,
Olivia (school friend)

Yes—Yes—Yes!!!!!!!

Monica March 13, 2007, at 04:22 p.m. EDT

We are so happy!!!!
  Our Prayers were answered!!!!!!
  We love you!!!!!

Monica
(cousin)

I Can't See What I'm Typing...

Simon March 13, 2007, at 04:28 p.m. EDT

I can't see what I'm typing... because my eyes are filled with tears—as Pam will tell you, I always cry at happy things rather than sad... thanks for sharing your news and making my day! This is just the best...
  But we'll still keep up the prayers and the fingers crossed and the support!

Love
Simon & Pam
(family friend)

God Has Answered Our Prayers!!

Amy March 13, 2007, at 04:33 p.m. EDT

I can't tell you how happy we are!! What great news!! Allison is singing and soooo happy. We will talk soon!

Love to All, Amy
(school friend)

Ally Is Writing This

Ally March 13, 2007, at 04:42 p.m. EDT

This is the best thing to me. You don't know how much this means to me. You may not be getting an E-mail but who cares. My mom was reading your care page and told me the news. I am sooooooooooo happy for you. I, Ally, is relieved you will be going home even though you won't be coming to school yet!!!

Good Luck at home

Ally
(school friend)

Praise God!

Leanne March 13, 2007, at 05:14 p.m. EDT

Praise God from whom all blessings flow!!! We are praising and thanking God for all the healing in your body and that you are able to go home! Enjoy sleeping in your OWN bed, and being in your own home!

Much love and continued prayers, Chuck, Leanne, Matthew and David (church family)

Praise and Thanksgiving!

Marchell March 13, 2007, at 05:17 p.m. EDT

Praise and thanksgiving for God's awesome healing power! God bless Julianna and the Smith family!

Marchell
(school friend)

Great News!!

Melissa March 13, 2007, at 05:37 p.m. EDT

We are so happy to hear your awesome news! We have been praying for you so much even though our names weren't on your prayer clock. God must have really been listening to us all! You are such a great kid!!

See you soon,
Matt, Melissa, Jessica and Leanna
(family friend)

3

There's No Place Like Home

CarePage Post March 14, 2007, at 08:48 p.m. EDT

Wednesday, Day 9

Dorothy was totally right... There's no place like home, there's no place like home... My Mom says "we went out of here like the wind, and we came home like the wind yesterday." What a whirlwind this continues to be.

When they told us the good results yesterday, and said we would be going home it was truly unbelievable.

Today, after totally sleeping in, we headed to King of Prussia to meet the team of doctors we will be working with there. I chose the King of Prussia CHOP Specialty Care Center for our outpatient services because one of the nurses clued me in that the Philly clinic is really overcrowded and waits can be long, and parking is terrible, etc. I asked one of the docs if we could try King of Prussia and change if we wanted, and she answered "you won't change." And after being there today, I think they were all right. The facility is wonderful, the doctor is really great, and the rest of the staff was wonderful as well. It's small, peaceful, and it is obvious that they want you to feel comfortable there. So we will be heading there on Tuesdays for the next 2 weeks and then more testing so we can get our roadmap for the next phase.

Julianna is pretty worn out still, but we are actually going to try and have her go to school for ½ day Friday. The doc really wants her back to her routine, not to be in the "bubble" I want to put her in. This is all such new territory and I think we are going to have to take it day by day.

We are busy trying to get adjusted to all this and getting prescriptions filled, and paying attention to Jeffrey, and making Julianna comfortable, so please accept my apologies, but I don't anticipate being able to return phone calls for a few more days.

We have some funny stories we want to share, but will do that in future posts. One last funny note... tonight at dinner when Jeffrey was done he said "I am excused" and he got up from the table. I turned to my Mom who has been taking care of him all this time and said, "Oh I see, there are some new rules in this house under Grandma's care—Jeffrey excuses himself from the table." She did tell us that her and Jeffrey have had some "secrets" while I have been gone—I will have to keep you posted on that as well.

As for prayer—keep it coming—please pray that Julianna's body will continue to respond well to the meds, and that she will stay healthy and free from all illness and infection.

CarePage Messages

A Miracle!

Donna March 14, 2007, at 05:24 a.m. EDT

this is such awesome news! I can't wait to tell annie (she still sleeping)—no one deserves a miracle more than you and your family Julianna!

Hope to see you really soon!

Donna
(school friend)

I'm So Happy

Annie March 14, 2007, at 08:09 a.m. EDT

Jules This Is Annie—

i'm happy that today you are going home. I can't wait to see you. I'll still miss you at school but maybe i can visit you at your house.

Annie
(school friend)

Thanks Be To God!

Clare March 14, 2007, at 09:08 a.m. EDT

We were so delighted to hear your good news Julianna! It has answered our prayers! We have tried to send messages before with some of Justin's jokes but it would not post. So we will send them on to you at home now. Hope you got Merlin's picture too. We shall keep on praying that you get stronger and stronger and can get back to your old routine and that we can see your happy face around here now.

Love Mrs F and Justin
(church family)

Another Answered Prayer

Lynne March 14, 2007, at 10:31 a.m. EDT

In a world where so many people detest our right to pray, this is proof positive that we are too blessed to be stressed and too anointed to be disappointed!

Aunt Lynne & Aunt Carolyn

What A Beautiful Day To Be Home!!

Amy March 14, 2007, at 02:19 p.m. EDT

Julianna and JoAnn,

I hope that you are home and enjoying your day. I am sure that God sent this beautiful day to welcome you home. Call if you need anything!!

Amy
(school friend)

Hip-Hip Hooray!:):):):):)

Melissa March 14, 2007, at 02:45 p.m. EDT

Dear Julianna,

I heard the big news! How does it feel to be in your own bed at night again? Today i am home sick with a fever and a bad cough so i am just resting and you know just chillin! So i felt like writing you! I am just so happy that you are safe and sound!:) i am still keeping you in my prayers and wearing the necklace you gave me for my birthday! In fact i am wearing it right now!:)what are you doing right now? Miss you lots!

From,
Melissa
xoxoxoxoxoxoxoxoxoxoxoxoxoxoxoxoxoxoxoxoxoxoxoxox-
oxoxoxoxoxox (school friend)

God Bless You...The Whole Smith Clan!!!

John March 14, 2007, at 04:47 p.m. EDT

I have been out of town for awhile and have not been able to do much of anything for you-all except to say a lot of prayers for your well being and for uplifting your spirits.

JoAnn: Thank you for keeping everyone appraised of your darling daughter's diagnosis and prognosis.

Julianna: Hang in there young lady. I am sure that it will all come out perfectly fine in the end.

> Hugs, John & Jeanne—Some Lower
> Mtn Road (neighbors)

Hey

Jessica March 14, 2007, at 09:05 p.m. EDT

Julianna,

I am so happy to hear you are home! You must be very happy. I have been really busy this week and I haven't gotten your package out, but I am sending it tomorrow so I hope it arrives at your house soon! I miss you tons and hope to see you soon!

> Love you,
> Jess (babysitter)

We're Soooooooooooooo Happy That You're Home!!!!!!!!

Patrice March 14, 2007, at 09:05 p.m. EDT

Dear Julianna,

We are so incredibly happy that you're home with your family! We hope and pray every day that you feel better soon!

> Love,
> Aidan and Katherine:-)
> (school friend)

There is No Place Like Home…

Susan March 14, 2007, at 09:26 p.m. EDT

Julianna,

Like your mom said.. There is no place like home. Praise God for all the prayers and that you are home. I'll continue to keep you in my prayers! JoAnn… you need something, call me. I know you have a good family support, but I'm here. Brian, maybe there is something I can help you with?
    Love to all!

Sue (church family)

It's a Miracle!

Laurelle March 15, 2007, at 06:46 a.m. EDT

We can't believe how wonderful the news is! You're all home again! Everybody's prayers have been answered!
    I'll spare you the silly jokes, this post!
    We are so happy to hear that you are getting better and were able to go home.

Love,
Laurelle
(cousin)

Hi to All

Amy March 15, 2007, at 10:52 a.m. EDT

We are so happy to hear that all is well at home!! You have our continued prayers!! We are a phone call away if you need anything!

Love to all, Amy
(school friend)

Hello

Ann March 15, 2007, at 11:34 a.m. EDT

Glad to read your emails and hear that things are going so well at home. We continue to keep you in our thoughts and prayers. If we can do anything at all, please give a call.

Ann and Family
(school friend)

Thursday

Linda March 15, 2007, at 03:01 p.m. EDT

Yea! You're really home! I prayed that all would go well and that you would get home like they said you would. It must be wonderful to back in your own place. Did I read it right? We may get to see Jules in school on Friday? Cailyn will be over the top excited! Of course our continued prayers are coming your way. I guess "storming heaven" really worked! What a blessing. Thank you so much for continuing to post progress. It is like Christmas morning when there is a new post to read!

Take care, love from our family
(school friend)

Wonderful To Hear You're Home!!

Lois March 15, 2007, at 07:18 p.m. EDT

Julianna,

Mrs. H told all of us that you were coming home, and we were all so happy and thankful to God!! And more good news—that you may come to school tomorrow!! I hope to get to see you and say hi! If not, I'm sure I'll see you soon.

Love, Mrs. S
(school teacher)

Great To Hear Your Home.!

David March 16, 2007, at 12:25 p.m. EDT

I was away on business and I am now checking my emails today. This is great news. Finally Julianna your home!!!!! The start of a new beginning.

Dave
(cousin)

CarePage Post March 17, 2007, at 10:22 p.m. EDT

Saturday, Day 12

We are all still in a major state of disbelief here at the Smith household. Julianna has really been tired and worn out until today. She never did make it to school on Friday. On Thursday I spoke to the counselor at her school and he told me that both strep throat and stomach viruses were going around the building. Plus once we heard the weather report I decided to give her the weekend to regain some more strength and stamina. At this point we are planning on her going ½ day on Monday afternoon. Then Tuesday we head to "clinic" for her chemo. Maybe she will go to school ½ day again on Wednesday, and we will see from there. We are definitely in "one-day-at-a-time" mode.

Part of Julianna's treatment is that she takes steroids twice a day. Apparently they are very effective in wiping out the leukemia cells. The docs kept telling us that she is going to have quite an appetite, and crave salty and spicy foods. At her last appt, the doc said to her "have you gotten up at 3:00am yet and asked your Mom to make pancakes?" Julianna and I just kind of looked at each other. Well... for the last 2 days Julianna's appetite has been pretty steady. I think she is eating about 5 meals a day, plus snacks in between. Luckily, so far, she is eating mostly healthy foods.

This morning at 6:45 am she came and told me she was dreaming about ham and would like to have some. I said we didn't have any and she said, "how about salami?" So at 6:45 am this morning she was sitting at our table eating salami. This is definitely going to be interesting.

On Friday, a dozen beautiful pink roses arrived here with a message, but it wasn't signed. I was wondering if anyone could claim them so that we can properly thank you. They are gorgeous and I must say we are getting pretty used to all the balloons and flowers in our house.

We still have some stories we want to share, especially Julianna, but I am tired—and these posts have space limitations, so I will have to write another day.

I did post 2 new pictures I think you will enjoy.

One last thing, today Pastor Jules did ask me about the round-the-clock prayer chain and I did tell him that you can all stop for now. Of course, you can still pray, but we are no longer expecting you to keep up that commitment. I will just say once again how that was *the* most important thing to Julianna (and me), and I don't think we will ever be able to fully convey our thanks to all of you—not only for the "prayer clock," but for all the prayers, thoughts, and love you sent our way.

Princess Julianna—so, so, so comfy in her own bed. Every time I tuck her in she has the hugest smile on her face.

Another one of Julianna's favorite comfy spots. Naps in the middle of the afternoon… Aaaaaahhhhhhh!!!!

CarePage Messages

School Again!!!!

Melissa March 18, 2007, at 07:49 a.m. EDT

Dear Julianna,

I can't wait for you to come back to school for 1 half day! Are you feeling better at all?
    Can't wait to see you!!

-Melissa
(school friend)

Welcome Home

Liz March 18, 2007, at 12:15 p.m. EDT

Hey Jules

We are so glad you are home, I know you must be too!!!
We think about you all the time. Hope to see you soon…

Love,
Aunt Liz
(family friend)

Love From Our Family

Amy March 18, 2007, at 12:30 p.m. EDT

We are sooo happy to hear how well things are going!!
Allison is looking forward to seeing you in school this
Monday!! It feels so good to be able to think of you back
in school with your friends. Enjoy the rest of the weekend
and those salami sandwiches!! Our prayers are with you!!

Amy & Family
(school friend)

Silly Jokes about Snow and Winter

Laurelle March 18, 2007, at 04:17 p.m. EDT

1. Where do snowmen keep their money? In snow banks.

2. What do you get when you cross a snowman with a
   vampire? Frostbite.

3. Where do polar bears vote? The North Pole.

Hope you're feeling better!!!

Love,
Laurelle
(cousin)

Glad You Are Home

Mary March 18, 2007, at 05:16 p.m. EDT

Julianna,

Hi! I am so happy to hear you are home! I have been praying for you, Mom, Dad & Jeffrey since I first heard from Aunt Linda. The prayer clock is such a cool gift and how awesome and thoughtful of your church family. I will continue to pray for you in the early morning before work—that God will sustain you with *His* strength and courage as the days go by. Enjoy your 1/2 day of school tomorrow.

Your mom's quilting friend, Mrs. L
PS... say Hi to mom for me. (family friend)

Hello to the Smiths

Beth March 18, 2007, at 06:19 p.m. EDT

Dear Julianna,

We are so glad to hear that things are going well for you. We are so happy that you are at home. There is nothing as comforting as being in your own bed and having all your favorite toys with you. We want you to know that we are thinking about you and hoping that your treatments go well. We are so glad that you can receive your treatments outside of the hospital. Please say hello to your mom, dad and Jeffrey for us. Have a great week!

Love, Beth,John,Hayley,and Jenna
(cousin)

Julianna, JoAnn, Brian and Jeffrey

Joan March 18, 2007, at 06:41 p.m. EDT

We are so happy that you are home and doing well. Let's hope all the days from now on get better and better. Our prayers have been and will be with all of you. We are hoping for a permanent remission and back to normal soon.

Our love to all of you, Aunt Joan
and Uncle George

My Little Piano Student!

Pauline March 20, 2007, at 11:24 a.m. EDT

Dear Julianna, I finally was able to get on your page. Thanks to Melissa, who helped me. I think it is great. I love seeing your pictures and reading about your progress. I think about you all the time, especially on Wednesdays at 4. I hope that one day you will want to come back. I will come to your house and give you your lesson whenever you are ready. Did you get the picture of Tiffy? She is beginning to get more used to me. I will sign off for now. I miss you and you are in my prayers. I went through what you are going through many years ago and I know that prayers work. I love you. Pauline and Tiffy

Dear Joann and Brian, How brave you both are. I am here for you should you need anything. My love and prayers to you both. Pauline

Dear Jeffrey, The skittle bowl is waiting. It misses your little hand. I know you are being a perfect little brother. Be sweet to your sister. I love you too.

Pauline
(piano teacher)

Salami For Breakfast

Mary March 20, 2007, at 02:25 p.m. EDT

Dear Mrs. Smith and Julianna,

I know that you made the best decision to skip Friday. Julianna, you didn't miss anything but yucky, cold weather.

We will work with you any way we can to accommodate your return to school. I know Julianna you must really miss your friends here at Buckingham.

I will still continue to say a little 6am prayer for you on work days.

Salami for breakfast...yum...yum!

Love,
Mrs. H
(school nurse)

CarePage Post March 21, 2007, at 10:05 p.m. EDT

Wednesday, Day 16

I have a lot to report so there may actually be 2 posts tonight if I can't fit it all in one.

First, I just need to put out another global "Thank You" for all the amazing cards, flowers, gifts, encouraging and heart-warming notes that continue to flow into the Smith household. Also, for those that sent cards and gifts to the hospital they have been forwarding them to us here at home. They must really be wondering in the CHOP mailroom who "Julianna Smith" *is* to warrant this amount of cards and gifts.

I do have a prayer request. At Julianna's appointment on Tuesday, the first person who analyzed her blood thought they saw "something." When the oncologist looked, she did not see anything. We have to return to the clinic this Friday to re-do the blood work. This, of course, means another "stick" for Julianna. The oncologist said we just "need to be safe rather than sorry." She told us not to lose sleep over it—yeah right! So, please pray that there is nothing there but healthy, normal cells. And please pray for Julianna's peace of mind. She was definitely anxious this past Tuesday in anticipation of her IV and chemo treatment.

Also, it continues to be a whirlwind here, so I am still having trouble getting to phone calls. Please accept my apologies.

As for what's been going on: Julianna had a really good day over the weekend, followed the next day by some bad pain in her back and her knees. The knee pain subsided, and the doc thinks it could have been her overdoing it in the snow on her "good day." The back pain is still there, most likely a side effect of the steroid. We are treating it with Tylenol and currently that is working.

She has been up a few mornings at 5:30 for a "snack" of ham or salami and mayonnaise. Our funny neighbors actually brought her some more ham and salami today. The sad part is that she will most likely be eating it tomorrow morning. My Mom did have a good idea that we let her bring some crackers upstairs so that she could just eat them at 5:00am instead of dragging me down to the kitchen. It did work, so I think we'll try it again tonight. Speaking of my Mom—she left today after completely cleaning my house. It's very sad that even Julianna said tonight at dinner "this is not Grandma's cooking."

Julianna did go to school ½ day Monday and ½ day today. She did very well. Needless to say her friends were very glad to see her. As long as they squirted first with the Purell they were allowed to hug her. Apparently there was a line to get to the Purell on Monday. Her school is being totally flexible with me. She will not make full days of school yet because she is still very worn out. They tell me just to bring her to school whenever we want, morning, afternoon, whatever—they will just be flexible.

4

You Owe Me That Chick

CarePage Post March 21, 2007, at 10:28 p.m. EDT

Funny Story #1

Julianna really wanted me to share this funny story with you...
Beginning early February, Julianna had blood work drawn twice
due to the high fevers that were occurring. She had been so brave
and both times I took her to WaWa to buy her a treat. It was on
a Wednesday that we were back at the doctor due to a fever of
103 degrees. Again, they did blood work. Again, I took her to buy
her a treat. The next morning, Thursday, the doctors' office called
and said we needed to have the blood work done again. She said
the lab couldn't process it—apparently, sometimes that happens.
She said we should go over to Doylestown Hospital and have it
drawn again because they could process the results very quickly
and the doc wanted it done right away. (We have since come to
realize that based on the results they saw from Wednesday they
needed it done again to be sure it was correct and not a bad test.)

Anyway, I broke out in tears having to make Julianna do this
again. Plus the stress of these high fevers. Anyway, we go to the
hospital and have the blood work drawn. We go to visit Julianna's
Aunt Linda that works there and then I took her to the gift shop
to buy her a treat.

She, of course, picks out this very cute fluffy stuffed animal
chick. I look at it, and I think the price says $54.95, plus she

already has plenty of stuffed animals so I say "no." I try and find her some other little treat, but she doesn't want anything. She goes back to the chick. I now see that it is actually $14.95, but I still say "no." She couldn't find anything she wanted so I said let's just go.

On the way to the car, I said to her that I usually just buy her a $3 treat after blood work, and since she didn't get anything this time, if she has blood work 4 more times I will buy her the chick. I thought this was funny and I laughed, but she didn't.

By the time we got home, the doc had already called with the results and said we needed to get down to CHOP. The first 12 hours at CHOP, Julianna literally had blood drawn almost every hour, plus she had 3 IV's put in, because the first one didn't work, etc, etc. Sometime the next day she looked over at me and said "You owe me that chick."

Needless to say, I had her Aunt Linda that works at the hospital get it for her, and I have since been convinced that one can never have too many stuffed animals.

CarePage Messages

Prayers from Florida

Kim March 21, 2007, at 09:52 a.m. EDT

Hello Brian, JoAnn, Julianna, and Jeffrey. We are *so* happy to hear about your quick response to the chemo! We have been praying for you during our family devotions. Now the kids will be able to see these great pictures and updates. What an answer to prayer! I'm always humbled when God answers the prayers of his people—we shouldn't be surprised, He told us to "Call upon me and I will answer thee".

We will continue to pray for you daily as this will be a roller coaster ride for *all* of you.

Lots of love!
Ray, Kim, Nate, Peter, and Olivia (cousin)

From Grandma's Friend

Fran March 21, 2007, at 09:55 p.m. EDT

Hello Julianna…You probably don't know me but you and your brother's picture hang on my refrigerator from Christmas to Christmas. I so look forward to receiving them each year. Your mom and dad are very thoughtful to send them to me. Your grandma Viv and I have been friends a very long time. You, your mom and dad have been in my thoughts and prayers. I wish you a speedy recovery and happiness for you and your family.

Fran
(family friend)

What A Great Memory!

Mary March 21, 2007, at 11:27 p.m. EDT

HI Julianna & Mom…

I am so happy to hear you are able to have some 1/2 days at school. It must be wonderful to see your friends again AND it sure sounds like they were so happy to see you. Your funny story about the chick just goes to show your have a very active memory! Keep up the good job. We continue to pray for you.

Mrs. L
(family friend)

Thursday

Linda March 22, 2007, at 11:53 a.m. EDT

Hey there! It was so good to see Jules in school yesterday:-) I felt like a little kid when I saw her! Please know that continued prayers are being sent your way for continued good news and a good report on Friday.

It was also good to see you back in some kind of normal routine at school. I hope you know that we'll all be there when your knees give out and you need someone to catch you:-) You are important in this too!

Take care for now,
Love from Linda (school friend)

Never Too Many Stuffed Animals!

Marlene March 22, 2007, at 12:38 p.m. EDT

Dear JoAnn, Brian and Julianna,

There is no such thing as too many stuffed animals. Maybe someday when Julianna is all better, she can gather some of the stuffed animals and give them to other children at CHOP. She can pass on the smiles.

Thanks for the funny story. She's a smart thinker! Sean and Carrie dropped off a purple bunny and flower the other day at your home. So that is yet another "stuffie!" We'll go with candy the next time!

Take care. We are praying, praying, praying...and thinking of you all constantly. Faith + Positive Thoughts = Miracles

Love to all of you,
Marlene, Sean, Carrie and Kate
(family friend)

We Can't Wait To See You!

Jeannie March 22, 2007, at 05:32 p.m. EDT

Dear Julianna,

It sounds like things are going well. We want you to know we think about you every day, nothing but happy thoughts. That stuffed animal story was great! That chick couldn't have found a better home. Tell your Mom she is doing a great job with the updates. Take care of yourself and we hope to see you soon.

Hugs and Kisses Love, Jeannie & Bruce
(family friend)

Love From Us

Amy March 22, 2007, at 07:28 p.m. EDT

Our prayers are coming your way for continued good news on Friday!!

So glad that you have been back to school with your friends.

We are always thinking about you!!

Hugs and Kisses from Allison!!
(school friend)

From Emma

Marchell March 22, 2007, at 07:47 p.m. EDT

Dear Julianna:

My Mom told me your funny story. I remember that I got a stuffed duck with a rain hat and rain coat from Doylestown Hospital's gift shop. I have an Aunt Linda who works at a hospital too! It was great to see you at school the last couple of days.

Love, your friend,
Emma (school friend)

Love The Funny Stories—Keep Them Coming

Chris March 22, 2007, at 08:46 p.m. EDT

JoAnn and Julianna,

Love the stuff animal story. I have visited the Doylestown Hospital gift shop several times and I do have to say they have a nice collect of soft and cuddly stuff animals. They also have my favorite sweet treat—Swedish Fish:) You are all in my thoughts and prayers!

Love,
Chrissy, Jim, Nicole and Katie
(family friend)

CarePage Post March 23, 2007, at 03:25 p.m. EDT

Friday, Day 18

Good news!! Another answer to prayer—Julianna's blood work looked fine today. What a relief!!!

So here is how the day unfolded: When we got to the clinic this morning, it was much busier in the waiting area than when we go on Tuesdays. They have mentioned to us before that Friday's are busy days there. Plus, there were women buzzing around and there were tables of fabric, and there were sewing machines set up. It turns out that one of the groups that donate the pillowcases to the hospital was there and they were letting the kids sew their own pillowcases. One of the women came over and asked Julianna if she would like to make one, and with a big smile Julianna said "Yes!" She picked out this great Easter fabric with Snoopy and Woodstock and a pretty pink fabric to go with it. Then, my quilting friends are going to love this, she sewed on a "Bernina" sewing machine. I was quite jealous.

A little while after they drew the blood work, a nurse came in and said, I want to be sure you know not to leave, the doctor wants to talk to you. I said, OK, and an immediate sense of dread came over me. I was so sick to my stomach—all the time acting normal and doing a Soduko puzzle with Julianna. The doctor finally came in and said everything was fine. I guess the nurse was just making sure I didn't leave, and I just read the worst into it. So we leave.

I made a wrong turn through all the construction trying to get on the Turnpike—this was the first time driving without Brian to the clinic—and I am totally going in the wrong direction. Meanwhile, I am trying to get home so Julianna can go to a birthday party she really wants to go to. I get Brian on the phone. I am totally panicked. I am yelling into the phone *"i don't know where i am!! There Is NO WHERE To Turn Around."* Now my phone rings, and I see it is the kids school. I can't answer it because I am trying to figure out where I am. I let it go to voicemail. When I retrieve the message it is Jeffrey's teacher saying that no one picked him up from school today. Brian was supposed to do that. I call Brian and tell him to call the school and get over there. I eventually find my way back to the Turnpike and go the right way this time. Tears are building up in my eyes—but for the millionth time I hold them back.

I did get Julianna to the party on time, Brian called and said he had Jeffrey—and I think since we had good news today I shouldn't be whining!

CarePage Messages

It's A Small World

Susan March 23, 2007, at 02:45 p.m. EDT

Hi Julianna,

I loved your funny story too! I was reading some of your notes from friends and family and I was very surprised to see that you are friends with Emma. She told you that she has an Aunt Linda that works at a hospital too. Well her Aunt Linda is my sister!

JoAnn... hope you are doing as good as you sound in your notes! It really is a small world isn't it. I can remember when both Julianna and Emma were little ones and I had Julianna in Sunday school. We are very close with Emma's family. Her mom Marchell is a sweetheart. Take care and know I think and pray for you guys every day. I check the CarePages daily to see how things are going.

Sue
(church friend)

Hello To The Smith Family

Beth March 23, 2007, at 06:05 p.m. EDT

Hello Everyone! We are so glad to hear that Julianna's blood work was okay today. I was thinking about all of you while at work today. I'm glad that Julianna is able to attend the birthday party and go to school as much as she can. I talked to cousin Cathy today. She had her baby on Tuesday. She had a little girl. They will be going to go home tomorrow. It just seems like yesterday that John and I were bringing Hayley and Jenna home from the hospital and it is almost 8 years now. Have a great weekend and thank you for keeping us posted on this webpage. Please know that we are thinking about you and hoping that all goes well. I also want to say that Hayley and Jenna really enjoy their Grandma's cooking also. They say "Grandma is the best cook and then comes you, Mommy." Take care.

Love, Beth
(cousin)

Hello From Mom Mom And Poppi

Roland March 23, 2007, at 08:31 p.m. EDT

Hi everyone

We loved the story of the chick..and are thrilled that the blood work was favorable today. Love you JoAnn and Brian. Love you Julianna. Love you Jeffrey.

Mother

Blessings… Bernina!!… Boo Boos!

Mary March 23, 2007, at 10:15 p.m. EDT

Julianna & Mom…

It is late in the evening and these are the words I can think of to sum up yours and Mom's… Dad and Jeffrey's day! A day in the life the Smith household! Please tell mom I laughed out loud about your experience with the Bernina. How thoughtful of those ladies being so giving you a chance to help someone else.

I am just so happy about your test results today. To quote a stanza from a great worship song…"What a *mighty* God we serve!"
Love to you, Jeffrey, Mom & Dad

Mrs. L (family friend)

Stay Strong Joann! Especially On The Turnpike!

Clare March 23, 2007, at 11:34 p.m. EDT

I am rejoicing with you about the good news of Julianna's test!

I probably was crying with you on the Turnpike today too!! I got lost trying to find 202 N to the turnpike after leaving a conference in Malvern. I was getting so frustrated and then hit the traffic at Valley Forge exit and with its construction it was a night mare. I nearly got hit in the side. When I got back and read your note it reminded me that: A little cry does us all good! Especially when you know others are with you in the stressful times and in joyful times We will keep praying that HE keeps you strong, JoAnn…

Clare and family
(church family)

CarePage Post March 24, 2007, at 11:12 a.m. EDT

Saturday, Day 19

There is a group at our church called the FTE (Family Time Event) team. They organize various family-oriented events throughout the year. Last year they sponsored our first annual Easter breakfast/egg hunt event. Last year, all proceeds from that event went to a fund for the victims of Hurricane Katrina.

Shortly after this journey began, our friend Tim from the FTE team approached us about this years breakfast and having it as a benefit for Julianna and our family. Our first reaction was to say "no," but we said we would think about it. After realizing that we really don't know what the road ahead is going to bring and what expenses we may incur, we decided to say "yes," with the provision that should we not need to use the funds we would make a donation to CHOP—I have a few ideas already of things I would like to donate—including some real coffee mugs, etc.

Tim suggested that I post this on the CarePage as a good way to let people know about the event. I feel a bit funny about putting this out there since it is benefiting us—I am hoping you all won't mind. As long as Julianna is well, we all plan to be there. Here are the details...

Please join us (and please pass this invitation on)...

Easter Egg Hunt
and
Pancake & Eggs Breakfast

A Benefit for Julianna Smith
Brought to you by
Bucks Central Church of Richboro, PA

Saturday, April 7th, 9–11 am
Northampton Township Senior Center
165 Township Road & Upper Holland Road
Richboro, Pennsylvania

Children should bring a basket for the egg hunt.
The Egg Hunt will begin at 10:30 am.
The Easter Bunny will visit with each child after the egg hunt!

All breakfast proceeds will be donated for the
support of Julianna Smith & the Smith family.
The Smith family are faithful members of our church,
and this benefit will support them while Julianna (age 8)
undergoes treatment for leukemia at Children's Hospital
of Pennsylvania.

Suggested Breakfast Donation: $5 adults, $3 kids

Enjoy a freshly-prepared breakfast,
bring the kids for the egg hunt,
and visit with the Easter bunny!

CarePage Messages

Great News!

Amy March 24, 2007, at 10:28 a.m. EDT

What a relief to hear that the test came back with good news!

Enjoy this beautiful spring day. We are thinking about you!

(school friend)

Great News!!!!

Pauline March 24, 2007, at 11:16 a.m. EDT

Dear Julianna, I am so happy to read your news and that things are going so well. It looks like all the prayers have helped, plus all the love sent your way. It looks like Spring is finally trying to get here. What a wonderful time of year. It sounds like you are able to do some fun things. That makes me happy. I am praying for you and I love you.

Ms. Pauline
(piano teacher)

For Julianna

Monica March 24, 2007, at 12:11 p.m. EDT

Hi Jules

It's a beautiful Spring Day today and as I was listening to the birds this morning and watching the horses on the hill, I thought about you and all the good news that we are hearing. We miss you and think about you all the time—say hello to Jeffrey for us—Can't wait til you are all better so we can see you and give you that big hug and kiss!!

love you—Monica, Dave, and the whole gang!!
(cousin)

Pancakes All Around!

Linda March 24, 2007, at 02:29 p.m. EDT

Happy Saturday!

I was so happy to learn that the blood work results were good yesterday. One day at a time.

My favorite meal of the day is Breakfast! What a wonderful excuse to have pancakes and syrup. I love the idea of sharing a meal for a wonderful reason with some wonderful people.

It is a real challenge to accept help when you are the one used to doing the helping. Thank you for allowing us that opportunity. It lets us to feel that we are doing something tangible to help in this difficult situation.

I didn't write it in my last post but I must say that I laughed out loud when I read about Jules "holding your feet to the fire" with the stuffed chick! Please tell us more anecdotes when you have the opportunity. I know your days are full and unpredictable so again—Thank You for keeping this page updated for us.

Love as always,
Linda and Family
(school friend)

Good News!

Susan March 24, 2007, at 04:49 p.m. EDT Thank God for the good news with Julianna's test and for her time to "sew". JoAnn… it's not whining, it's sharing and you have no idea how I would have handled that situation… very badly. I'm one of those..take her out of Newtown and forget it, except of course LBI! Hope to talk to you soon.

Love,
Sue
(church friend)

Hi Everyone

Tina March 25, 2007, at 05:14 a.m. EDT

Dear Julianna, Jeffrey, JoAnn, and Brian,

Hi, I've been meaning to get in touch sooner, but I just recieved my mom's email about these CarePages today so I checked it out as soon as I could. I wish I was a little closer to home so I could come see you guys but I guess it's kind of impossible for about another year. I've been trying to get some Japan souvenirs together to send but I don't get too much time to shop (work *all* the time!!)but I'll get around to it soon. Just wanted you to know I was thinking about you guys and I'm praying for you Julianna! I hope you feel better. By the way, how's your chick doing? I love my stuffed animals, too… I have 4 now! Well hang in there guys, I miss you!

Love, Tina
(family friend)

I Love Breakfast!!

Amy March 25, 2007, at 06:48 p.m. EDT

Hi to all! What a great idea! We would love to attend the breakfast and egg hunt!!
    Talk to you soon!

(school friend)

Too Old for the Bunny?

Deborah Finn March 25, 2007, at 07:34 p.m. EDT

I thought I was too old for the Easter Bunny until I learned he'd be hoppin' for Julianna. I'm looking forward to high-fivin' that big-eared furball. See you at the breakfast!

Bruce, founding Pastor of Bucks Central Church, on behalf of Debbie, Karrie, Brian and Kelly

Annie Will Be There!

Donna March 25, 2007, at 09:42 p.m. EDT

Julianna,

What fun! We can't wait for the breakfast and the easter egg hunt! Get ready…we are pretty good at the "hunt" thanks for letting us know!

Donna & Annie
(school friend)

Sending Love...

Erica March 25, 2007, at 10:04 p.m. EDT

Dear Julianna,

Ally's mom told us about your CarePage...what a cool website devoted to the one and only Julianna! We are just thrilled to hear that you are feeling better these days. You are such a beautiful and strong girl. You've been so brave, Julianna.

Jared and I talk about you every day, and he was thrilled to see you at school last week. May you feel stronger every day. Jared has some funny jokes he wants to share with you... keep your eye out for another letter from him this week!

With love,
Mrs. C (and Jared, too!)
(school friend)

It's Good to Be Home

Laurie March 26, 2007, at 11:16 a.m. EDT

Julianna,

Ken and I are so glad you are home and getting better every day! And always remember to hold your mom and dad to their promises!!!!

Love, Laurie & Ken
(family friend)

Happy Monday, Julianna

Lynne March 26, 2007, at 01:42 p.m. EDT

I just wanted to drop you a short note to let you know that now, in addition to all the people from our very big parish praying for you, the people from Our Lady of Lourdes in

Lancaster, PA are praying for you too. Aunt Carolyn and I visited some friends there this weekend, and we brought Cara & Mia too, so they could see their Mommy and Daddy. What a loud weekend we had, 5 barking dogs and 4 laughing goofy adults. Everyone is starting to have a little fun, now that you are home. We love you, and we will visit soon. I have a bit of the sniffles, so I am staying away, but only physically. I am with you in spirit all the time!

CarePage Post March 27, 2007, at 10:01 a.m. EDT

Tuesday, Day 22

We had a busy weekend so I have not had time to write—sorry Rachel. (Rachel is my friend from church who told me on Sunday that she is "addicted" to this Care Page. She said she is checking every hour to see if I have written anything.) We had a good laugh about it, but the truth is that I really enjoy writing these—so it is nice to know people enjoy reading them.

Julianna has been feeling well—just the usual tiredness. She got to go to "Dilly's" this weekend—which is a great little hamburger stand near the Delaware River. It just recently opened for the season—and they have the best curly fries with cheese. It is kind of a famous place in this area and one of our favorites. If I make it back and forth to King of Prussia today without getting lost—I may take her there for a treat afterwards. Oh, did I mention they also have really, really good soft-serve ice cream??

Sunday we went to a family birthday party on Brian's side. We have 5 birthdays in February/March among the immediate family of cousins and aunts. Julianna and Jeffrey have 3 new cousins—so it was like musical babies at the party. I was in a bit of a funk that afternoon. Jeffrey and I had gone to church in the morning which was emotional for me to see everyone—in a good way. Interestingly enough, my take away from the sermon was

"God is not your last resort—but should be your 1st resort." Also, the notes in my Bible from a previous sermon said that we should please God in our lives on a daily basis—even through hardship. I decided this is definitely easier said than done, but it certainly was good for me to be reminded of this.

Julianna has many friends at school, and this year there are 3 girls in her class that are her special pals. I think I may have mentioned them before—they are Cailyn, Ally, and Annie. We decided that yesterday—Monday—Julianna would wear a "fundana" on her head to school since her hair is starting to fall out. A friend had sent Julianna 2 of these fundana's and they are adorable!! They are basically a better designed bandana for full coverage. Julianna was going to wear one that has Hershey kisses and red lips all over it. Cailyn's Mom, Linda, suggested we bring Julianna and Cailyn to lunch at their favorite place "Catherines" and then Julianna and Cailyn could walk into school together for the afternoon wearing their fundana/scarf accessories. Julianna is still only going to school ½ days. When we showed up at the restaurant, even Linda was wearing a bandana—it was black and white and was actually a pirate bandana—yes I believe she is a huge Johnny Depp/Pirates fan. Anyway, we had a fun lunch. Getting into the car to go to school Julianna had a huge smile on her face. I said to Linda these are the moments I live for these days– to see Julianna smile. When Julianna came home from school she said Ally and Annie were also both wearing bandanas. How cool is that!!!! What a great day.

5

We Are "Normal"

CarePage Post March 28, 2007, at 02:06 p.m. EDT

Wednesday, Day 23

I just wanted to fill you all in on yesterday. First, we made it to King of Prussia and back without getting lost. That was very exciting, but don't think it means I am set, because given my directionally-challenged brain I can still get lost the next time. Julianna, who it turns out I did scare on our last trip when I was screaming into the phone at Brian in a complete panic, said "Mom, to go home the *right* way, you go *right*." OK then.

We did go to Dilly's as her treat, which is the only way I could talk her through the IV. The truth is it just isn't fun being a human pin cushion, and trust me, it isn't fun being the Mom of a human pin cushion either. They did discuss with me that they are going to put a "port" in for the next phase. They will do that under sedation either in her upper arm or chest, and then they just put numbing cream there and can administer the meds that way. One of the nurses said the kids really prefer it.

The social worker from CHOP is going to Julianna's school today to talk to her class about leukemia. At first I was resistant to this, but since they keep telling me how this is going to be a 2-3 year process, and lots of "stuff" happens, and her doctor was raving about what a great presentation this is for the kids, I decided to say "yes." The focus of the school counselor with the kids has been "how to be a good friend to Julianna," and this will be the same focus.

I had a long talk with the social worker and it turns out everything Brian and I are feeling these days is normal. That was re-assuring. We are both still in a "fog" and there are times, like while driving, that I question if this is really happening—normal. Most days I can't even do things like read the newspaper because I really don't care about things like the Iraq war at the moment— normal. (All right, I do have to admit I read about the autopsy results of Anna Nicole—I am sorry, and I shouldn't be admitting this, but that is still fascinating to me—9 different prescription drugs in her system!!!) Some days we are really not in the mood to make "small talk" with people—normal. The social worker did say that most people, within a few months, do "recover" from all this and this just becomes part of who we are. Please pray this will happen for us sooner rather than later.

Tuesday April 3rd is Julianna's next appt. It is scheduled for 10:00am for a spinal tap and bone marrow biopsy. This is easy on her because she is sedated. I have sat through 2 of these so far— they are excruciating for me. Please pray that all will go smoothly for all of us. It will take about a week for the full pathology results, but we should have preliminary results that same day. Please pray, pray, pray for good results.

I did learn yesterday that the correct terminology is that Julianna is "on her way to remission." Apparently, they like to use the word remission as a way to give families hope. I can't remember how the doc at CHOP exactly worded it because I was stunned to be even hearing the word at that point, but I know now that she is "headed for remission."

Let me end today with this: For the 3 weeks that my Mom ran the Smith household—which does include keeping up with Jeffrey—she lost 10 pounds. Brian and I were thinking that if people are interested we could take applications to sign up for the "Manage the Smith House Weight Loss Plan."

CarePage Messages

Wazzzzzzup Is In The House

Marie March 28, 2007, at 08:35 a.m. EDT

Julianna,

Uncle Eddie, Aunt Marie and Boomer are all pulling for you.

I love your Web Site—you must be really special.

I'm so sorry we couldn't make it to the birthday's. I am working every weekend now and it has made it tough on party's. I was reading about your "chick" and can't wait to see it. But I think I would have asked for a real one. Or two.

Aunt Marie, Uncle Eddie & Boomer

Bandanas All Around

Linda March 28, 2007, at 09:05 a.m. EDT

Happy Wednesday!

I hope that yesterdays treatment went well and that Julianna is not too tired again.

I know that Cailyn, Ally, Annie and Honor were all thrilled to wear bandanas and scarves to support their friend on Monday. It is rare that we (well at least I) have the opportunity to wear all the scarves that have been collected over the years. I love the idea of wearing them to let Julianna know just how very much we are with her in her work to get to the other side of this diagnosis.

Hopefully more kids will join in and we'll get a chance to see some wonderful styles of scarves and bandanas!

Take care,
Love from Linda and Family
(school friend)

Send The Application

Monica March 28, 2007, at 03:01 p.m. EDT

Send me an application—I've been trying to drop 10 pounds for over a year now.

Love you Julianna
(cousin)

Happy Wednesday, Julianna

Lynne March 28, 2007, at 03:52 p.m. EDT

Well, I guess I can take about 10 of those weeks, and then I will (maybe) be ready for shorts this summer! Sign me up! and *good job* on giving mommy directions. She can use a co-pilot, we all can.

Love you,
Aunt Lynne

April 3rd—Got It!

Stephanie March 28, 2007, at 04:11 p.m. EDT

Hello, dear friends! It's wonderful to be able to stay in touch this way. I've got April 3rd 10AM on my prayer calendar! And please know, that if I was anywhere in the area I'd be getting one of those applications!

Love to you all!
Steph (family friend)

Any Time You Need Me!

Jeannie March 28, 2007, at 05:42 p.m. EDT

Hello Smith family,

We are so glad things are moving along positively! Any time you need me for anything, especially the weight loss program I am available, just give a call. I'm sure you will get those directions down perfectly as long as you have Julianna for a co-pilot. We will keep the prayers coming your way. Thanks for the update.

All our love, Jeannie & Bruce
(family friend)

Sign Me Up!!

Amy March 28, 2007, at 06:08 p.m. EDT

I could really use a weight lose program like that!!
    We were so glad to hear that things went well on Tuesday. Give me a call if you ever want company for the drive!! Allison is looking forward to Julianna being in school for lunch and recess on Thursday. We are sending prayers and love your way!!

Amy and Family
(school friend)

CarePage Post March 29, 2007, at 09:05 p.m. EDT

Thursday, Day 24

I just wanted to write a quick update tonight because I have a few things to share. First, as it turns out Julianna is not going to be going to school full days. She is very tired and when I discussed it with the doctor on Tuesday we agreed that 1/2 days for now is all she can really handle. So we have a tutor coming in the morning for just an hour and then she goes to school at 1:00. I do have to admit it is nice not having to wake up to an alarm these days. We are going to keep this schedule for the next few weeks anyway.

Yesterday I got an email from Julianna's teacher saying the following: Some impressive news… I just wanted to let you know that Julianna scored a 99% on the third grade computation task for our portfolios—she missed a 1/2 point for labeling an answer incorrectly! I am so proud of her hard work and she was thrilled, too. (Mom is proud too!! and relieved that we are staying on track with school.)

In the same email her teacher said the number of bandana wearers continues to grow and even a boy wore one yesterday. It turns out the kids are just being so sweet. Many third graders are wearing bandanas or scarves—not just the girls in Julianna's class. (There are 3 third grade classes.) Today I even saw another third grader on the bus wearing one. How blessed we are to be part of a school with such sweet and wonderful kids.

I am off to bed—Jeffrey started yesterday with a fever, cough, and sore throat. At 6:00am this morning he came to get me. He was crying because he didn't feel good and he said he was having a heart attack. He is definitely not the easy-going patient Julianna is. So please pray for his quick recovery, and please pray that the rest of us stay healthy.

Good night…

CarePage Messages

Hi JoAnn

Susan March 29, 2007, at 08:48 a.m. EDT

JoAnn, I just wanted to take a minute and tell you I'm with Rachel and "tune in" to your CarePage basically everyday to check and see how you are all doing.

Love, Sue
(church family)

Smiles…

Erica March 29, 2007, at 10:20 p.m. EDT

JoAnn,

Thank you for sharing Jeffrey's heart attack comment…I literally laughed out loud when I read it.

Jared came home from school and said it is National Bandana Month in honor of Julianna;-) He will be wearing one tomorrow. I'm glad to hear it raises her spirits, too.

Erica
(school friend)

From Basketball Maggie's Mom

Suzy March 30, 2007, at 06:13 a.m. EDT

JoAnn and Julianna, Maggie and I too are reading your updates all the time! Wow! What an effect you are having on our world Juliana! Maggie has become an expert on leukemia. Mostly she just tells people about how God is taking such wonderful care of her teammate from hoops. JoAnn, you are daily in my prayers. Your writing is wonderful. We are keeping Jeffrey and Brian up in prayer too. Even though we just got to know you, you are in our hearts. Your sister in *Christ*, the tie that binds us all together.

Suzy
(family friend)

Jeffrey is Still *Too Funny!*

Lynne March 30, 2007, at 12:16 p.m. EDT

Hi there, and happy Friday! Please tell Jeffrey that he is in our prayers so he will be getting better just like his sister. That's too much funny! (hope he gets the pun!)

Love to all, and hope to see you next Saturday,
Aunt Lynne

Hi Julianna!

Anna March 31, 2007, at 10:54 a.m. EDT

Hi Juliana,

Just sending you my love and kisses.

Grandma Vivian was just giving me an up-date.

Glad to read that you did so well on your portfolio work.

Tell mom, dad, and Jeffrey—I am keeping you in my daily prayers.

Love to all,
Cousin Anna

p.s. Christie and her husband, Louis, might be able to come for the Pancake Breakfast because it is only a short distance from their house in Huntingdon Valley.:)

Hello to the Smith Family

Beth March 31, 2007, at 04:44 p.m. EDT

Dear JoAnn, Brian, Julianna, and Jeffry,

Thank you so much for keeping us updated. We think of you often and are glad to hear that Julianna is able to go to school. I was also thrilled to learn that they have such stylish hats or scarves now. I have to wear a hat at all times while working in the operating room and some of the styles and fabrics are so much fun now. I can just imagine the pretty designs you have to choose from. We will hold you in our thoughts for this coming Tuesday. I am so glad to hear that Julianna will receive sedation for her tests. Take care and thanks again for keeping us posted.

Love,

Beth, John, Hayley, and Jenna

Hello From Buckingham

Leeann April 01, 2007, at 09:41 p.m. EDT

Hello, Julianna,

I just wanted to send you a little message to let you know that you are in my thoughts and prayers. Mrs. H and Mrs. F keep us all updated on the excellent progress you are making. And the representative from CHOP did a great job when she spoke with our third grade class. We are all so very proud of you! You are a brave and strong little girl. It is just delightful to see you back at Buckingham. Your third grade friends in my class get very excited when they know you're coming. And they just love supporting you by wearing bandanas too:) You have fabulous little friends and a marvelous mommy too. I can't help but notice how big her smile is every time she brings you in to school.

Hugs & Kisses, Mrs. S
(third grade teacher)

6

The Infamous Kidney Stone

CarePage Post April 02, 2007, at 11:21 a.m. EDT

Monday, Day 27

OK, brace yourselves. You will not believe the weekend we had. Let me start with telling you that on the way to the hospital for the first time I was trying to tell Julianna that we should look at this like an adventure. She was totally not buying it. I am sure she thinks of an adventure as something fun and that is why I couldn't convince her. Even during our stay at the hospital, when something would happen, I would say, "see this is part of our adventure." When we got home, she was still not convinced, so I looked up the definition of adventure. Here it is, according to Webster's: 1 a: an undertaking involving danger and unknown risks b: the encountering of risks 2: an exciting or remarkable experience 3: an enterprise involving financial risk...

So on Friday night, Julianna kept waking up and saying crazy things kind of very fast and as if she was delirious. I would calm her down and she would sometimes cry because she was aware of what she was doing but couldn't stop. I called the oncology doc at 2:00am and was told that the meds can cause this "mind-altering state" especially at night. Some kids react more with moodiness, but this is also a side effect. They said as long as I could calm her down to just ride it out and watch her carefully the next day. I did figure out that if I hugged her tight and sang to her she calmed down immediately. I think we had our last episode at around 3:00am.

Needless to say we stayed very calm and quiet on Saturday. The kids babysitter, Jessica, came over for a nice visit, and we all loved seeing her. We introduced her to Dilly's fries because we had some that we brought home and I have a feeling when Jules feels better that her and Jess will be making a lot of Dilly runs.

Saturday night we all slept fine!! Halleluiah!! Sunday morning while walking from one room to another, Julianna started to cry in pain from lower back pain. I immediately called oncology at CHOP. I spoke to a nurse and they were suspicious of a urinary tract infection. She started to show other symptoms so I called CHOP again, and they said we better head down and get her checked out. Luckily we have great friends and neighbors who were able to care for Jeffrey for us.

We were at CHOP most of the day. She really wouldn't eat. She was so exhausted she could hardly keep her eyes open. They ran all kinds of tests. Of course they had trouble getting an IV in her and she was pricked in 2 different places and they kept going in and out. They finally had to call in the "IV Team" who used a special light and the IV went in quite quickly. This of course raises the question of why the IV Team just doesn't do all the IV's to begin with. I will be asking this question tomorrow and will let you know the answer. All the tests actually came back fine. No UTI, her blood counts are really looking good. There is no reason to admit us, they finish giving her the fluids through the IV, and they send us home. Her back pain continues but all her other symptoms have gone away.

She was up every hour on the hour through the night due to all the fluids she had received. We are totally relaxing today and hope to have an uneventful day. For all our "prayer warriors" out there, please pray for calm days and nights, and please pray for strength for all of us—mine is definitely slipping and I need a boost. And don't forget about the prayer we need for tomorrow. Specifically pray for the nurses and doctors and the precision they need to perform these procedures.

As for this "adventure"—no matter what Julianna says, I think our experiences to date really reflect that definition... but I wish they didn't.

CarePage Messages

Monday Message

Linda April 02, 2007, at 12:59 p.m. EDT

OK. Adventure seems to be the word that fits here. Good luck trying to "sell" that to Julianna!

Thank you for the update on your weekend—you've been in our thoughts and prayers. I'm so happy that she did not have to be admitted to CHOP and was able to come home. Hopefully you all are taking it easy today and getting some much deserved rest. It is supposed to be a lovely afternoon with great temperatures so enjoy a seat out on your patio with a nice cuppa something and relax:-)

Getting past tomorrow will be a great relief. Hopefully you'll get your roadmap for the next phase and it won't be an unknown anymore. Prayers for an uneventful day are coming your way! As always, you're on our minds so if you need something that we can provide, please let us know. One day at a time is the phrase that comes to mind despite the road map. Do what you can—one day at a time.

Looking forward to good results tomorrow:-)

Much love,
(school friend)

Prayers And Thoughts

Monica April 02, 2007, at 03:09 p.m. EDT

Hi guys

Whew…that was some weekend. I'm sure glad everything calmed down—Thank you God!! We'll all be with you tomorrow in thought and prayer—keep us posted—

Love you Jules—
Monica and everybody!!!
(cousin)

Hi There Julianna

Lynne April 02, 2007, at 03:30 p.m. EDT

I just wanted to let you know we are rooting for you tomorrow, as we do every day. Please stay strong. So sorry you had a rough weekend, let's hope that is the end of that and it is smooth from now on.

Hugs and kisses,
Aunt Lynne, Aunt Carolyn, Mia & Cara

What An Adventure!

Amy April 02, 2007, at 04:04 p.m. EDT

I hope that you will not have an adventure like that for a long time! We will be praying for quiet days and nights and that all will go as planned on Tuesday!! Just try to remember that your friends are out there, thinking about all of you and sending good thoughts your way.
    Love from the Fells

Hugs and kisses from Allison!!!!
(school friend)

Hello to the Smith's

Jeannie April 02, 2007, at 07:06 p.m. EDT

Thanks for the update! We will just keep praying for more positive adventures. Keep your chins up and hopefully the weekends to come will be brighter. Thanks for sharing these moments with us.

Love to all, Jeannie & Bruce
(family friend)

CarePage Post April 03, 2007, at 08:02 p.m. EDT

Tuesday, Day 28

Yes! Yes! Yes! Today's preliminary results from the bone marrow test look very good—the marrow looks clear of all leukemia cells—this what we hoped and prayed for. We will have the "full pathology" report in a few days, but they like to at least tell you how things look initially.

Julianna did so well today through the procedure. Of course the worst of it was trying to find a vein that is not bruised, beaten, or broken. That took quite some time and was a bit stressful. When they finally got it done, I said to her I would go buy her whatever she wanted. She asked for a hot dog from Target and a new bathing suit. On the way home, I got her exactly those 2 things. This reminds me that one of the nurse practitioners last week was talking to me about not over-indulging Julianna through this process. I can't remember why we got on this topic of conversation, but I had to bite my tongue. At the moment, I will pretty much give Julianna whatever she asks for. I laugh to myself almost every morning as I watch her lick whipped cream off her plate like a puppy dog. Things I would *never* let her do before are now everyday events. I am sure at some point we may need to back off on this a bit.

So, I was not planning to actually sit it on today's procedures. I thought I would just stay until they sedated her and then leave the room, but Julianna really wanted me to stay. Brian left the room even before they sedated her—we do not allow him near anything after the shower curtain incident. Julianna was actually awake through most of the procedures today which was quite interesting. She chatted with the nurses about the beach because the procedure room is totally painted in a beach scene—it is actually very cool. Anyway, it all went very smoothly. I just love the nurses and her doctor at King of Prussia. I can't tell you how much they just care and are good at what they do.

We both had a nice nap today, and are actually just about to eat a late dinner, so I am signing off for now. Thank you all—we truly gain strength when we know that all the people who care about us are sending thoughts and prayers our way. I even said to Julianna at 10:00 that probably 5,000 people were praying for her at that moment—I know she loves hearing things like that, so thanks for being there for us.

CarePage Messages

Every Single Day<3

Jenna April 03, 2007, at 12:44 a.m. EDT

Hello there…sorry I didn't leave a message sooner. I just wanted to say hi to the family and let you know that you are in my prayers every single day. I hope that things continue to look up for you. I hope to see you on Saturday, I miss you all very much. I also must say I looove the canopy over Julianna's bed:)

"Angels are watching over you
when times are good or stressed.

Their wings wrap gently around you,
whispering you are loved and blessed."

Love, Jenna
(family friend)

Prayers And Luck For Today

Donna April 03, 2007, at 07:18 a.m. EDT

Just wanted to let you know that the we are praying for all of you...for rest, calm, comfort and skill (on the part of the doc's and nurses). Good luck today...

By the way we are also praying for a clear and easy path to King of Prussia...

Annie sends lots of hugs to you Jules!

Donna and Annie
(school friend)

I Am Praying For You

Kim April 03, 2007, at 11:59 a.m. EDT

I just wanted to drop a note to let you know that I am praying for you all. I pray that you get the sleep that you need JoAnn and Julianna too. I know that at this time it is impossible to see the Lord working in all of this but He is and one day I pray that you can all look back at this time and be able to see the blessings. Right now there is so much stress, fatigue, fear etc. I pray that the Love of God would just hold you up and surround your family and that you would feel His peace. He is in control and we must just trust in Him. I pray for you all to get some much needed rest and I pray that your day goes smoothly.

Love,
Kim and Family
(cousin)

Always Praying

Jessica April 03, 2007, at 05:01 p.m. EDT

I really enjoyed seeing you guys over the weekend! I missed everyone so much. I am looking forward to a Dilly's trips too!

I am praying for Julianna today like always. I hope everything goes well.

See you this week hopefully!

lots of love,
Jess (babysitter)

Happy Tuesday Night

Linda April 03, 2007, at 09:34 p.m. EDT

:-)

I am grinning. So very happy to hear the preliminary results. Cailyn left the house with her prayer intentions today and I'm sure that around 10am we all bowed our heads and prayed. Storming heaven once again! I hope that you have a restful night and a peaceful day tomorrow.

I'm sending big huge happy cyber hugs your way!

Love from our family
(school friend)

Yee Haw!!!!

Virginia April 03, 2007, at 10:56 p.m. EDT

That's wonderful news! We're so happy we can't stand it! Much, much love coming your way from Newtown.

Jules, Virginia, Guy, and Wilbur
(pastor)

Wonderful!

Donna April 04, 2007, at 07:22 a.m. EDT

Yahoo! Well obviously all the thousands of prayers are working!!!

I am so happy that your "adventure" has taken a very positive note. Julianna you are such an amazing little girl... do you think maybe you got it from your Mom?

Annie is still sleeping but I know this news will put a big smile on her face!!! Lots of love and big hugs are comin your way!

We will continue to keep you in our prayers...

Donna and Family
(school friend)

You are a Princess

Marie April 04, 2007, at 08:24 a.m. EDT

Brian, Jo, Juliana & Jeffrey

We're all praying for you!

And Juliana you are so courageous. I know how hard it is for you but you are doing a great job. Keep up the good work. I love your Princess Bed.

Aunt Marie, Uncle Eddie, Boomer,
Anthony & Louise

Fantastic!!!

Amy April 04, 2007, at 08:32 a.m. EDT

Allison and I were reading this together this morning and are so happy!!!! God is smiling this morning!!
    Have a great day!!

Love, Amy & Family
Hugs and kisses from Allison!!!!!!!
(school friend)

Great News

Laurie April 04, 2007, at 09:26 a.m. EDT

What great news! We are so happy everything went well yesterday. Our thoughts and prayers continue.

Love you. Laure & Ken
(family friend)

Great News!

Maryann April 04, 2007, at 09:40 a.m. EDT

Hi Julianna,

What wonderful news! Thinking about you & keeping you in our prayers!

JoAnn,

Enjoy reading your updates!

Love,
Maryann, Mike, Carolyn, Laura & Michael
(cousin)

Finally Figured Out The CarePage!!!

Diane April 04, 2007, at 10:51 a.m. EDT

Whoaaaaa!!!! What great news! We will keep praying and wishing for the best days!

Love, Diane W and Family
(school friend)

Praise Be To God!

Mary April 04, 2007, at 11:15 a.m. EDT

Hi Jo, Julianna, Brian & Jeffrey...

Mr. L & I are so happy for you, Julianna, about your preliminary results. You are such a brave girls with all the "sticks." We continue to pray for God's strength for you and painless ways for the nurses and docs to care for you. Resurrection Sunday Blessings,

Mrs. L
(family friend)

Hello from Pauline and Tiffy

Pauline April 04, 2007, at 11:40 a.m. EDT

Dear Julianna, I don't know what happened to my first message, but it just never happened. It's a very rainy day, which isn't too bad, but I don't like the cold. I send you a really big Hug and Tiffy sends you a big Lick. She is not happy about the rain because her tummy is so close to the ground that she gets all wet. I want to wish you a wonderful Easter and also Jeffrey and your Mom and Dad. I am praying for you and know that you will be just fine. I am having my family pray for you, and they are about 52 people. I am one of eight children and one of my sisters,

Ruth, has 10 children. Take care and know that I Love you Julianna and I Miss Seeing You!

> Pauline and Tif too
> (piano teacher)

Thankful

Ann April 04, 2007, at 11:53 a.m. EDT

Good morning! Just a note to say that we are very thankful that the initial results from yesterday are promising. We kept you in our thoughts and prayers throughout the day. Melissa and so many others continue to wear their bandanas every day-even when you are not able to be in school, Julianna. Have a restful day and know that we care and are very proud of all that you and your family are doing each and every day.

> Fondly, Ann and Family
> (school friend)

Praise God!

Lynne April 04, 2007, at 01:52 p.m. EDT

What wonderful news! We are beyond happy. Like happy squared; no, make that happy cubed. on third thought, happy to the nth power, yeah that's more like it...
    We will continue to pray and give thanks!

Stay brave and keep smiling!!

> all our love, Aunt Lynne
> and Aunt Carolyn, Cara & Mia

Happy Day!

Jeannie April 04, 2007, at 11:46 p.m. EDT

Julianna,

It sounds like your doing a great job! Your mom and dad should be extra proud of you. We will keep praying for many more happy days to come.

All our love, Jeannie & Bruce
(family friend)

Go Jules!!!!

Jean April 05, 2007, at 07:31 a.m. EDT

Yeah Aunt Jean figured this message thing out. I love these care pages. I am up to date and don't have to bother you with phone calls. We are all praying for you. We love you!!! Oh and Julianna I would shoot big at this point when you want things go for it girl I doubt your Mom will say no. Morgan sends her love as do Meagan and Mandy. We are thrilled that your tests are turning out so well. *We* are here if you need us!!! *LOVE YOU!!!*

Aunt Jean

Yippee!!!!!

Chris April 05, 2007, at 10:03 p.m. EDT

Glad to hear the great news on the test results. You are one brave girl. We are so happy for you. We will continue to keep you in our prayers.

Chrissy, Jim, Nicole and Katie
(family friend)

CarePage Post April 08, 2007,
at 05:24 p.m. EDT

Easter Greetings from 3S06—Oncology Unit at Children's Hospital. Certainly not where we would like to be spending Easter Sunday—but here we are. The truth for me is that based on some things that were happening at home—I am actually happy to be here—turning all this over to the experts is a relief for me. I understand we had an amazing turnout at the Pancake Breakfast yesterday. Most people have been using the word "heartwarming" to describe it. I cannot begin to tell you the disappointment for me and Julianna to miss it. We were on our way there, but ended up at the ER instead. Thank you all for your show of support. I hope to hear all about it in detail and maybe see some pictures soon.

As for what's going on... First the good news, Julianna is officially "in remission." I double-checked the terminology with the doctor this time. This is very good news and the best outcome of the first phase of treatment. We still have a long road ahead, but we can feel positive about her initial response to treatment. As for why we are here, Julianna has had some pain issues that are not resolving, she has had more of those mind-altering episodes, and today she is developing a fever. We spent 11 hours in the ER yesterday—horrible, horrible, horrible!!!!! But at midnight last night we got comfortable here in a room that is at least familiar to us. She has undergone some tests and will undergo more today and tomorrow. Things are checking out good—which is good on one hand—but doesn't help to figure out the issues she is having. As always, the docs here are confident we will get to the bottom of this all.

All right all our prayer warriors—here we go. Please pray for strength for all of us—even Julianna, my "trooper," is starting to break down a bit. Please pray for peace of mind for Julianna through all these tests. Please pray the docs figure all this out and can easily fix things. Please pray that our road ahead would be smooth and we would have continued good results. And, of course, please pray for anything else that you think would help us. I will keep you all updated as I am able.

CarePage Messages

Happy Easter

Linda April 08, 2007, at 02:10 p.m. EDT

Happy Easter Smith Family:-)

I hope that you are enjoying a restful Easter Sunday. You've been on our minds these past few days. Yesterday we had a lovely time at your church breakfast. I saw a bunch of folks with cameras taking pictures so I'm sure that you will get to see these snipits from the day soon. Your pastor is such a wonderful speaker. He said a lovely prayer—"after breakfast grace" I think he called it. He said such wonderful things about Julianna. We all had positive thoughts being sent your way about that time.

I hope that things are settling down a bit and that you're not in the middle of more "adventure."

Have a blessed Easter and know that you are never far from our thoughts and prayers.

Love from Linda and family
(school friend)

Prayers For Comfort And Strength!

Donna April 08, 2007, at 08:19 p.m. EDT

Hi Guys—

Well…we are so happy about the news of 100% "remission" but our hearts ache for all the pain and discomfort you are going through right now…

Our prayers are focused on comfort, strength and as swift a path through this as possible!

Big hugs and lots of love from Annie!

All our love and prayers.

Donna and Family
(school friend)

Happy Easter

Liz April 08, 2007, at 08:20 p.m. EDT

Dear Jules

Happy Easter...I wish you were home, but I know you will be soon. You are constantly in our prayers and our thoughts. We love you.

Love, Aunt Liz,
Uncle Andy, Jake, Tea and Nathan
(family friend)

Sunday Night

Linda April 08, 2007, at 10:07 p.m. EDT

Thank you so much for updating us all in the middle of this adventure of yours. I kinda had a feeling...I'm sure that it is a great comfort and relief to have the doctors and nurses at CHOP looking out for you. Hopefully you don't have to think as hard trying to figure out what to do next like at home at 3AM!

Remember that we are off until Thursday. If there is anything that we can do—any of us—name it. If company would help, let us know. We would be happy to bring a treat down and sit for a while. Whatever you think would be helpful. In the meantime, we are saying our prayers for your strength, Jules comfort and the docs wisdom to figure out what is going on so you can come back home.

We love and miss you,
Linda and family
(school friend)

CarePage Post April 09, 2007, at 07:52 p.m. EDT

So, the plot thickens here at 3South. We found out at 9:30 last night that Julianna has a kidney stone. It's small, it has worked its way close to her bladder, and as of last night I thought we were going to wait and let it pass. The team of urologists just left—it was very much like a Grey's Anatomy episode—all different levels of docs stand around and the attending doc asks questions and they feel her back and tell him what they think it is, etc. The feeling now is that they are afraid to let it go because they don't want bacteria backing up behind it—that could be dangerous for her. So—if it doesn't pass on its own—they will have to do a procedure tomorrow to help it along. P*lease, please pray* that it passes tonight or tomorrow morning first thing. I really don't want her to have to get another procedure.

She had her first MRI today. They set her up with headphones and a movie. I thought we were going to be fine. She stayed still for the entire hour. After we went into a waiting area for the nurse to come get us she started crying. She said they forgot for a long time to hit the "play" button on the DVD and she was just staring at the first screen of the movie for a long time. Of course, at the time she couldn't tell us. Uuuggghhhh!!!! When we told her nurse on the floor what happened, she went and grabbed Julianna all kind of movies to watch in her room. They did say everything preliminarily looks good though. We are hoping at this point that the "episodes" were triggered by the pain from the kidney stone. Even the male doctor said that women who get kidney stones say it is worse than childbirth.

Julianna is also getting her first blood transfusion tonight. Her platelet count has gone below where it needs to be. This is apparently very common for kids like her. But it's another thing I need to swallow.

I am feeling very sick to my stomach these days. Please continue to pray for us all.

CarePage Messages

Our Prayers Are With You

Carol April 09, 2007, at 09:02 a.m. EDT

So glad to hear you are in remission and we have been praying for strength for you through all those tests. We pray the doctors will find the root of these problems also and that you will be home soon.

Carol & Bob
(family friend)

Always In Our Prayers!

Jeannie April 09, 2007, at 09:32 a.m. EDT

We are all so very happy to hear the word remission. We are all praying that Julianna moves past the troubles she is having swiftly. Be strong and keep doing what you are doing. Your strength is definitely shinning through.

All our Love, Jeannie & Bruce
(family friend)

Praise & Prayer for Julianna

Mary April 09, 2007, at 11:08 a.m. EDT

Julianna, JoAnn & Family,

An old hymn of faith speaks words of encouragement far greater than I can ever say, so my message to you all is from it:

What A Friend We Have In Jesus...

Have we trials and temptations? Is there trouble anywhere?...(2a)

Are you weak and heavy laden encumbered with a load of care?...(3a)

Can we find a Friend so faithful who will all your sorrows share?..(2b)

In His arms He'll take and shield you, you will find a solace there...(3b)

We praise the Lord for the word "remission" and continue to pray for you all, knowing God is the great Physician equipping your doctors to "do their thing!"

Lovingly,
Mary and family
(family friend)

Thinking Of You:)

Diane April 09, 2007, at 11:17 a.m. EDT

We are so thankful to know you are in remission!!!!We know you will get through this tough time like a true hero. We will keep praying that each day gets easier for you! Peace and Happiness,

Diane W and Family
(school friend)

Thinking Of You!!

Amy April 09, 2007, at 03:00 p.m. EDT

Our prayers are with you!! Allison is sending a big hug you way! Stay strong. If there is anything that we can help you with, just yell our way!

Love Amy and Family
(school friend)

Praying

Jessica April 09, 2007, at 08:47 p.m. EDT

I was very sad to hear that you guys were back in the hospital. I am praying that things go well.

I came across this Irish Blessing the other day and it made me think of you, so I thought I would send it your way...

May God give you...
  For every storm, a rainbow,
  For every tear, a smile,
  For every care, a promise,
  And a blessing in each trial.
  For every problem life sends,
  A faithful friend to share,
  For every sigh, a sweet song,
  And an answer for each prayer.
  Hope to see you soon and I hope you start feeling better!
  I love and miss you so much,

Jess (babysitter)

Prayers & More Prayers

Barbara April 09, 2007, at 09:23 p.m. EDT

JoAnn & Julianna,

You are in my prayers every night, but I will add the daytime too. I tend to look at the postings as the glass half full. I only see answers to questions and positive feedback. Keep looking for the good answers and they will come.

All my Love,
Cousin Barbara

Monday Night

Linda April 09, 2007, at 09:30 p.m. EDT

Hey there friends,

So…a kidney stone. Yup that really hurts. I've had two and they are painful. I slept through the first (had the procedure) and passed the second on my own. Do they have any idea why she made a kidney stone? Is that a side effect of the disease /treatment or is it a coincidence and it's totally unrelated…I wonder.

We will continue with prayers for strength for your family. The wisdom for the doctors prayer worked! At least you know what's going on and what needs to happen.

Again—remember that we are available for whatever you need. Just let us know and we'll be there—OK?

Prayers are on the way all around.

Take care,
Love, Linda and family
(school friend)

PS—Cailyn sends cyber hugs to Jules:-)

Sending Positive Reinforcement

April 09, 2007, at 10:18 p.m. EDT

Josie—I like to believe I sent strength over the phone the other day & hope it comes over the internet as well. You've all done terrific so far & you have to just keep talking to yourself that better days are coming. All my Angels in Heaven are watching out for us. Don't show Jule you're nervous—take deep breaths (that's why your stomach hurts) and make sure you're eating. Love & big squeeze hugs to you both from Mommy & Pops

Hi!!!!!

Dawn April 09, 2007, at 10:51 p.m. EDT

Hi everyone!!!! Sounds like one thing after another... which makes me so sad for you!!! Continue to hang in there and be strong...it may not seem like it now, but before you know it, this will all be in the past and easier days will be here!!! You are all on my mind continuously!!! And even though I am not a prayer warrior, I do pray for you!!!

Much Love! Cousin Dawn XOXO

Yikes!

Jeannie April 10, 2007, at 12:12 a.m. EDT

Hi Jules,

We are really glad they figured out the problem behind your pain. I want you to know I also had a kidney stone. At times it could be so uncomfortable. I hope things move along quickly and you feel better soon. You just hang in there, you are a real trooper. We love you and are thinking about all of you.

All our love and prayers. Jeannie & Bruce
(family friend)

Praying Every Day...

Christine April 10, 2007, at 05:26 a.m. EDT

Chach (Nickname for JoAnn),

Know that Kevin and I keep you in our prayers every single day... I pray you have the strength of 10,000 women (just how many men that must be equivalent to is amazing!!!!!!)... to be everything you need to be for your precious Julianna... You are stronger than you think... oh, and take deep breaths and eat—like your mom said!!!!!! We love you guys... take care...

Chrissy, Kevin, Abby, and Nathan
(family friend)

Ps. I know we're far away—but you know if there is *anything* you need, we'll do it...

Rock/Stone Collection

Christine April 10, 2007, at 05:32 a.m. EDT

Julianna,

I know you are a very handy girl, but really, making your own stones!!! Have Jeffrey pick up some rocks outside for you if you need to start a collection!!!!! We hope and pray you feel better today... All of us pray for you every day... we want you well...

Love you bunches—Chrissy, Kevin, Abby & Nathan
(family friend)

Wow!

Amy April 10, 2007, at 12:01 p.m. EDT

We are so glad to hear that they found out what was causing the pain! We hope that by the time you read this it
has passed and you are feeling better!! We are sending you
prayers and all of our good thoughts your way! Allison's
bed time prayers are always being sent your way! She is
sending big hugs and much love! We are here if you need
anything at all. Please know that nothing you could ask for
would ever be too much!

Love from Amy and Family
(school friend)

So Sorry!

Donna April 10, 2007, at 12:40 p.m. EDT

We are praying and thinking of you all! You may not see
it clearly yourself (or feel it) because you are in the middle
of it but joann, you are amazingly strong. Jules you are the
sweetest hero we know! Annie's and all our prayers will ask
for more and more strength,,comfort (lots of it) and some
calm for all of you.
  Ditto to what amy said—please yell when we can help
out with anything…nothing is too much to ask.
  Annie Sends Her Hugs And Love!

Donna and Annie
(school friend)

Hang in There

Susan April 10, 2007, at 01:05 p.m. EDT

I'm so glad the doctors finally figured out what was causing
your pain. I've been praying for this! I prayed the minute

I read about the kidney stone and as the other messages posted say.. by the time you read this I hope it's gone! Keep us posted and know the prayers are continuing!

Sue
(church friend)

JoAnn and Julianna

Rose Marie April 10, 2007, at 07:11 p.m. EDT

We are praying for you all the time and have all our friends praying too! We women have a lot of strength and endurance. We can get through anything, *we will get through this, believe me, with the grace of god!!*

We love you and pass on our strength and endurance as well.

Hugs and kisses, Auntie Ro and Uncle Ed

Julianna

Rose Marie April 10, 2007, at 07:14 p.m. EDT

How about that, you have a friend with almost our name!! Wait till I tell Christian. He went to school with a girl whose name was spelled Seese, she grew up in Heights.

Love, Auntie Ro

Stones are not so funny!!!

Marie April 10, 2007, at 07:36 p.m. EDT

Julianna,

You and my Sister, Toni should sit down and write some books. Up and down the hills you both go. Yikes. I'm having trouble just keeping up with the both of you. Toni had two surgeries for her kidney stones and stents for one of them during her pregnancy. I'm so sorry you are going through all of this too.

I sent you a little package at the house, to give you something to do when you're traveling back and forth. I hope you get it soon and like it.

Aunt Marie

Power Of Prayer

Diane April 10, 2007, at 08:23 p.m. EDT

Claire and I just wanted you to know that you can count on us to be your faithful, relentless prayer warriors. We have had lots of "practice" and are honored to hold your entire family up in our daily (several times a day) prayers. We pray for your complete healing, strength and peace and that *God* would surround you with legions and legions of guardian angels. *He* promises to never leave or forsake you!!!! (and *He* never breaks a promise!!!) We love you!

Diane and Claire
(school friend)

Hi Jules

Karen April 10, 2007, at 08:29 p.m. EDT

Hi Jules, Sorry to hear you are back in the hospital, we wish you well and hope to see you at school soon. I hope you liked the teddy bear. Aimee says hi.

Lots of love from Emily
(school friend)

CarePage Post April 11, 2007, at 01:03 p.m. EDT

Just a quick update… all right maybe not so quick as there is a lot to report. Yesterday Julianna added an ultrasound and the operating room to her list of things on this adventure. The stone did not pass. They put a stent in the passage from the kidney to the bladder which is where the stone is currently residing. Hopefully this will open it up enough for the stone to pass. Please keep praying for this to stone to pass. While they had her sedated they performed the other 2 procedures she was going to be having this week—the spinal, and YEAH they put in her port. This is going to make her life so much easier because they will no longer have to go digging around for a good vein to put in an IV. This port can stay in for the next 2 years if necessary. All of this made for a very long day yesterday and she ended up having to go 24 hours without eating. She was so, so hungry and it was so hard for her to have to go all day without eating. Our Pastor sat with Brian and I last night for the 4 hours it ended up taking in the OR—this was such a comfort on so many levels. She did want to eat last night so we were up until midnight eating cereal, and yogurt, and pudding, and beautifully colored Easter eggs—that we colored in the hospital on Monday,

As for the mind altering episodes—she has not had any since Saturday in the ED. (Did you know the ER is now referred to as the ED—Emergency Department, and what I knew as CAT scans are now CT scans—hmmmm.) Anyway, the neurologist (sorry for the Grey's Anatomy reference again—but he could definitely be a McDreamy) said all full reports from the MRI look normal—which is very good, so he and the oncologist are suggesting at this point that the episodes were either pain induced or a reaction of an 8 year old to everything that has been happening. We are letting it go for now.

We had a decent night sleep—probably the best we have actually had in weeks. I let her have potato chips with her breakfast this morning. We are waiting on a few more things and we are actually going home. I am looking forward to putting this one behind us and hopefully having a little bit of a quiet stretch.

Thanks for all the encouraging and funny messages via CarePages. They definitely make me feel "not so alone" in all of this. By the way, for today anyway, my stomach is feeling better.

CarePage Messages

Wednesday AM

Linda April 11, 2007, at 08:11 a.m. EDT

Good morning Smith Family:-)

I hope that this finds you closer to resolving some issues with stones and rocks and the like. It sure would be nice to hear that you are home already—tucked in your own warm bed!!

You are on our minds and in our hearts. Our prayers ask for strength for your whole family to deal with this latest bump and strength for whatever lies ahead. We are so fortunate to have CHOP so close to us and your team sounds like they are skilled and caring. It must be a relief to know that you are in such capable hands.

However—I can feel your stress from here! Is there anything that we can do to help you? Please let us know if there is.

Cailyn is hoping to see Jules back in school soon. We all miss her smile:-)

Take care & know that we are all thinking of you and praying for you.

Love from Linda and Family
(school friend)

Welcome Home

Roland April 11, 2007, at 01:18 p.m. EDT

Hello from mom mom and poppi and jeffrey who wants to stay here for infinity. He is becoming a Lojek..What a blessing to have him and God is answering my prayers again and you are coming home. Right now he is at Mandys school with Aunt Jean reading to the kindergarten class. Life is good. See you soon.

Love Mom.

Peaceful Thoughts:)

Diane April 11, 2007, at 03:03 p.m. EDT

Well, when Julianna does something... she sure does it 100%!! A Kidney stone!!! How in the world did this happen? I am so glad you all can take a deep breath and come on home. I have faith that Jules will pass the stone and be up and running. Courtney and I and the rest of the crew will keep up with positive thoughts and prayers.

(school friend)

Smith's Adventure

Jeannie April 11, 2007, at 03:36 p.m. EDT

You guys really don't mess around when you go on an adventure. We are glad to hear things are moving along. We hope Jules has a speedy recovery from this hospital stay. We continue to send lots of prayers your way.

All our love, Jeannie & Bruce
(family friend)

Faithfully Reading And Praying

Deborah January 19, 2008, at 09:45 a.m. EDT

I love your care pages updates and pray every time there is a request in one of them. Even though I don't get to see you, know that Julianna and the rest of you are in my prayers. God's grace will carry you through this difficult and faith stretching time...

All my love, Deb
(church friend)

Hi Julianna

Monica April 11, 2007, at 05:47 p.m. EDT

Hi Jules

I'm glad things are moving along (except for that silly "stone!!!")

I hope it passes real soon and then you'll feel as good as new.

Grandma keeps telling us all about your adventures—and her adventures, too!! We miss you and are all praying for you, Mommy, Daddy and Jeffrey! See you soon—love Monica and everybody

(cousin)

Hello to Julianna!

Beth April 11, 2007, at 06:11 p.m. EDT

Dear Julianna,

We have been thinking about you and are so sorry that you had to spend Easter at the hospital. We hope that your kidney stone passes and that you will feel better. We are so glad that you got a port inserted because that will make it so much easier for you to get your medications. Hayley and Jenna are on spring break from school this week. We went to Washington DC for Tuesday and Wednesday. We walked around all day on Tuesday to see the monuments and the memorials and then today we went to the National Museum of Natural History and saw lots of neat things. Please know that we are thinking about you and hoping that you come home from the hospital soon. Say hi to your Mom, Dad, and Jeffrey for us.

Love,
Beth, John, Jenna, and Hayley
(cousin)

Praying You Home!

Mary April 11, 2007, at 06:41 p.m. EDT

Hi Julianna, JoAnn and all...

Appreciate the updates and want you to know I am praying you home! Julianna, tell Mommy she isn't the only one being in-serviced on medical terminology! I too recently learned the change in ER to ED and CAT to CT! Ahhhhhhh a terms, they are a changin'!

Mrs. L.
(family friend)

Hi

Amy April 11, 2007, at 08:20 p.m. EDT

Wow, that is a lot of news! We hope that the kidney stone passes quickly! Allison can't wait to see you Julianna!!! She misses your smile and hugs in the morning at school! We pray that you will be home soon so that we can visit! Remember that whenever you feel good enough for a visit, where ever you are, just call and we will be there with bells on!!! Our prayers are coming your way along with our love and best wishes!!

Love from Amy and Family
(school friend)

Really. Like Dr. McDreamy?

Donna April 11, 2007, at 08:50 p.m. EDT

JoAnn-you are amazing...you even found a silver lining in this "adventure"...

Thanks for the updates JoAnn! You all certainly deserve a break! We are praying for the stone to pass very quickly, painlessly and for you all to catch up on some much needed rest!

All our love and prayers continue to flow your way!

And again—whatever you need please don't hesitate to ask!!!

Annie sends hugs!

Donna and Annie

Hi Juilanna from Mrs. D at Holy Nativity Pre-School

Josephine April 11, 2007, at 09:33 p.m. EDT

Hi Juilanna, you sweet, sweet girl. Myself and the other teachers at Holy Nativity are praying for you. I hope you pass your stone soon! Just know that I love you and that I am keeping you and your family in my thoughts and prayers! Tell your wonderful Mom we send our love and to Jeffrey and your Dad too. Please let us know if we can be of any help. You will be hearing from me soon! I LOVE YOU!

Love, Mrs. D
(preschool teacher)

Just Wanted To Say Hi

Jessica April 11, 2007, at 09:38 p.m. EDT

Hey guys!

I am very happy to hear that McDreamy said everything looked good (hey at least the doctors are cute!) I am also very happy that you guys get to go home!

I hope Easter egg dying went well, Brian told my mom he was going to bring eggs for you guys.

As always I am praying! Hope to see you soon!

Love And Miss You,
Jess (babysitter)

Thinking & Praying For You

Rebecca April 11, 2007, at 10:52 p.m. EDT

JoAnn,

I am Mitzi's mom and wanted you to know that I and my Ladies Bible Study of the Covenant OPC Church having been praying for Julianna, you and your family since we heard about Julianna.

We have been also encouraged and offered praise for the progress and the news that Julianna could go home, & continue treatment.

We will continue to pray and offer our encouragement.

Thinking of you,
Sue (Mitzi's mom)

Hello Julianna From Daniel H

Helene April 12, 2007, at 09:24 a.m. EDT

Hi Julianna, I'm really glad you are feeling better. We miss you at school. I had alot of fun at your Easter egg breakfast, I sent pictures of us to show you what it was like. Well, rest up and I hope to see you at school soon.

Love Daniel H
(school friend)

Praise God!

Donna April 12, 2007, at 09:33 a.m. EDT

Dear Juliana,

Praise God, all is going well and you finally got to eat! I am watching the rain pour down and praying that kidney stone would just swim downstream and land (splash!) in the bladder. It is raining so hard, a squirrel was looking in our front door when I went to get the paper this morning. He was very wet and bedraggled and he almost came right inside! We are praying and thinking of you all.

With much love, Donna and Dan
(church family)

Thinking Of You

Phyllis April 12, 2007, at 12:35 p.m. EDT

Dear Julianna,

Sorry to hear about your kidney stone. Mr. P had a stone many years ago that didn't want to come out. He also ended up in the hospital. Sometime during the night the stone passed into his bladder and the pain got better. When he came home he passed the stone about 2 days later. To this day we still have it in a special box. Hope yours passes soon also. You and your Mom, Dad and Jeffrey are in our thoughts and prayers every day.

Love,
Phyllis and Lou P (Grandma's friend)

The Twins Spent Seven Hours Testing Today Too!

Marie April 12, 2007, at 07:53 p.m. EDT

Julianna,

Me and my sister spent all day at the Pediatrician's office, then Monmouth Medical Center for ultrasounds and blood work. So, while I was tending to the twins and my sister's needs all day—I thought of *you*. And wanted you to know we were thinking about you as well. It wasn't such a good day, hang in there. This too shall pass.

Aunt Marie

7

Not Coping

CarePage Post April 16, 2007, at 09:28 p.m. EDT

Hi all. I just wanted to let you all know what's been going on…

Wednesday: came home from hospital—*Yippeee* for Julianna. *Yikes* for the rest of us.

Thursday: Jules started her day vomiting. This sent me over the edge. I was supposed to go to parent/teacher conferences. I had to call the teachers and cancel. I couldn't even get the words out. I got Julianna's teacher's voicemail, but poor Jeffrey's teacher answered the phone. I was a mess, but she was very comforting and understanding. I realized at that point, that I was going to need to call in reinforcements—and that's what I did. All those people who have been offering to help are now going to get their chance. A friend came right over and helped me cope.

Friday: Julianna woke up with a nosebleed. Yes, I know you are tempted not to believe this, but it is true. It was minor—luckily. My sister, Julianna and Jeffrey's very special "Auntie A" came for a visit and sleepover. Julianna was actually great this day. They spent a lot of time bird watching, and giggling, and reading, and doing crafts.

Saturday: Jeffrey was up in the night twice with serious nosebleeds. We almost went to the ER, but Brian and I were not spending a 3rd weekend in the ER. Jeffrey has a history of these, and we had them under control, but I think with this lingering winter and the dry heat we need to step up our efforts—which we have and he's been fine. My Dad and brother came for most of the day and the kids had a great, fun visit.

Sunday: Julianna continues to do good. She actually had a friend over for a few hours in the afternoon. This was really good for her. Around 9:00 or so she felt hot to me and she had a 100.1 degree fever. This causes me some uneasiness.

Monday: 1:30 in the morning Julianna has some "burning" issues, a headache and a 101.4 fever. This is not good, but I decide not to call the ER because I know they are going to make us go there. At 8:00 am her fever is back to 100 something, and at 10:00am it is 99 something. A friend comes to help me out. I decide to call the doc and let them know what is happening. Of course, they say we need to come in. My friend kindly drives me because I am hanging by a thread. They gave Julianna some IV antibiotics through her port—which was very cool. I was told that if she gets a fever at 101.4 or higher again I am to call immediately and get her to the hospital. So now we are going to start a list of people willing to be on call in the middle of the night to take Julianna and I to the hospital, this way Brian can stay here with Jeffrey. I can't drive downtown to CHOP in the day, never mind in the middle of the night. At 8:30 tonight Julianna had a fever of 100.1. I am now going to bed and going to pray all night that Julianna's fever goes down because if she is well, we are going with her class to the King Tut exhibit tomorrow. I packed a bag for the hospital just in case, and I told her that since we are packed and ready we probably will not have to go. I will let you know how it turns out.

We think she is passing tiny, tiny particles that are the kidney stone, but we don't know for sure.

I am too tired to even think of what to ask you to pray for—but I am confident you will all come up with something. Good night.

CarePage Messages

Nosebleed Remedy

Marie April 16, 2007, at 09:48 p.m. EDT

Nicholas gets these so often now that sometimes even I get scared. A fellow nurse turned me on to a saline gel called "Ayre". It's hard to find sometimes because the pharmacies don't stock a lot of it. But Nicholas puts it in his nose at night before he goes to sleep and it cut down on the amount of times we are waking up in the middle of the night with heavy bleeding. We noticed that now it's more like when he doesn't remember to use it—we are seeing the recurring bleeding. Try it, it's not painful for them just inconvenient.

Aunt Marie

We Will Continue To Pray

Donna April 16, 2007, at 10:00 p.m. EDT

Big hugs to all of you from the Devaney home! Our thoughts and prayers are still going strong for all the Smiths...
Annie sends hugs and kisses to Jules!

Prayers and hugs—
Donna and Annie!!!
(school friend)

Prayers Are In Our Hearts For You And Your Family

Helene April 16, 2007, at 10:06 p.m. EDT

Dear Joann,

I'm sorry for your tough day.

We here are keeping you in our prayers and asking god to give you the strength that you all need at this time.

God is with you!

Helene
(school friend)

Monday Night

Linda April 16, 2007, at 10:23 p.m. EDT

Oh man…God doesn't give us more than we can handle. I bet you just wish HE wasn't that confident in you!

I can't believe Jules is in fever mode again. I thought of you guys today and talked about the class trip tomorrow. I so hope that you get to go to the museum instead of the hospital:-)

I'm happy that there is a port in place for ease of giving medications. That's tons better than trying to find a good vein.

Thank God for friends. What a great idea to get a list together of potential "on call" people. The reality is you will likely need us more than you want—but we'll be here for you.

I'm off to say my prayers. Rest well.

Love from Linda and Family
(school friend)

Praying For A Peaceful Night

Clare April 16, 2007, at 10:25 p.m. EDT

I am just back from a flying visit to England. So now I have had a chance to catch up with all the postings and you have certainly had a challenging week. So I will get back to doing my prayer walk (with the dog) each evening and concentrate on Julianna. I shared about Julianna and the family with my cousin in England and she is going to prayer for you along with her church. So you will have someone praying for you in the long hours of the night, because of the time change (5 hours).So it will be like a prayer clock going around the world.

We love you-take care

Clare (Mrs. F)
(church friend)

Do Not Grow Weary In Doing Well...

Mary April 16, 2007, at 11:15 p.m. EDT

Hi Jo… & Julianna,

This verse from Galatians 6:9 is my prayer for you. I can't even imagine the weariness of your lives. I commend you for leaning on those in your circle of family and friends to help you and stand by your side. I will continue to pray that God lifts you up at your weary mommy moments and Julianna at your weary Julianna moments as only HE can.

Your quilter friend, Mary

Always In Our Thoughts!

Jeannie April 16, 2007, at 11:39 p.m. EDT

Dear B,J,J, and J,

We are sorry to hear you guys are having such a rough go of it. If there is anything we can do to help out, please don't hesitate to let us know. You are always in our thoughts and we are praying for more days with a little sunshine!

Love to all, Jeannie & Bruce
(family friend)

CarePage Post April 17, 2007, at 09:50 p.m. EDT

King Tutankhamun Rules!!! Yes, Julianna (and I) made the field trip today. It was so great for her. I told everyone today that if we didn't make it there they were going to have to sedate *me*! Luckily it all worked out and I had a very happy child today.

Our clinic day has moved to Wednesday so we head to King of Prussia tomorrow where Julianna will be sedated and get a spinal. I haven't had time to even post details on this phase of treatment but I will try to do that soon.

I continue to be exhausted so I need to go to sleep for now. I just wanted to let you all know about Julianna getting to go to the King Tut Exhibit today.

CarePage Message

Cool—Prayer Walk

Christine April 17, 2007, at 06:18 a.m. EDT

Chach (Nickname for JoAnn),

I love the idea (Clare's idea) for a prayer walk... Jack the dog (you member Jack—114# of pure love!!!) always takes *me* for a walk now each day... and instead of focusing on "stuff" I'm going to spend that time praying for you... We love you guys... keep hanging in there... if only by that thread (which is actually made up of prayers and thoughts and caring—so it is stronger than anything here on earth)...

Chrissy, Kevin, Abby & Nathan—oh, and your new prayer partner—Jack

(family friend)

Hot Potato—Cool Cucumber

Christine April 17, 2007, at 06:23 a.m. EDT

Julianna,

We know you are one hot potato—but you need to stop having those fevers girlie!!!! Think about being a cool cucumber instead of a hot potato…All of us think of you every day… and now you have a new prayer partner—do you remember Jack the dog???? You take care and know that we all love you…

> Christine, Kevin, Abby, Nathan, and good old Jack
> (family friend)

Count Me In!

Linda April 17, 2007, at 09:10 a.m. EDT

You can call me anytime of the night and I will drive you anywhere—I have that portable GPS, so odds of me making a wrong turn are slimmer than ever. Hang in there, even if just by a thread. Allow the good thoughts to take over. This is one of the 4 agreements, by Don Miguel Ruiz, I am not sure if you have ever read that book. I think the 4th agreement may help you a bit, it is Always Do Your Best. "Your best is going to change from moment to moment; It will be different when you are healthy as opposed to sick. Under any circumstances, simply do your best, and you will avoid self-judgment, self-abuse, and regret." So, please don't beat yourself up. You are doing great! better than great, actually, and don't feel weak for asking for help. Jesus asked that his friends stay awake with him while he prayed. Even He asked for help in a trying time. We love and support you all, and pray every day that the road of this adventure will be paved and the potholes filled.

Nose Bleeds—Yuk

Pam April 17, 2007, at 03:37 p.m. EDT

I have always had bad nose bleeds (still do sometimes). When I used to work in a pharmacy (another life ago!!) the pharmacist told me to soak a cotton ball in Peroxide and push it up the nose. Sounds weird and sometimes feels a bit weird as it fizzes a bit but it often works well.

I think the idea is that it cauterizes the area a little.

I'm sorry we can't help with the night driving (I'm as blind as a bat at night!!) but all our thoughts are with you and Jonathon gives us lots of updates too!!

We're sorry to have missed you at the breakfast- what a turn out. We saw Brian from across the room but then had to leave.

We hope summer comes quickly and we can get back to the routine of sitting out on your beautiful patio and sharing.

Pam
(family friend)

Hi

Amy April 17, 2007, at 05:35 p.m. EDT

We were so happy to see you at the trip today!! We hope that you enjoyed your time out of the house and with friends!! Just call us day or night for whatever help you need. Prayers are coming your way!!

Lots of love, Amy and Family
Allison is sending a hug your way.
(family friend)

You Are Stronger Than You Realize!

Susan April 17, 2007, at 05:57 p.m. EDT

JoAnn,

Though you feel like you are hanging by a thread, I truly believe you are stronger than you realize. One day and sometimes one step at a time. Count me out for those drives too… I don't know where we would land, but maybe just maybe you'll think of something you would want me to do, other than pray. My little niece Molly just asked me today if my friend Julianna was still in the hospital. I told her I had been checking the CarePages and would check today. She came to the breakfast benefit and has asked for Julianna often. I know she is saying her prayers for her. I'm praying for *sleep* for all of you, no fevers, no nose bleeds and no hospital trips for awhile! Hang in there in the meantime!

Love,
Sue
(church friend)

It Was Nice To See You Both Today!

Marchell April 17, 2007, at 07:24 p.m. EDT

JoAnn,

Emma was glad to see Julianna at the King Tut exhibit, and it was nice to finally meet you, too! I had no idea the last few days were so trying for Julianna and your family; as Pooh says "you are stronger (and braver) than you know." Forgive yourself when you feel overwhelmed, and don't be afraid to ask for help when you need it.

One summer at church, when Emma was in preschool, they made a collage on construction paper with the words "Trust in God, There will be enough." (I think Amy taught class that day). I had it framed and it's hanging in our kitchen. I often look at it and remind myself to Trust in God when I don't think we will have enough (patience, money, time, faith, energy, etc. etc.)

Trust in God, and of course, we will keep praying every day.

Marchell
(school friend)

Julianna

Cailyn April 17, 2007, at 09:05 p.m. EDT

Hi how are you doing, I don't really know what to say but hi all you people out in the world *please pray for julianna*!! thank you

your friend

Cailyn bye now!!! Really get off its nine 0 clock leave me alone are you looking at my message how rude of you ahhh your looking at me. STOP now ok now i am mad ahhhh-hhhh this is so embarassing ok i am ok now bye every one bye bye, a.k.a by

Reply: wow...

Linda (Cailyn's Mom) April 18, 2007, at 07:06 a.m. EDT
It really does make a good case for parents monitoring kids while posting messages—doesn't it?
It was late...she was tired...punchy...I dunno?

(school friend)

Hi Jules

Roland April 17, 2007, at 09:32 p.m. EDT

I'm so glad you got to go on the trip today..I can't wait to hear about it.

I was praying you would be able to go and feel better.

I'm coming to mind Jeffrey tomorrow morning. Hope I see you.

love mom-mom

King Tut, Huh?

Linda April 18, 2007, at 09:01 a.m. EDT

Sooo glad you got to go…alli could think about was Steve Martin on SNL. too funny. Please let us know if this weekend is good for a visit, i am finally cold-free!

Aunt Lynne

Go Julianna!

Wendy April 18, 2007, at 09:28 a.m. EDT

Hi Julianna, JoAnn, Brian and Jeffery—

We are sooooo happy that you were able to go on your class trip to the King Tut exhibit. Very cool! We are keeping all of you in our thoughts and prayers. Please let us know if we can help out in anyway.

Love—Rick,
Wendy & Rusty
(church friend)

King Tut Was Great!!!!

Amy April 18, 2007, at 02:34 p.m. EDT

Really the great part was seeing you there Julianna!!
  We hope that today went well!!

Love from Amy and Family
(school friend)

Great News!

Jeannie April 18, 2007, at 04:34 p.m. EDT

We were so happy to hear Julianna enjoyed her field trip!
Maybe sometime we can hear all about it. Let's hope we
have many more happy days to come.

Love to all of you, Jeannie & Bruce
(family friend)

You Go Girl!!!

John April 18, 2007, at 07:10 p.m. EDT

It's been awhile since I posted a note. Sorry.
  I am happy that you are geting around and that things
seem a bit more sunny and bright.
  You are in our parayers.

—John & Jeanne
(neighbor)

No News?

Linda April 20, 2007, at 08:13 a.m. EDT

I hope that means it is all good—I miss the posts, JoAnn…
taking a break, are you? A well-deserved one.

Aunt Lynne

Hope Things Are Well

Susan April 20, 2007, at 06:01 p.m. EDT

Hi All,

I've been thinking of all of you and hoping things went as good as can be expected on Wednesday. I'm so glad you *both* made the exhibit and you finally met Emma's mom Marchell! I hope to hear how things are going soon. Prayers are still coming your way!

Sue
(church friend)

Saturday AM

Linda April 21, 2007, at 10:45 a.m. EDT

Hello friends!

I hope that this sunny Saturday morning has a smile on your face as you wake up:-)

Paryers are coming your way for continued good updates and restful nights. Remember that we are available whenever you might find yourself in need.

I think that everybody was so happy to see Jules on the field trip. It does them as much good to see her up and moving around as it does Jules to keep in front of her friends!

Call anytime for anything—OK?

Love always,
Linda and family
(school friend)

CarePage Post April 22, 2007, at 10:24 p.m. EDT

I am getting some grief for going so long without an update—sorry. I am told people are concerned and get worried—some more than others (you know who you are—Lynne.) Although our days have been relatively quiet, I still can't seem to get even 2 minutes to write an update. Being a full time nurse to an 8 year old is very demanding you know. Add to that a 6 year old who is definitely showing signs of "our situation" and you see my reason for not updating sooner.

While Julianna is mostly doing well, everyday it seems to be something. Friday she had back pain from her spinal on Wednesday. This has never happened before, so of course I am on pins and needles. Saturday night into Sunday she started to have a high fever—nearing that 101.4 magic mark which means a trip to CHOP. Again, I am on pins and needles. Tonight at dinner she has a fever again of 100.7 and a headache—yes pins and needles. Do you see a pattern here???

In between the pins and needles, we have had some nice, normal moments. A family that used to attend our church came to visit on Friday night. Their daughter, Jessica, who is now 27, had a childhood cancer 20 years ago. They all came to chat with us. Jessica and Julianna spent I think it was close to 2 hours in Julianna's room talking. I can't even tell you the difference in Julianna's spirits before and after that time. I knew Julianna needed this and I was so glad when she said she wanted to meet and talk with Jessica. I have a feeling this relationship is going to mean so much to Julianna.

Saturday Julianna spent a good part of the day doing crafts and giggling with her friend. It was so good to see her be with a friend. She has not been to school for weeks now and I think this is not good for her. Hopefully she will get to school some this week. She is going to have to have an outpatient surgery this week to remove the stent. We don't know if she actually passed the stone. We won't know for sure until they test her this week. Once I know the day for the surgery I will post a prayer request.

Just to update you all on where we stand with treatment. I started these posts detailing them by day #. That was because the first phase of treatment—which is all we knew at the time was 28 days and that's how we were tracking everything.

We finished that phase and went right into the week of pain preceding the kidney stone diagnosis. That was actually supposed to be a quiet week for Julianna as she had a break from all medications. It was unfortunate the way things turned out. The Wednesday that we left the hospital after the kidney stone was actually Day 1 of this next phase which is called "Consolidation" and will also last 28 days. It consists of weekly spinals and a med that she takes orally once a day. I am not sure I will ever get used to watching my daughter lay curled up like a ball on a table while the doctor sticks huge needles in her back. It's hard to even describe what I am feeling during these. A friend came with us to clinic and that did make the trip a bit more social which was a nice change. I do remember hearing once, I think it was from my cousin who is an OR nurse about how during surgery they chat about movies, etc. I remember thinking that was kind of crazy, but here we were during the procedure talking about American Idol, etc. Anyway, this should be an easier phase but the kidney stone really has made things complicated.

Some of the meds have caused Julianna to have weakness in her legs. We are going on Tuesday for an evaluation for physical therapy. The good news is that we are going to a place where a friend from church works. We are hoping she will get to work with Julianna. Also, they have aquatic therapy that Julianna is excited about, so we are hoping that may work out for her also.

So that's my update for today. I will post again as I can.

CarePage Messages

Sunday Night

Linda April 22, 2007, at 11:07 p.m. EDT

Thank you so much for the news:-) I know it's tough to find a minute to compose your thoughts but we do worry when it is quiet!

Prayers tonight for a quiet and restful night. If that thermometer number creeps up, remember you're not alone. Call one of us on your list and we'll get you where you need to go.

I'm happy that Jules got some social time. Little girls need to be little girls together and laughter is one of the best medicines! It also sounds like your friend's daughter from church is going to be a light in Julianna's world.

Take care,
Cyber hugs and kisses to all from Linda and family
(school friend)

Thank You For Allowing Us To Visit

Denise April 22, 2007, at 11:46 p.m. EDT

Hi all!! What a feat, I figured this out and just read the entire web page. It was so wonderful to spend time with you on Friday evening. I hope it was good for you to just visit with old friends who feel your pain, hate that you are all going through these very difficult days, but *promise* it will be better very soon. Jess enjoyed her time with Jules and it gives her such joy to be able to help her in any way. Even though it was all 20 years ago, we all felt like it was yesterday. Right now your memories are horror stories. In God's infinite mercy, 20 years from now, these will be beautiful memories of miracles, love, support of family and friends and above all *His* faithfulness. You are all in our thoughts and prayers daily. We are here for you no matter what time or what need. Be well, Julianna. Be at peace, Brian and JoAnn. Enjoy the beautiful weather, Jeffrey—Josh wants to know when you can come over his house???

(church friend)

Thanks For The Update

Donna April 23, 2007, at 07:05 a.m. EDT

Thanks for the update JoAnn-We appreciate getting news whenever possible! We are continuing to pray daily for Julianna and the whole family-there are also the continued prayers from London by Joe (Annie-Rose's Dad) which cover some of the overnight hours! Good luck with the procedure this week to remove the stent and keeping the fever down!

Lots of hugs and kisses from Annie to Jules!

Donna and Annie
(school friend)

Just Checking In On You:):):)

Melissa April 23, 2007, at 08:26 a.m. EDT

Hi Jullianna! How are you doing? Did you like the King Tut field trip? I did! Olivia and I got matching bandanas and we are wearing them today (Monday). This week is turn off t.v week and that means no webkinz either. Right now in school we are finishing up our Egypt unit. Have to go to school now! I am still keeping you in my prayers every single day! Hope you get better soon!

Your Friend,
Melissa (school friend)

Have a Sunny Day!

Pauline April 23, 2007, at 09:25 a.m. EDT

Dear Julianna and Jeffrey, Just want you both to know that I miss seeing you on Wednesdays!!! I hope that I can come for a short visit one of these days. Julianna, I am praying for you everyday!

JoAnn and Brian, I am here to help. Please,please feel free to call for anything! Nights are always best.

Pauline
(piano teacher)

Hi, Julianna

Jeannie April 23, 2007, at 05:55 p.m. EDT

We are hoping every day will get a little easier for you guys! We always try waiting patiently for your updates. We can only imagine how hectic it is for you all. Remember we are always available if you need us for anything. Love to all, Jeannie & Bruce

"The guardian angel's of life sometimes fly so high as to be beyond our sight, but they are always looking down upon us."

(family friend)

Thank You For Your Continued Updates

John April 23, 2007, at 07:01 p.m. EDT

It is great to read all of the bright spots...and the low points that you pen on these wonderful updates. If nothing else, this will be a wonderful journal for the future. If not for you per se then for your beautiful daughter. I love the story of the 27-year old daughter of a church friend who came and spent two hours with Julianna. And the joy I read of the "attitude adjustment" when the little chat was over.

Hugs all around.

—John and Jeanne
(neighbor)

CarePage Post April 24, 2007, at 05:04 p.m. EDT

Well, if you thought you felt sorry for me before, wait until you read this. Yesterday—Monday—Julianna was well enough to go to school for the afternoon. This meant that I was going to have 2 ½ hours to myself for the first time in many weeks. I am not complaining, really, just stating the facts. Anyway, what I did during that time, you might guess the following: nap, cry, take a walk, stare into space, get a massage… nooooooooooooo, with my first free time in weeks I cleaned the upstairs bathroom and vacuumed a bit. How pathetic is that. Alright, I did actually sit on my patio and sip some soup broth for 10 minutes while my scrubbing bubbles were still hard at work. I know I should be thinking "oh normalcy," that's a word the docs and social workers like to use a lot, but…what I am thinking is "I *need to hire a cleaning lady!*!!!" Of course, when I mention it to Brian he looks at me like I have 2 heads—OK well that's back to a bit of "normalcy" anyway. For today's 2 ½ hours I actually sat and had some Cappuccino and made a phone call—and then I continued to attempt to organize my very disorganized house.

As for Julianna—which is what you really want to know—it turns out we have to go to K of P (King of Prussia) tomorrow for blood work or what everyone refers to as "counts" and downtown on Friday for the surgery. We really thought they were going to combine all this into one trip on Friday, and they are combining the stent removal and the spinal, but it is a blow to us to have to make that trip tomorrow for counts. Oh well... we will have to make the best of it. Our friend is going to drive us which makes me and Julianna very happy. This same friend also had us get some books on tape from the library the last trip we took together and Julianna just loved this, so she will probably spend the time in the car doing that.

This morning we went for Julianna's physical therapy evaluation. This is going to be really good for her. Before we went she said, "Mommy, this will be the first place I get to go where they are not going to stick me with a needle." Unbelievable, the life of Julianna these days, although for her it is just a matter of fact statement. Again, I hear the words of the doctor in my head—don't overindulge, don't overindulge, hah!! Actually just the other day I bought her the Betty Crocker cake decorating kit that she keeps seeing on TV—she really wanted it, what was I to do. Luckily, she hasn't been wanting anything extravagant because then it might really pose a dilemma—or not.

So, as for some prayer requests... the nurse called today to say that a third grader has come down with strep throat, so pray that Julianna stays healthy. Please pray that her counts are good tomorrow so that everything can proceed for Friday. Please pray for no fevers, no fevers, and no fevers. Please pray for the surgeon and oncologist on Friday—that all will go well with these 2 procedures and that Julianna will do well with the anesthesia. Until next time...

CarePage Messages

Happy Tuesday!

Linda April 24, 2007, at 11:32 a.m. EDT

I hope you are having a good day. We are so glad we got to see you all on Sunday, it was a nice visit, and we look forward to many more of them. Sorry for spazzing out about the lapse in time between updates, I will try to be more patient, as long as you write one a day:):):)

How is Jeffrey's allergy? Please tell him he is honking like a goose from the Migration DVD. I was trying to remember where I heard that sound, and it finally came to me. Talk to you all soon,

love and prayers,
Aunt Lynne and Aunt Carolyn

Just Another Little Note

Linda April 24, 2007, at 11:36 a.m. EDT

I just realized that the last post was number 221. Do you realize that is 221 would-be phone calls? These care pages are wonderful!

Tuesday PM

Linda April 24, 2007, at 06:00 p.m. EDT

Two days in a row to have Jules in school!!!! That is exciting news. I know that Cailyn loves seeing Jules back at her desk:-)

I'm sorry that you need to make two trips this week. It really sounded good to combine everything into one trip. I'm glad that your friend will go with you tomorrow. I know it changes the feel of the day.

We're praying for no fevers and good counts tomorrow. Stay well with no Strep!! Keep us posted on how things go on Friday. There will be lots of prayers coming your way—do you have a procedure time?

Thank you so much for posting these updates. They are such a great way to stay in touch with you without being intrusive! Like Linda F. said—221 posts!!! Wow—you'd be on the phone alot:-)

Take care,
Love from Linda and family
(school friend)

Scrubbing Bubbles Rule!

Christine April 24, 2007, at 07:43 p.m. EDT

Chach (Nickname for JoAnn),

I'm with you on the scrubbing bubbles—I bet all of those fuzzies in the bathroom took a serious beating with all of your anxieties and worries!!!! Take that—scrub-scrub!!!! Take that!!!! I think it would be enjoyable to "control" something for a while—since everything has been out of your control… I'm so glad you've been able to maintain a bit of humor through some of this… My prayer walk with Jack has been going well… I *need* to pray as he's dragging me along! Know that we all think of you all every single day—and not a day goes by that we don't pray for all of you…

We love you guys… Chrissy, Kevin, Abby
& Nathan (family friend)

"Positive Thoughts"

Jeannie April 24, 2007, at 07:56 p.m. EDT

Hello to the Smith's,

We will definitely keep you in our prayers. We hope everything goes well for you on Friday. We are really glad to hear Jules has been to school. Take care and hopefully you will have lots more down time to come.

Love you guys, Jeannie & Bruce
(family friend)

We're Storming Heaven—as requested!

Joan April 25, 2007, at 08:27 a.m. EDT

To the Smith Family:

Just letting you know there are lots of prayers coming your way even from those you haven't met personally—however, once a Buckingham Knight—always a Buckingham Knight and the families who need prayers within that community will always be included in ours.

Even though we may not know each other, I'm confident that all our prayers for Julianna and your entire family have certainly made their way together up the stairs to heaven.

Blessings, good wishes, strength and continued support from our Family—Joan, Robert & Cameron

(Buckingham Elementary alumni)

PS—Romans 12:12 has always been a comfort to our family in times like these..."Rejoice in hope, endure in affliction, persevere in prayer..." God Bless!

(friend of a friend)

Prayers for Wednesday and Friday

Donna April 25, 2007, at 01:09 p.m. EDT

Annie has been so happy to see Jules in school...we are praying Strep stays far from the Smith house!

Good luck on Wednesday and Friday-I hope it is a little less stressful having a friend with you.

Prayers continue going strong from our house to yours!

Donna & Annie
(school friend)

Prayers Coming Your Way!!!

Amy April 25, 2007, at 03:17 p.m. EDT

We were so happy to see Julianna in school this week!! Allison just loves seeing her smiling face!! Let's hope that the strep throat stays away from our classroom and far, far, away from the Smith's house. You are always and will always remain in our prayers. We will be thinking about you.

Amy and Family
(school friend)

8

Our Village

CarePage Post April 26, 2007, at 12:10 p.m. EDT

Here are some words I haven't uttered lately, "We had a *great* day yesterday." Julianna's "counts" were fabulous yesterday—her doctor couldn't be more pleased. Her doctor also approved her for aquatic physical therapy which made Julianna extremely happy. She has also been fever free. My friend drove us to and from clinic, so I got to relax on the ride and drink my coffee on the way there—it was very nice.

Add to all that the fact that I got home to a phone message from a friend from church who said the company she works for would like to offer us complimentary housekeeping twice a month. I played the message 3 times to be sure I was hearing it correctly—and not having my own "mind-altering experience."

As I sat on the couch with tears in my eyes, I thought of my first few days in the hospital when I saw signs everywhere for a meeting they were going to have called "It takes a Village." I didn't get to the meeting, but the description talked about how it is so important when you have a seriously ill child to let others help you. The message was loud and clear that you can't do this alone. I am thinking how fortunate we are to have a "village" of caring people who are willing to do whatever we ask or do what they know we need—because while all we are going through at times seems unbearable, it is beyond my imagination to think about going through this without the support we have. We will be forever grateful for our "village."

As for tomorrow—I will know later today what time the procedure is going to be. They take the youngest kids first, so I have a feeling we might be a bit later. I will post as soon as I know the time. Yesterday her doctor did say if she didn't pass the stone—we don't know it she did, and they can't retrieve it, they will have to put in a bigger stent. We are praying she has passed the stone, and would ask for prayer for that also.

I am off to get Julianna ready for school. Her school is having a bake sale today to raise money for the American Cancer Society, so we need to get there early to make some purchases.

I wanted to end with this quote that my sister-in-law sent me while we were in the hospital, and then I came across it again yesterday in a CHOP calendar called "Courageous Kids." There is no author listed, but in the calendar this is listed as a quote from a 9 year old cancer patient: "Yesterday is history, tomorrow is a mystery. Today is a gift. That why we call it the present. Live and savor every moment."

CarePage Post April 26, 2007, at 04:57 p.m. EDT

Just wanted to let you know that our "arrival time" at CHOP tomorrow is 6:45 AM. *Yikes!!!*

I have no idea how long the prep time will be before the actual procedure. I will try to post as soon as we get back home to let you know how it all goes. Thanks for keeping us in your thoughts and prayers.

CarePage Messages

Good Morning

Linda April 26, 2007, at 08:47 a.m. EDT

We hope yesterday went well, and are praying for an easy time tomorrow. We also pray that these diseases are eliminated, so that this *adventure* is not endured by any more children, their families, and friends. And a special prayer for those going through it without the strength of this support group. As for the *normalcy*, that is making me angry—this shouldn't be normal,it is unacceptable. ok, i guess my venting is done, thanks everyone.

Aunt Lynne

Woo Hoo!! Good Counts!!!!!!!!

Linda April 26, 2007, at 01:33 p.m. EDT

We have a winner!
Thank God and keep asking, because HE delivers!

(family friend)

Yippppeeeeeeeeeeee!!!

Marie April 26, 2007, at 01:36 p.m. EDT

Oh Smith Family,

We are all so happy to hear some *good* words from you.
We'll keep praying and looking for more of the same.

Jersey Shore Smith Family

Praise And Thanksgiving For Your Improvement

Jane April 26, 2007, at 03:50 p.m. EDT

Have been praying and am so glad to connect on this message board
You are so so special and we rejoice to hear your improvement.
We all love you.

Aunt Jane

J

Linda April 26, 2007, at 04:12 p.m. EDT

I love to hear happiness in your written words!

I can't tell you how happy Cailyn, Annie & Ally were to be buying baked goods today at the school. They were sitting in the cafeteria saying that "this very cupcake is going to help Julianna!!" It is so great to hear them so happy being able to help. I've said it before but it is so true—it is such a gift to be able to help someone else. I'm grateful to the 4th grade classes for giving our kids the opportunity to experience how good it feels to help. Directly or indirectly—those cookies and cupcakes help someone that they know.

Having Jules back in school for three days this week is another gift! The kids were thrilled to see her:-)

We are praying for an easy Friday. Whatever best case scenario is—I'm asking for that!!

Congratulations on the scrubbing reprive:-) Spend your quiet moments relaxing on your patio—not with your head in the tub!

I know we are all looking forward to an update tomorrow after the procedure…(hint hint!) Thanks for keeping us informed. We are so happy to know that it's been a good few days!

Take care, Love
from Linda and Family
(school friend)

What Great News!!

Amy April 26, 2007, at 05:13 p.m. EDT

I was so glad to read your latest update! Help with the house work, how great is that!!!! We will be thinking about you at 6:45 tomorrow morning and will be saying a prayer.

Allison is so happy to see Jules in school and wanted me to send a special hug and kiss her way!

Love to all, Amy
(school friend)

I'll Be Up & Praying!!!

Christine April 26, 2007, at 05:34 p.m. EDT

Chach (Nickname for JoAnn),

I still get up with the chickens—so I'll be thinking about you guys and praying for you... You might just get to see a beautiful sunrise! No matter what, God is faithful... hang in there.

Love ya, Chrissy,
Kevin, Abby & Nathan
(family friend)

Sending Strength Your Way

Marlene April 26, 2007, at 05:48 p.m. EDT

Hang in there and know that we are continuing to think about and pray for Julianna daily. Sending sunny thoughts your way!

Love, Marlene, Sean, Carrie
and Kate (family friend)

Triumph Through The Trial

Kim April 26, 2007, at 07:24 p.m. EDT

Hello again. Even though we may not post a message very often, we do pray for you daily. I can only imagine how tiring it is to face these struggles! We pray that you will have small victories each day, and that your relationship with the Lord will only strengthen through this whole process.

Love and prayers,
Ray, Kim, and the kids (cousin)

Wonderful News (Well Not The 6:45 Arrival Time)

Donna April 26, 2007, at 09:05 p.m. EDT

It was so wonderful to hear the positive news after Jules tests on Wednesday and the wonderful gift of house cleaning-talk about the perfect gift! We will all be praying for positive news and the passing of the stone!!!
Hugs to Jules from Annie!

Donna and Annie
(school friend)

Looking Forward To A Great Friday!

Jeannie April 26, 2007, at 09:42 p.m. EDT

We were real happy to hear Julianna had a great day. You will be in our thoughts and prayers tomorrow as always. We look forward to another great day.

Love to all of you
Jeannie & Bruce
(family friend)

Great News and Prayers Continue

Susan April 26, 2007, at 11:33 p.m. EDT

I'm so happy to hear some good news and it seems joy in you JoAnn. I'll be up early as usual getting ready for work and I'll start my day with prayers for Julianna. Your "village" is probably bigger than you can even realize. I pray you feel God's love and peace tomorrow.

Love, Sue
(church family)

CarePage Post April 27, 2007, at 02:24 p.m. EDT

Great news!! Julianna is stone-free and stent-free. Everything today went very well and very quickly. We left here at 5:15 this morning. I had Julianna sleep in her clothes so we could roll her out of bed and right into the van. The urologist explained everything about how if the stone was still there and they couldn't break it up they would have to re-stent, and I had to sign forms for possibilities of all kinds of oscopy's. They wheeled her away and once more I prayed—please let the stone be gone!!! It was not much later when the urologist came out and said there was no stone, and they took the stent out—and she did great. The oncologist went in and performed his set of tricks—on to recovery—and now home. Needless to say, Julianna is already napping and I am about to join her. I am hoping for some quiet days, so don't be concerned if you don't hear from us for a few days.

CarePage Messages

Thinking Of You Always

Melissa April 27, 2007, at 09:14 a.m. EDT

We are keeping up with all of the events in your continuing adventure. You are making us all so proud because you are so courageous. We pray for you as a family each evening at dinner and also at night before bed. Someday we'll have to have a visit. Please keep us on your "village" list so we can help out if needed.

Lots of Love,
Melissa, Matt, Jessica and Leanna
(family friend)

Great News

Susan April 27, 2007, at 02:49 p.m. EDT

I woke early a few times this morning and prayed each time that the stone would be gone. Thank God it was! Prayers for a quiet and peaceful weekend.

Love,
Sue
(church friend)

Great News!

David April 27, 2007, at 03:01 p.m. EDT

Glad to hear Julianna's doing well.

(cousin)

Friday Afternoon

Linda April 27, 2007, at 03:46 p.m. EDT

Thank God.

I couldn't be happier for that news!

Talk soon,
Linda
(school friend)

Wonderful News!

Jeannie April 27, 2007, at 03:47 p.m. EDT

We are really happy to hear your great news. Now for a little R&R, you guys certainly deserve it. Take care of yourselves and lets look forward to many more brighter days to come.

All our love,
Jeannie & Bruce
(family friend)

Praise The Lord!

Debra April 27, 2007, at 04:25 p.m. EDT

Praise the Lord for your wonderful news! We are all relieved to hear the positive update. We celebrate this victory with you, and look forward to many more on your road to recovery!

Blessings,
Debbie (church friend)

Praise the Lord!!

Carol April 27, 2007, at 06:58 p.m. EDT

So glad to hear she is doing so well and the stone is gone. We are praying for her and the entire family every day. Hope you have a good weekend with sleepful nights and no fevers!

Carol
(family friend)

Good News Spreads!!

Clare April 27, 2007, at 08:47 p.m. EDT

What wonderful news and answers to prayer. We heard all the way from Michigan, Julianna and JoAnn, where we are staying. We said some prayers during a wakeful night too and God heard. Now just go and enjoy a few days of rest-you deserve it and you do not have to get out the Scrubbing bubbles! Just relax in God's Loving Care.

All our love,
Clare and Family
(church family)

So Grateful

Pauline April 28, 2007, at 10:08 a.m. EDT

Dear Julianna, How terrific that the stone was gone. God really does answer prayers! And so many people are praying for you. Have a great day! I Love You!

Pauline and Tiffy (of course!)
(piano teacher)

Hello to All

Amy April 28, 2007, at 03:10 p.m. EDT

What great news!! Allison sends hugs and kisses and is so happy to hear that everything went well, as are the rest of us. Enjoy the weekend!! You all deserve some quiet time.

Love and prayers from Amy and Family
(school friend)

J

Jenna April 28, 2007, at 03:58 p.m. EDT

I was extremely glad to hear the good news. I'll be praying every day for you Julianna:) and I hope things continue to go well.

(family friend)

Greetings from Grapevine, TX

Linda April 28, 2007, at 08:20 p.m. EDT

Sooo happy to hear the great news—no stone, no stent, sounds like a country western song! we are here until Tuesday, and blessed with a laptop our department ordered, so I can keep up while we are away.

Enjoy the weekend! we love you,
Aunt Lynne & Aunt Carolyn

Wonderful News!

Donna May 01, 2007, at 08:49 a.m. EDT

How great for all of you especially Julianna!! We are all so thrilled that everything is looking up!

Annie has been so happy to have Jules in school so often.

Our prayers will continue for more goodness your way!

Donna and Annie
(school friend)

Sooo…New????

Linda May 02, 2007, at 12:29 p.m. EDT

Hey there Julianna,

We hope you are feeling better and better, and that the treatments are getting a bit easier to go through. Hang in there! We love you!

Aunt Lynne and Aunt Carolyn,
Cara & Mia too

Hellooooooo Is This Thing On?

Linda May 03, 2007, at 12:25 p.m. EDT

Gee, I thought someone was aware of how crazy I get when there aren't any updates??? and I thought you were going to just put a line out here… Hoping and praying it is all good.

Love,
Aunt Lynne & Aunt Carolyn

CarePage Post May 03, 2007, at 02:35 p.m. EDT

Today we have achieved a big milestone—Julianna has been in school all day. Its 2:30 and I haven't gotten a phone call yet to say come pick her up. She has been doing very well. We have had quiet days—as I had hoped—with just a few bumps along the way.

Julianna recovered well from her stent removal on Friday, and we even went sneaker shopping on Saturday because, of course, she needs new sneakers for physical therapy, and apparently her

Dad needed new sneakers too because he got a pair also. Then we even had a little lunch out after we finished shopping.

Sunday Julianna woke up feeling good again and we thought we would try to get to church. She was excited about the thought of seeing everyone and she said it would probably be like her first day back to school and everyone would want to hug her. She thinks this is pretty cool. More than halfway through the church service Julianna and her Sunday school teacher walk into where we are and Julianna is crying. I bolt up from my chair and take her out. Brian follows after us. She is crying and says she is sick to her stomach. I get her home. I tell Brian to stay because if we pull Jeffrey out, and he doesn't get to have light saber fights with his friends after church, we are going to have 2 crying kids on our hands. I assume someone will drive them home. We get home and Julianna gets quite sick, but she feels so much better. She takes a nap and she feels great again.

I don't know what caused her upset stomach. I have a theory, but no scientific proof, so I won't get into it. Anyway, we were supposed to go to a family birthday party, and Julianna really wants to go—so off we go. We had a really nice time and the kids had a great time being with their cousins.

Tuesday, Jeffrey ended up having his nose cauterized. I had made an appointment with the ENT after that last horrible bloody nose—just to see... Anyway, apparently there was some big blood vessel up there and he cauterized it. Jeffrey was an excellent patient while we were there. Stayed like a soldier the whole time. Halfway home and for most of the afternoon he cried and whined like crazy. I work very hard at being patient with him.

Wednesday we went to clinic. My Dad came to take the ride with us. He is a 4 time cancer survivor so he has some experience in this area. I also decide to bring Jeffrey because he has been getting upset the last few times we've gone to clinic, so I think he should come and see what he thinks he's missing out on.

Our first stop is vitals and he has to step on the scale and get measured too, etc. Next the blood draw room. Jeffrey brought a tiny penguin stuffed animal and he is telling the nurse that his penguin is very healthy. They prick Julianna's finger and squeeze blood into a vial. Jeffrey watches at first, and then he buries his head in my leg. Next we go to what they call the "day hospital." It is a large area with separate stations equipped with a big chair, smaller guest chairs, a dvd/playstation set up, etc. Of course, Jeffrey wants to play playstation (because he doesn't play it enough at home.) Next we go to an exam room and this is where Jeffrey starts bouncing off the walls. We barely get through the exam and the nurse practitioner suggests we go back to the day hospital to get Jeffrey something to do. We are getting settled back there and Julianna's doctor walks over. At this point, Jeffrey is climbing with his feet up my Dad's body and flipping over. I introduce him to the doctor and tell her this is why you haven't met Jeffrey before. Now he is being bad because he wants to go to the cabinet and get a different playstation game. This is reminding me of the one *and only* time he came to the hospital and was just as crazy. In the hospital, at one point, we turn around and he is in the hazardous waste garbage. I am thinking…this might be Jeffrey's one and only visit to clinic also.

CarePage Messages

Thank You!!!!

Linda May 03, 2007, at 03:08 p.m. EDT

Phew…once again, had me worrying. Sounds like a breezy time for all. Ha Ha Ha. Jeffrey is such a trip… and you are quite the storyteller. We are so glad things are going better, and a full day at school! that is more than a milestone, it is like a mega-milestone. Thanks so much for updating, We love you all, and continue to pray for more miracles for our Julianna and her family.

Love to all, Aunt Lynne & Aunt Carolyn

From Karen and Family

Karen May 03, 2007, at 04:01 p.m. EDT

It was great to see Julianna, with her big smile, in school this morning. All the girls were so excited to be with her and to show off their matching bandanas, which were so cute. We're hoping to see more of Julianna in school.

Love, Karen, Mike, Aimee and Emily
(school friend)

Jeffrey And Dyl Could Be Brothersssss

Cathy May 03, 2007, at 04:03 p.m. EDT

I am sooo thrilled to hear about school..and that she is doing well...However, Mr Jeffrey sounds just like my Dylan...Dylan loves his cousin Jeffrey and they are twoooo *Peas In A Pod*..I send the biggest hugs to you & Brian and the family...we think about you all sooo much and are continually wishing you all well...

lots of love cathy
(cousin)

Looking Forward To Seeing You.

Mary May 03, 2007, at 07:25 p.m. EDT

JoAnn & Julianna, Jeffrey & Brian...

I am looking forward to seeing you on Saturday.

Blessings,
Mrs. Landis
(family friend)

Yea!

Debra May 03, 2007, at 08:05 p.m. EDT

Hi Julianna. Congratulations on making it through a full day of school! Have a great weekend, enjoy the beautiful spring weather, and rest up. JoAnn, it sounds like Jeffrey is ready for a full day of school too… to wear off some of that energy.

> May God bless you all,
> Debbie
> (church family)

Hello to the Smith Family

Beth May 03, 2007, at 08:24 p.m. EDT

Dear Julianna, Jeffrey, JoAnn, and Brian

We are so glad to hear that things seem to be going smoothly. We are glad to hear that Julianna is able to get to school. You must really enjoy seeing your friends and teachers. Please know that we are thinking about you and hoping that you can continue to go to school and that your clinic visits go well.

> Love, Beth, John, Jenna, and Hayley
> (cousin)

Great News!

Jeannie May 03, 2007, at 09:30 p.m. EDT

Hi everyone,

It sounds like things are starting to settle down some. We are real happy to hear that. It was nice to hear Julianna made it through a day of school. We would love to get to see you guys soon. As for monkey boy what were you thinking? Just kidding, lol. We hope you guys have many more quiet days.

All our love, Jeannie & Bruce
(family friend)

Wow!!!

Diane May 03, 2007, at 09:49 p.m. EDT

I have to say...I am exhausted reading about all that you did in one day!!!But...what a good day! I bet you both enjoyed a really nice nap! Question is did Jeffrey? I am thrilled that everything is moving along without to many bumps in the road. Were still thinking about all of you with the most positive and peaceful thoughts!

Love, Diane and Family
(school friend)

Friday AM

Linda May 04, 2007, at 09:06 a.m. EDT

Happy sunny Friday:-)

I hope that it was a restful night and that the day is starting well. I know that Cailyn was giggling leaving the house today hoping to see Jules for another whole day. She sure did enjoy playing that "dictionary game" yesterday!
      Take care and I'll catch up with you soon.

Love
Linda
(school friend)

This Is For Brian

Linda May 04, 2007, at 11:50 a.m. EDT

Happy Birthday!

We didn't want to miss out on putting a special prayer request here for you to continue being strong through this adventure. We love you B!

Lynne & Carolyn

Hi to All

Amy May 05, 2007, at 12:15 p.m. EDT

Allison was so happy on Thursday and Friday to see Jules in school *all day*!!!!! Allison just loved their lunch and recess time together. Enjoy this beautiful sunny weekend!!

Love from Amy and Family
Hugs from Allison!!!!

9

Real Chicks

CarePage Post May 06, 2007, at 05:54 p.m. EDT

The "chick" story continues. Yesterday, Julianna and her Dad (and her Auntie A) went to the local feed store where Brian buys our bird seed, etc. I knew it was what they call "chick days." I didn't even think to say "don't come home with any chicks." Julianna walks in the house with a cardboard box and the biggest grin on her face. I said to her, I meant to tell you not to bring any chicks home. She answered, "We wouldn't have listened anyway." OK then. I am definitely outnumbered on this one. I have posted some pictures so you can see the chicks too.

Julianna's Betty Crocker cake decorating kit arrived just in time for Brian's birthday. It was very fun, but it takes a ton of icing and a ton of time. I posted a picture of her and Brian and the cake.

I also posted a picture of Julianna under the most beautiful garden quilt. A friend from my quilting group, who is a very accomplished artist/quilter, made this just for Julianna. As you can see, it is just gorgeous, and we are quite honored to have it.

Speaking of quilts... many years ago my friend Lynne and I were in a quilt shop near her home. Somehow we got talking to the owner and we learned about an organization called "Quilts for Kids." It is based locally, and the story is that the woman who started it was in a warehouse where they were going to be throwing out all these designer fabrics. She thought something could be done with all this fabric, and "Quilts for Kids" was started.

Last year, Jeffrey's pre-school made a quilt for this organization because one of his teachers was involved in a quilting group. At that same time, my quilt group came upon a lot of fabric and we donated it to this organization. I knew that the quilts were donated to area hospitals, and I believe given out to police officers to use if there is a child involved in a car accident, etc. Our last stay in the hospital when Julianna went to the OR to have the stent put in, and the port placed, and her spinal—the patient rep came out to me and handed me a beautiful quilt for Julianna. It was made by a girl scout and donated to "Quilts for Kids." I looked at the patient rep stunned. I told her I knew of this organization and have donated to them—I was never thinking I would be on the receiving end. I said I feel funny taking this. Of course, she insisted I take it. Once Julianna was recovered from her surgery, I showed her the quilt. We talked about it and agreed we should donate it back for a child who does not have "quilting connections." Julianna had also received a beautiful comfy, flannel quilt from another friend while she was in the hospital the first time. I was so proud of her for deciding to give this quilt back.

I know I have been doing more rambling lately than giving updates about Julianna's progress. In the next post, I will tell you all about her next phase of treatment which starts this Wednesday. In general, she is doing very well. Except for the weakness in her legs, she is just about back to normal. Right now she is jumping on the trampoline.

As for her biggest concern in the past—her hair. It has not completely fallen out, but it is definitely thin. Her teacher wrote a nice note the other day about how great it has been to have her in school full day. Here is what she wrote: "Julianna had a nice first full day back at school. The girls had a ball playing Pictionary on the board during recess! It was so nice to hear them all being so silly. Julianna had her bandana off during recess and when the kids started coming back in one of the girls asked her if she was going to put it back on. She said 'I don't really feel like it.' I was so proud of her and her classmates—there was not one stare, mention of her hair, mention of the missing bandana. Math went on as normal!"

Isn't that amazing!!!

All right, enough chatter—I will write again soon detailing her "roadmap" for the next 2 months. Thanks for reading.

Julianna with all her balloons, a new Pooh, and a new
Vermont Teddy Bear named Hugs. Every person
who walks into our house spots the balloons and says
"whoooaaa."

Julianna's first professionally decorated cake—using her
new Betty Crocker Kit.

Julianna with her real chick "Miss Red."

Julianna in one of her favorite outside spots with a brand new garden quilt made especially for her by a friend of her Mom's.

CarePage Messages

Hello to the Smith Family

Beth May 06, 2007, at 09:01 p.m. EDT

Dear JoAnn, Brian, Julianna, and Jeffrey,

Thank you so much for taking the time to keep us posted. You say "thanks for reading," and I want to thank you for taking the time to write. I am so glad that Julianna is able to get back to school. I know how concerned Hayley and Jenna are when they miss things at school. Please know that we are thinking about you and wish you well in the coming weeks.

Love, Beth, John, Jenna, and Hayley
(cousin)

Hello To All!

Jeannie May 06, 2007, at 09:33 p.m. EDT

Wow, Julianna it was nice to hear you donated a quilt that would go to someone else. That was so kind of you, you are truly a special girl! We are so happy to hear things are looking up. It was great to hear you were at school all day, we bet you truly enjoyed it. Well I guess your mom is very excited about the new additions to the family. Take care and thanks for sharing.

Love to all, Jeannie & Bruce
(family friend)

Happy Monday, Julianna

Linda May 07, 2007, at 09:31 a.m. EDT

Wow! that cake looks so professional! I bet it tasted good, too. we are so glad you are feeling well enough to jump on the trampoline, bake a cake, shop for chicks...getting better every day!
thanks for the updates JoAnn, you are amazing!

(school friend)

Chicks

Wendy May 07, 2007, at 10:25 a.m. EDT

Hey Julianna—

The chicks are soooo adorable...and they are alot of fun! They quickly learn that you're their "Momma" and will follow you everywhere. The cake looks great! Very professional...you have so many wonderful talents.

Hugs and Kisses—
Rick, Wendy & Rusty:-) (church friend)

Hey There

Susan May 07, 2007, at 11:01 a.m. EDT

Wow, Julianna you are amazing! That cake looks awesome. Take good care of your chics! JoAnn..thank you for your updates and I for one don't consider it rambling, but great that we can truly "hear" how everyone is doing. I love the pictures, especially the one of Julianna and Brian! Take care and good luck this week!

Love,
Sue
(church friend)

Baby Chicks

Pauline May 07, 2007, at 11:45 a.m. EDT

Dear Julianna, What a cute addition to your family. I guess you'll have plenty of fresh eggs when they grow and become Hens. Enjoy them while they are so cute. I am so happy to see that you are doing so well. You look great... also, what beautiful quilts you have. I miss you and Love you and you are always in my prayers!

Pauline
(piano teacher)

Happy (belated) Birthday Uncle Brian

Marie May 07, 2007, at 10:49 p.m. EDT

Brian,

I'm so sorry we missed your birthday. I'm sure you heard the details but we wound up in the Bahamas to celebrate Eddie's 50th from Anthony!

Julianna,

You are your fathers daughter! You'll have to get Daddy to explain that to you. I always tell everyone that it's a good thing I married Uncle Eddie and *not* your daddy!!!! I'd have a petting zoo by now for sure. But I'm still hopeful. We will have to visit and get you to make a birthday cake for Uncle Eddie and your Daddy so we can celebrate all together. Nicholas is looking at all your pictures with me and says "hello."

Aunt Marie

Wow, Chicks!!

Amy May 09, 2007, at 06:01 p.m. EDT

Allison is going to want to live with you now! What a cool Dad!!
Enjoy your new pets, we can't wait to hear what their names are.

Love from Amy and Family
(school friend)

CarePage Post May 10, 2007, at 10:28 p.m. EDT

On Wednesday, Julianna and I made our way—yet again—to King of Prussia. They checked her counts and said she was fine to officially start her next phase of treatment. This phase is called "Interim Maintenance." It goes for 2 cycles of 28 days and is supposed to be a phase where her body gets to rest a bit. We knew they would be accessing her port so I had to apply cream to it before we left and then wrap it with Saran Press and Seal. This is very hysterical but this press and seal sticks to your skin very well and comes off much easier than those large band aids they normally use.

She received an IV Push of chemo at clinic and will be on a variety of oral medicines. On Wednesdays she has to swallow 17 pills. She did really great with this, but if you can remember to pray for her on Wednesdays in particular that would be great. She swallows 4 with breakfast, and 13 with dinner. The plan is that we don't go back to clinic until June 6th... of course because we just can't seem to catch a break—we did find what appears to be a "bullseye" on Julianna's neck the other night. The doctor confirmed that it appears to be a bullseye. It is not the exact typical bullseye but she said who knows what a bullseye looks like on an immune-suppressed kid. They are testing her for Lyme's Disease. They were going to start treatment even before the test results but the antibiotic reacts with one of her chemo drugs so we are in a holding pattern for the moment. The problem with this is that many times the test comes back negative even if you have Lyme's Disease, so we are very concerned about this.

When we left the clinic yesterday we went shopping for bathing suits for Julianna—her doctor and I teased that at her age bathing suit shopping is still *fun*!! Then we decided to both have pedicures and she also got a manicure. We had such a good time sitting in the massage chairs having our pedicures—although they had to use power tools on the bottom of my feet, and she decided the pedicure actually hurt a little bit—but the massage chair was definitely goooodddddd. I am not sure but I think stress was oozing out of my body while I was sitting there. Julianna has "Egypt day" at school tomorrow and a birthday party featuring a red carpet theme on Saturday—so her pearl blue fingers and toes are going to be just great.

Julianna has been having physical therapy twice every week. Once "on land" and once in the pool. She really likes it—although today she worked out too hard in the pool and exhausted herself. Her Dad made her a strawberry smoothie in his new smoothie machine—so that made her all better. I am supposed to be doing exercises with her each day and today I learned how to stretch her calf muscles—I am hoping to fit that in in-between insurance paperwork, and dispensing and crushing up medications—uuggghhhh!!!

Except for the Lyme issue, Julianna has really been feeling good and we are hoping for this to continue through this "rest" period. So, if all goes well I will write on a weekly basis to keep you updated. At this point I do think it is safe to say "no news is good news." If we hit a bump of any sort I will write—otherwise assume all is well…

CarePage Messages

So Good To See You And Mom!

Mary May 11, 2007, at 12:18 a.m. EDT

Julianna & JoAnn…

It was nice to see you at PCS quilt auction. You both look like God is taking care of you! I will especially keep you in prayer on Wednesday. Actually, that is kinda cool because we have chapel at school on Wed. and it will be an extra reminder!! Kudos on the "Quilt for Kids" quilt. How awesome to be a giver, receiver and giver again on such a memorable project. Enjoy that new quilt from Mom's quilt friend!

Love Mary
(family friend)

Hi Julianna!

Pauline May 11, 2007, at 04:27 a.m. EDT

I am so happy to hear that you are doing so well. I will pray for you about the Lyme's…that you don't have it. I found a bulls eye on Tiffy's tummy so she will have to go to the

Vet. I will be gone for one week to visit a friend who is sick, in Germany. I leave on Mother's Day. I know you will do something special for your Mom...she is the Greatest! Draw her one of your super pictures!

Love to you. Pauline
(piano teacher)

Thinking About You Guys...

Christine May 11, 2007, at 06:12 a.m. EDT

Hey there Smith's—just wanted to get a quick note off to you and say that we're thinking about you all of the time. The prayer walk with Jack is still going strong... he's still pulling me every morning. Julianna: I just *love* your new chicks... they are adorable... I have 8 new ones too—maybe they can hang out together some time... the plane ride might be tough on them though... How many do you think I can fit in a suitcase????? What kind did you get? I got Isa Browns and Barred Rocks this go round. My Arracaunas are still laying colored eggs—mostly light green. Sounds like you're feeling a titch better—*yeah*... and oh, my you looked *lovely* in the picture where you are relaxing out on the patio under your beautiful quilt. I want to come to your spa too!!!! It looks like the service is fantastic. Take care and know that we pray and think of you all of the time.

Love, Chrissy, Kevin, Abby, Nathan and old Jack
(family friend)

Happy Friday!

Linda May 11, 2007, at 02:14 p.m. EDT

JoAnn, thanks for the update—our prayers will be for no Lyme and continued improvements.

Julianna, blue nail polish???? how chic!

I bet your fingers and toes look like Rita's water ice, right? *yummy*!

Have lots of fun and continue to get better every day. be brave with all those medications. They are working, so every time you take them say *'Do Your Stuff!'* and they will. We are going on a vacation, so I won't be near a computer (*Yippee*!!! and *Boo Hoo* at the same time) until we get back on 5/21. We will miss you, and we will visit soon after we get back.

We love you!
Aunt Lynne & Aunt Carolyn

Happy To Hear From You!

Jeannie May 11, 2007, at 06:05 p.m. EDT

Hi everyone,

Well we hope you have a good resting period. We are sure you all need and deserve it. Pedicure and manicure are the best I'm sure you enjoyed that a lot. Hope all goes well with the bull's eye. You certainly get your share of extra happenings. This too shall pass. We will definitely keep you in our prayers, always. Take care and hope to see you soon.

Love to all, Jeannie & Bruce
(family friend)

CarePage Post May 12, 2007, at 10:07 a.m. EDT

I really did not want to be writing this soon... but we did hit a bump and Julianna wants me to make a request for prayers because she said "it always works." She woke up yesterday crying that her tongue hurt. We have learned that she has a very high tolerance for pain, so when she cries it means it *really* hurts. I was not making a trip to King of Prussia—I just couldn't bear to for some reason, and luckily her doctor was willing to go with what I was telling her I saw. So the diagnosis is mouth sores—a side effect from the chemo—although her doctor was very surprised that she would have them given the medications she is currently on. She said Julianna is definitely challenging her because she does good with the tough stuff and struggles through what is supposed to be the easy stuff.

Luckily, she made it through "Egypt Day" Friday morning and then spent the afternoon on the couch pretty miserable. We got some "Magic Mouthwash"—that is really what it's called. It numbs the tongue so Jules doesn't really like it, and we have to be careful so she doesn't bite her tongue by accident. Doesn't this all sound like fun???? We are very good friends with the pharmacist now, and he calls us after the doc calls in the prescriptions so we can get them right away. The kindness is never-ending—so that does make up for the fun we are *not* having.

She slept great—which I was so grateful for. She is in pain but the Tylenol with codeine is definitely helping that. We didn't even need a prescription for that because—imagine this—I already had that in our medicine cabinet—along with some morphine (that I need to keep locked up so I don't get tempted to take it. Ha-Ha!)

She is feeling good now—we are hoping she can make it through the red carpet party and enjoy herself.

As for the Lyme's—there are a few tests they run. The first one came back negative, and we are now questioning whether she really has a bullseye. We are holding off on treatment until the tests are all back.

So... for those of you so inclined, please pray that we can keep her comfortable through these mouth sores and that they go away really, really quickly. Thanks!!!

CarePage Messages

Great To See You At Egypt Day

Donna May 12, 2007, at 09:25 a.m. EDT

It was so good to see you at Egypt Day! Julianna did a great job as did all the kids!

Hope everything stays calm and the Lyme meds don't cause any undo discomfort!!

Your right those blue sparkly finger and toenails scream "star on the carpet!!!" JoAnn how come you didn't go with blue?

Well based on "no news is good news" we will pray we don't hear from you here for a while!

Have a great Mother's Day...I am sure Jules would agree you deserve special hugs on Sunday!!

(school friend)

Love From The Fells

Amy May 12, 2007, at 11:01 a.m. EDT

Our prayers are coming your way!! I hope that by the time you read this Julianna will be feeling much better and will be getting ready for the party. Allison is hoping to walk the red carpet with you Jules!!

Enjoy your Mother's Day!!!

Amy
(school friend)

Prayers are coming!

Jeannie May 12, 2007, at 11:59 a.m. EDT

We definitely always have you all in our prayers. We will have some extra ones coming your way. We hope all these bumps in the road will be over with quickly.

Love to all of you, Jeannie & Bruce
(family friend)

Lots of Ice Pops Jules…

Marie May 12, 2007, at 02:28 p.m. EDT

Jules,

Tell Mom to get you lots of ice pops and Italian ices for the mouth sores.

Aunt Marie

P.S.

Marie May 12, 2007, at 02:29 p.m. EDT

Jo,

Happy Mother's Day

Marie

I Spotted You At The Fair!

Suzy May 12, 2007, at 04:41 p.m. EDT

Hi Julianna! I spotted you at the Plumstead fair last Saturday and you look *great*!!! I talked to your mom for a brief moment, and she looks *great* too. You must be making it pretty easy on her. I hope you had fun at the fair. Did you get any water ice from Chubby's at the fair? It was *yum*!!! We are just praying and praying that everyone was *wrong* about the bullseye and you *DON'T* have lyme's. We will just look forward to that good news!

Love, Mrs. M and Maggie
(from basketball)

CarePage Post May 18, 2007, at 08:58 a.m. EDT

It is Friday morning and finally Julianna is almost pain-free. She still had the mouth sores on Monday so we made a trip to K of P to be sure it wasn't anything else. Her doctor is very cautious—which I appreciate—but I sure wish K of P was closer. Luckily, we had some friends willing to drive us because I had been having a few emotional days—I just couldn't seem to pull it together. Having other people around really helps me—so we are lucky to have lots of people willing to hang around with us. The doctor confirmed that it was just mouth sores. I had a friend call and recommend an over-the-counter product called "Rincinol P.R.N" that her family has used for mouth sores. She felt it was more effective than the Magic Mouthwash. We had great luck with the Rincinol—so if any of you ever have to deal with mouth sores you might want to try it. Anyway, the doc gave us a new prescription for Tylenol with codeine. She also told us that the other Lyme's test came back negative. She said the "bullseye" could have been just the actual tick bite. We are letting this go for now.

Tuesday, Julianna woke up in a lot of pain. She said the back of her legs, her lower back, and her neck hurt. Of course, this sent me into panic mode. I called K of P. When I explained the symptoms, the nurse casually said, "oh that's the Vincristine—when did she get that?" I said Wednesday. She said it was nerve pain, a side effect of that drug. I was practically jumping for joy. I was so happy that it was that and not something much, much worse. She said give her pain meds—how convenient she was already taking Tylenol with codeine for the mouth sores. She also suggested a warm bath—we did that and it helped.

The pain got less and less each day, but Julianna hasn't been able to get to school all week. I am getting good at stretching her legs out—and that really helps her. Plus, she cons me into a lot of back rubs—which also helps her.

She has a lot going on this weekend—so it is fun for her to have things to look forward to. I did post 2 new pictures—one from "Egypt Day" and one of her in her "Red Carpet" outfit.

It's been a long week, and we are going to just continue to take it easy and relax… again, I am hoping not to write unless we hit a bump…but that didn't work out so well last time…

Julianna at Egypt day.

Red Carpet—*Here I Come!!!*

CarePage Messages

Jack Needs *Your* Prayers!

Christine May 18, 2007, at 09:19 a.m. EDT

Julianna,

Hey—do me a favor—your prayer buddy, Jack, is staying at the vet today and having some surgery. We found a lump on him as big as Texas and they are going to take care of it... So—as much as he prays for you—send up a little one for him OK?

I was thinking about your trips to King of Prussia... it has been a long time since I've been out that way—but if I'm not mistaken, there is a good mall out there—so maybe you can squeeze some shopping in at the mall!!!!

Know that we think about and pray for you every single day—oh, and Mom, Dad, and Jeffrey too. I pray for strength and courage for all of you.

Got to thinking about the bullseye too—*so* glad to hear it wasn't Lyme's... that would have been a drag... but I wonder if Jeffrey didn't draw the bullseye on you to make you a target—be *careful*!!!!

Love you mucho—
Kevin, Christine, Abby, Nathan,
and old Jack (Family Friend)

Hi Julianna

Monica May 18, 2007, at 09:35 a.m. EDT

Hi Julianna—wow—I just had a chance to see the new photo's Mommy posted—you looked so beautiful on Egyptian Day—Just like an Egyptian princess!!! And the same for your Red Carpet outfit—WOW—you looked smashing!!!! I am glad you feel a little better—I had sores in my mouth once and it was so uncomfortable. I remember I couldn't eat because it hurt so much. Samantha is getting her first communion tomorrow—she's excited. Dylan is also coming—He keeps saying he's going to Sam's "Reunion". Ha—He's so funny. I hope Jeffrey is good—we love you—feel good!!

Monica and everybody!!
(cousin)

Hello

Susan May 18, 2007, at 11:53 a.m. EDT

I just wanted to say hi and thank you for the update. I check often to make sure things are going okay. I'm glad to hear the sores are getting better. Rest up and enjoy your weekend!

Sue
(church family)

Happy Things Are Going Well!

Jeannie May 18, 2007, at 02:51 p.m. EDT

It sounds like things are moving in the right direction. Thanks for keeping us posted. Well, we were wondering who the red carpet star was hiding behind those foster grants. The Egypt outfit was great, we expected nothing less. It looks like you had some great days Julianna!

Love to all, Jeannie & Bruce
(family friend)

Hi To Everyone

Amy May 18, 2007, at 05:05 p.m. EDT

Hi Jules,

Allison wants to say hi and she misses you!!! She hopes to see you at school next week.
Just remember that we are here if you need anything! Prayers and love are coming your way!!!

Amy and Family
(school friend)

The Dark Glasses Certainly Do It For You Julianna!!

Clare May 18, 2007, at 09:44 p.m. EDT

On our walk last night i looked up at the stars and thought about you-Julianna and so I said a little prayer to make those mouth sores go away. You said "the prayer always works" and you are *right*! Because next day we get this message from your Mom that you are almost better from the pain of the sores. Merlin and I will go out tonight too and do the same so that the back pain goes and Mom gets some rest. You really look like a movie star in the photo. Take care-we will keep on praying for you.

Mrs. F, Justin and Merlin
(church family)

Hello to the Smith Family

Beth May 21, 2007, at 04:33 p.m. EDT

Dear Julianna, Jeffrey, JoAnn, and Brian,

Thanks for the update. We are sorry to hear that Julianna has not been able to make it to school. You must really miss all of your friends there. Hopefully with summer coming you'll be able to visit with your friends outside of school. Hayley and Jenna are finished with school on June 5 and they have a swimming party to go to that day. We join the University of DE pool every year and the girls cannot wait for Memorial Day Weekend when the pool opens. It's been kind of chilly here so we wonder if we'll be doing any swimming. Take care and know that we are thinking about you.

Love, Beth,
John, Hayley, and Jenna
(cousins)

*Helloooooooo...*we're back!

Linda May 22, 2007, at 06:04 p.m. EDT

Just a short note to say we are back from our cruise, and yes, everyone we spoke to on Princess Crown are praying for continued progress on your adventure. We were sorry to hear about the pain and the mouth sores, but glad that they are getting better. the pictures look wonderful, but we can't wait to see you in person.

Take care and keep smiling!

We love you,
Aunt Lynne & Aunt Carolyn

Hoping All Is Going Well…

Linda May 29, 2007, at 08:59 a.m. EDT

…just checking in…a week and 3 days is about long enough between updates, don't ya think?:):)

(school friend)

10

Lots to Share

CarePage Post June 01, 2007, at 09:27 a.m. EDT

Have I really not written since May 18th???? Julianna is doing so, so good!!! We have tons to tell, some great heartwarming stories, and pictures, and of course a prayer request, but I have to come back when I have more time. It will hopefully be later today, but I don't want to get in trouble for not posting so I thought I would at least write this for now. Love to all, J and J

CarePage Post June 01, 2007, at 03:17 p.m. EDT

So, here's what's been going on since May 18th:

Julianna has had some really great days and we have lots to share. We have had some minor issues so I will get those out of the way first. One was what appeared to be "restless leg syndrome" for a few nights. This is not something the doctors' office has ever seen before as a side effect—so we are not sure what to make of it. It happened several nights—but we got through it by exercising, stretching, and massaging—sometimes until the wee hours of the night—oh yeah, and some nights we gave up and had Julianna take Benadryl, but it was short-lived and we hope it stays that way. Julianna and I agreed that as long as it wasn't painful—which it wasn't—we could easily deal with it. (I am thinking; however, that I might be able to add physical therapist and masseuse to my list of qualifications.) Our only other issue is that sometimes Julianna is having trouble sleeping. Insomnia is a side effect of some of her meds, but I think it is more of her schedule being out of whack lately. Certainly not a big issue and not one we are worrying about right now.

This phase of treatment we are in is two 28 day phases that are almost identical. We finish the first 28 days this coming Tuesday. On Wednesday, June 6th, we go to K of P and Julianna is going to get an IV Push of one of the more severe chemo drugs, she is going to be sedated and get a spinal, she will start her 5 day run of the steroid drug, and she will take those additional 9 pills as she does every Wednesday. I am growing concerned as this day draws near because these past 3 weeks have been the easier part of the treatment plan, and so this seems like a lot to me. Additionally, her birthday is quickly approaching, and we are hoping to have her celebrate with her class on Friday June 8th and with a few friends on Saturday the 9th. So... we need all the prayers and positive thoughts you can send our way, so that her body can handle this on Wednesday and she can celebrate her birthday as planned.

As for all that she has been doing...we all got to go visit Julianna and Jeffrey's Grandma and Grandpa over Memorial weekend for a few days. We went to one of our favorite restaurants. We got to go to an annual Memorial party (with my family)—and both kids even danced the chicken dance and the hokey pokey, and we attended a picnic (with Brian's family) where the kids played games, and were on the swings, and played in the creek. Julianna and her cousins even netted some fish from the creek, and Jules got to bring them home and put them in our pond.

One of the highlights for Julianna was Field Day this past Wednesday. The chemotherapy makes her super sensitive to the sun and the doctors words, "the last thing this kid needs is a sunburn", ring in my ears every time we walk outside. Julianna also seems to really not be able to tolerate the heat that well. I was trying to convince her to skip Field Day, but that wasn't happening, so I had to shed my paranoia and figure out a plan. I have purchased a case of sunscreen, (well, maybe not quite a case), so I was prepared in that respect. I asked Julianna if I could bring her a chair with a small umbrella hooked to it like I use at the beach. She said that would be OK. At the last minute, I grabbed a second chair—thinking of her pregnant teacher, or a friend, etc. Well, the day could not have worked out any better. She was able to participate in a few events. She took pictures and video using her new digital camera that her Gramps gave her as an early birthday present. Her teacher sat with her some, and one of her friends –who had a bicycle accident over the weekend—sat with her because she couldn't be in the sun either. The third grade girls, and parents, and the school staff, could not have been sweeter and constantly came over to visit. It was truly an extraordinary day. I have posted some pictures—go have a look.

Happy Julianna at Field Day.

Julianna and Cailyn Playing Tetherball.

Julianna and Her Very Special Pals—Annie, Cailyn, and
Ally at Field Day.

Silly Jeffrey at Field Day.

CarePage Messages

How Are The Chicks?

Ravenna June 01, 2007, at 10:08 a.m. EDT

JoAnn—thanks for posting the update, I'm happy to hear all is going well. Julianna was in my dream last night. Please give her a big hug from me.

love, Ravenna
(family friend)

Thank You!!!! For The Update...

Linda June 01, 2007, at 12:39 p.m. EDT

So glad to hear that you are feeling better, Julianna. We want to come visit, maybe bring the girls for a few minutes. I will call and see if that is a good idea or not. or, maybe you can stop by after Church on Sunday. Please let us know.

Aunt Lynne

Thanks Again

Linda June 01, 2007, at 04:52 p.m. EDT

The update is so positive, we couldn't hope for more. Positive vibes to all, and prayers, prayers, prayers.

(school friend)

Great Field Day!

Denise June 01, 2007, at 05:41 p.m. EDT

The Smith Family,

We are so happy to hear things are going better. We have all of you in thoughts and prayers. Happy almost birthday Julianna! Great pictures too!

Love & thoughts,
Neil, Denise, Isabella, Victoria and David
(school friend)

Hello to the Smith Family

Beth June 01, 2007, at 07:12 p.m. EDT

Dear Julianna, Jeffrey, JoAnn, and Brian,

Thank you so much for your update. We are so glad that things are going ok. We are glad that Julianna was able to participate in Field Day. Hayley wants to write something now-I'm glad that you are out of the hospital and able to do things. I hope you don't have to take the treatments too much longer. I really miss you. Now Jenna wants to say something—I hope you aren't scared. I know I was but the nurses are really nice. I miss you. I'm glad that you are ok. Please keep us posted and take care.

Love,

Beth, John, Jenna, and Hayley (cousin)

Yea Jules!

Lindva June 01, 2007, at 08:43 p.m. EDT

Happy stormy Friday!

Hopefully you are nestled in watching the light show outside through the windows.

I'm so happy to see the pictures of Jules at Field Day. What a great idea to bring along the chair & umbrella

—just like going to the beach. It was hot enough to imagine yourself at the beach too!!

I know that Cailyn is looking forward to spending some time with her buddies next weekend. Big prayers are coming your way for an uneventful treatment session on Wednesday as well as no after effects to interfere with any plans.

See you soon,

Love as always,

Linda and Family (school friend)

Hello to the Smith's!

Jeannie June 01, 2007, at 09:15 p.m. EDT

Hello everyone,

Thanks so much for the update! It sounds like you guys have been quite busy. We were happy to hear Julianna made it to field day! We are sure there was no other place she would have wanted to be. The pictures were great. We will be expecting to see more pictures now that we know Julianna got such a great gift from Grampa! We hope to hear more great stories in the near future. Thanks for sharing.

Love to all, Jeannie & Bruce
(family friend)

CarePage Post June 02, 2007, at 03:36 p.m. EDT

I wanted to tell you a few very heartwarming stories. Julianna and I talk a lot about how many wonderful experiences we are having—that we would *not* be having if this did not happen to her. The truth is, we sometimes still do say we wish this wasn't happening; however, that is clearly overshadowed by the generosity, love, and genuine care we have been experiencing these past few months. I have about 5 stories to share to date. I will post them each individually as I write them. I hope that they warm your heart and make you feel as good as they have made us feel. I can't help but think of the scene from "How the Grinch Stole Christmas" where his heart grows and grows at the end of the story—I think to 10 times its original size. That's what it feels like to me every time we experience something amazing—which is good, because it definitely makes up for the times where I feel like my heart has been ripped to shreds—like one of those wind socks that you see at the beach with all the long streamers hanging from it. I definitely prefer the Grinch feeling. Well, happy reading...

Story#1

A friend from church asked her Mom—who is a very accomplished seamstress—if she would make some fundanas for Julianna. When we received the fundanas we were amazed. Julianna was especially thrilled because not only were they made from great summer fabrics—including Pooh and butterflies—she made 2 of each so that Julianna could share the matching one with a friend, Plus, they were this great design with padding across the top that makes them especially comfortable and they look especially cute. I told my friend this is the only bandana that I have looked good in. When I emailed to thank my friend, she sent me back this explanation of how her Mom came to get this pattern:

"she went on line to a company called Nancy's Notions where she gets a lot of her sewing supplies. She found the pattern for the fundanas but it wasn't available to order online. So she emailed them to find out if she could purchase one. The contact for Nancy's replied back that they were no longer available, but that she had one that she would make a copy of for my Mom and mail to her for her personal use. My Mom replied back and explained to her why she wanted the pattern and the lady dropped it in the mail to my Mom that day and told my Mom she would be praying for Julianna. With the help of my Mom's 8 year old next neighbor as a head model, she tweaked the pattern to get the fit she was looking for."

Julianna thought this was a very cool story and she is always happy to hear how many different people are praying for her. A few weeks later, we received yet another gift of more fundanas—including a very fun patriotic star one—which Julianna wore ALL of Memorial weekend—you can see a picture of it in the photo gallery. There were also more fun Pooh and summer fabrics—2 of each again, and 2 larger size ones for me!! I cannot tell you the joy in Julianna's face when she received these fundanas. She also tells me everyday how the girls seem to only wear these now—that's how much they like them too!!

Julianna in her patriotic fundana and her Muffy bear in
her Betsy Ross outfit.

11

Supersibs! And Flashes of Hope

CarePage Post June 02, 2007, at 03:47 p.m. EDT

Story #2

One night last week Julianna decided she wanted to set up Brian's iPod for her to use. I thought this would be a good idea because she is starting to get into music, and I thought she could try to use it when they are sedating her and when she is at physical therapy working out on the various machines.

Of course, it was taking very long to set everything up on my computer for the first time. Now she is really into it and really wants to get it done. So we are working away buying music, uploading cd's, creating playlists, etc., etc. Most of the time, Jeffrey is being a pest and driving me crazy, and not doing what he is supposed to be doing—like eating his dinner. (Brian was not around this night.) So, of course I lose my temper with him, and punish him to his room.

The next day I do my best to explain things to Jeffrey and to apologize because I really was not fair to him. Later that day a box arrives in the mail for Jeffrey. He is super excited because he *loves* to get mail. He is opening the box at super speed. Inside is this big, beautiful, gold trophy from an organization called SuperSibs. It looks just like a typical sports trophy. The top is a big gold "V" with a torch and flame, and the SuperSibs logo. The bottom has his name on it, and it says "For your Strength, Courage &

Love—*you* are a SuperSib!" He is over-the-top excited, and I get a chance to really tell him what a great brother he is and how proud I am of him—and I get to redeem myself a bit. I am so grateful to this organization—they obviously know what families need—but *wow!*—the timing could not have been more perfect. I have posted a picture of Jeffrey with his trophy.

Jeffrey with his SuperSib Trophy—"For your Strength, Courage & Love—*you* are a SuperSib!"

CarePage Messages

Hello Again!

Jeannie June 03, 2007, at 03:00 p.m. EDT

Congratulations to Jeffrey! What a great gift. There are certainly a lot of good people out there and they picked the perfect time to show how much they care. We bet you are certainly proud of your son. Thanks for the great story.

Love to all, Jeannie & Bruce
(family friend)

Lots Of Prayers For Wednesday's Treatments

Donna June 04, 2007, at 09:15 a.m. EDT

Thanks so much for the update and heart warming stories of kindness from near and far. Annie has been so happy to see Jules at school and Field Day…man Jules you are one tough kid that was a *hot* day!

We will continue to pray for you all and especially that the Wednesday treatments go "painlessly" during and after!

Lots of prayers from Donna and Family
(school friend)

Thinking of You:)

Diane June 04, 2007, at 12:35 p.m. EDT

What a great idea to bring an umbrella and chairs for field day. I know Claire love the idea. My dad was a little envious too. So you are up for another great adventure at KOP! We will say a prayer and think positive thoughts! I know you will be super strong mentally and physically.

Thoughts and Prayer, Diane W and Family
(school friend)

Howdy!

Lisa June 04, 2007, at 05:10 p.m. EDT

Hi Julianna,

I'm glad to hear that you are feeling well. It was nice to see you at school today. I hope that you can attend Market Day on Friday! I hope that your treatments continue to go well.

Karlynne
(school friend)

CarePage Post June 06, 2007, at 10:02 p.m. EDT

Whew!!! What a day—everything went mostly smoothly and we are at home resting.

My good friend offered to drive us today—which always immediately alleviates some stress for me. We arrived at clinic, and Kim (the receptionist at the front desk) told us the pictures had arrived. I never had a chance to tell this story, but during the second week of our first stay at CHOP we had this amazing experience. First, Julianna had a bone marrow procedure in the morning which was a bit of an ordeal. We got back to our room and the CHOP teacher was there. I went off to make a few phone calls. I came back to the room to check on Julianna and the teacher said the photographers where just there. I looked at her quite puzzled and she explained that there is a professional childrens photographer (Flashes of Hope) that comes to the hospital once a month and photographs the children. She said the photographs are in black & white and are some of the most beautiful photographs she has ever seen. I went in the hallway and saw the photographers. They were just about to go into the next room, and they said they would come back.

The photographers did come back and explained that they would love to photograph Julianna—and me. Of course I said no to photographing me. They said "all the Moms say that." They insisted, so I said they better have some really good touch-up tools. They said "all the Moms say that too." Anyway, we had such a fun photo session. Julianna got so into it. She was really posing and being a ham. They asked us what were some things that were special to us and to her. We hugged and cuddled and did Eskimo kisses with our noses. They photographed Julianna with her blankie and one of her stuffed animals, and in front of her prayer clock. The photographer loved the idea of the prayer clock and asked to be put on it so she could pray for Julianna too!!

So back to today… we went to the "day hospital" area of the clinic after Julianna got her vitals. Megan, one of the nurses, came over with the pictures. She said wait until you see these. She said her and Julianna's doctor both looked at them through tears in their eyes. She said you are not going to believe it—they are just amazing. She handed us the 8 x 10's and said we should look at those first. I can not even begin to tell you the emotions I felt when I looked at the pictures. It was truly overwhelming. Once I cleared the tears from my eyes I was able to focus again and look at the stack of proofs. Other nurses came over that hadn't seen them yet, my friend was also feeling the emotions, and another Mom came over too to have a look. I have put a few of the photos in the photo gallery—the smaller size will not do them justice, but hopefully you can still enjoy them. One of the nurses said to Julianna, "cancel all the plans you had of what to be when you grow up, because you should be a model."

Anyway, after all that we went to the exam room. They have a new and improved needle they use to access the port. The nurse sticks Julianna and she can't get the needle in the right place. She poked and prodded a bit and now Julianna is crying. The nurses really don't like to ever hurt the kids, so she takes a break. Then she decides to just go with one of the other needles they have used in the past so that we don't cause more pain. She gets that needle in and it is still not working. She tries a few things and she is saying that sometimes after a month a clot can form. I am trying hard to remain calm, but inside I am panicked think-ing—*now what*!! I am so glad my friend is there because there is enormous comfort in not being alone. Another nurse comes in and they determine the port is slightly tilted and they maneuver the needle one more time and blood starts flowing—*Yipppee*!! Everything from there went smoothly, and now we just wait and pray for no side effects. I am out of space and energy so I will say good night.

Flashes of Hope took beautiful and touching photographs that captured both the innocence and uncertainty of an 8 year old Julianna who had just been diagnosed with cancer. Regrettably, they denied permission to share the photographs in this book.

CarePage Messages

Well, Here We Are On Wednesday

Linda June 06, 2007, at 04:45 p.m. EDT

Praying today was okay and that the treatments continue to work—

we love you all,
Aunt Lynne & Aunt Carolyn

Hugs All Around

Ravenna June 06, 2007, at 10:17 p.m. EDT

thank you for the update, JoAnn—I guess I needed to cry like this. I've been thinking about you all, all day long, with much concern.

Lots Of Love To J. J. J. and B,
Ravenna (family friend)

Beautiful Photos!

Erica June 06, 2007, at 10:56 p.m. EDT

Dear JoAnn and Julianna,

What gorgeous photos!!! You brought tears to my eyes. Julianna, you are just beautiful (and your mommy is, too;-) Thank you for sharing such candid stories, JoAnn. I'm so glad today went well. Thinking of you both.

Erica
(school friend)

Photos

Jennifer June 07, 2007, at 12:35 a.m. EDT

Those pictures are absolutely breathtaking! I agree with your nurse, Julianna—you should definitely become a model when you grow up!

(cousin)

Pictures!

Jessica June 07, 2007, at 02:15 a.m. EDT

The pictures are so beautiful, they brought tears to my eyes too!!!

I am hoping that I can come visit soon! I have been so busy since work started and the weddings this week, but hopefully sometime in the next week or so. I miss you guys a whole lot and I loved vegging out on the couch with Juls!

I really hope to see you soon! As always you are in my heart!

All my love, Jess
(babysitter)

Wow

Christine June 07, 2007, at 05:16 a.m. EDT

Julianna & Chach (Nickname for JoAnn)—

Gorgeous… just gorgeous… I see beauty, strength, and courage… It just radiates out…

Julianna—you must have prayed for old Jack—he had to go to the vet 3 x—with lots of procedures, but is now fine—he's back to his prayer walk for you—and loving it!

How are your chickens? Mine look all grown up now… no eggs yet—but I'm hoping maybe in July…

Well—ta ta for now to you princesses… Have a wonderful and blessed day…

> Love, Chrissy, Kevin, Abby &
> Nathan—and Jack (woof)
> (family friend)

Thanks For Sharing!

Donna June 07, 2007, at 07:08 a.m. EDT

Wow it is amazing the power and emotion that can be delivered through photos…I am certain there isn't a dry eye viewing your Care Page today!!! You are both so beautiful, vulnerable and powerful in those photos.

We are very happy it went "relatively" smoothly yesterday and will continue prayers for no side effects!

> Hugs from Annie and Donna
> (school friend)

Pictures

Sue June 07, 2007, at 07:38 a.m. EDT

The Flashes of Hope Pictures are truly beautiful. Thank you for sharing.

> (church family)

Wow!

Linda June 07, 2007, at 08:25 a.m. EDT

Those pictures are truly amazing. Thank you so much for putting them out for us to all share. Of course I was crying—no surprise there…even Cailyn was a bit misty eyed looking at them! I saw love & trust in those photos. A picture really does say 1000 words. You are both beautiful:-)

Thanks again,
Linda (school friend)

You Look So Beautiful!

Pauline June 07, 2007, at 08:37 a.m. EDT

Dear Julianna, I love the photos from Flashes for Hope. You look amazing in all of them and I especially love the one where your Mom is hugging you. I wish Claus were here to see them. He would definitely get out his camera. I know he sees them! I really miss you and hope that one day I can come for a visit. Tell Jeffrey that he is a Super brother. I know it is difficult for him,but he is doing his best, I am sure. I don't suppose you have any room on your prayer clock for me, but if you do, please let me know the time. I am praying for you anyway.

Lots of Love, Pauline
(piano teacher)

Ths Most Beautiful Pictures I Have Ever Seen

Michele June 07, 2007, at 09:28 a.m. EDT

JoAnn & Julianna, Your pictures are amazing, You can't help but feel the love from them and of course they brought tears to my eyes...

(family friend)

Nose to Nose

Marie June 07, 2007, at 09:28 a.m. EDT

Nose to Nose is my favorite!

I would have that blown up 50x30.
Always thinking about you all.

Aunt Marie, Uncle Eddie, and Nicholas

Beautiful People

Wendy June 07, 2007, at 10:47 a.m. EDT

Well you guys did it to me again. Here I am with tears in my eyes at work looking at your beautiful Flashes of Hope photos. You both could be models and look fabulous. But most importantly, the beauty of your love is so wonderfully captured in those photos. Thank you for being such wonderful role models of love and faith.

Hugs—Wendy
(church family)

I Am Right There With You, Wendy

Linda June 07, 2007, at 12:11 p.m. EDT

Talk about heart strings being pulled! *Phew*! these are so beautiful. I love them all, but my favorite is the hug.

Thanks for sharing. Now I have to go sob.

The Photos Are Beautiful!

Debra June 07, 2007, at 03:37 p.m. EDT

You girls are beautiful. Julianna, you should be a model… absolutely stunning! We are still praying for you, and looking forward to seeing you in church!

Love, Debbie
(church family)

Truly Beautiful

Barbara June 07, 2007, at 06:43 p.m. EDT

The pictures are just wonderful and brought tears to my eyes also. How many wonderful people there are in this world that support us in our need. I'm still praying for you all.

Love,
Cousin Barbara

Hello to the Smith Family

Beth June 07, 2007, at 08:26 p.m. EDT

Dear Joann, Julianna, Jeffry, aand Brian,

The photos are beautiful! Thank you for sharing them with us. As I was reading your update I was hoping that we would get a glimpse of the pictures that you were describing. I am so glad that the nurses figured out what was wrong with the port. I can just imagine the anxiety that you feel when you are waiting for the blood to flash back. Hayley and Jenna had their last day of school on Tuesday. This year went by so quickly. Now we start the rotating child care schedule. They are either with me, John, John's Daycare, Grandma, School Daycamp, and Gymnastics camp. These girls have a variety of activities to keep them occupied this summer. We are also spending one week in Sea Isle City. We think of you often and hope that things continue to go well.

Love,
Beth, John, Jenna, and Hayley
(cousin)

The Photo's

Monica June 08, 2007, at 10:37 a.m. EDT

Thank you—the photo's are wonderful and heart warming—Julianna, you are one beautiful little model, but I always knew that!!!!

If anyone needs a good stock tip—it's Kleenex Tissues.

Keep sending the emails—we are all praying for you and we love you, too.

Love Monica and everyone!
(cousin)

CarePage Post June 08, 2007, at 10:09 a.m. EDT

Story #3

Don't put those tissues away just yet. I have some time as I am relaxing with Julianna—she is quite worn out so we are taking it easy. It's a good chance for me to get caught up on another story I wanted to share.

This is a story about an amazing labor of love by an art teacher, a very special class of third grade children, and various school staff members. Apparently, shortly after Julianna's diagnosis, her classmates were expressing their concerns about Julianna to their art teacher—Mrs. N. The art teacher felt she wanted to be able to do something to help the kids through this. She had the idea that they could make a quilt for Julianna. She went on a hunt for fabric—including Pooh fabrics—as the kids had told her what a huge Pooh fan Julianna is.

From there she got the kids to pick fabrics, and design and make their square. She then ironed on the fabric and also sewed down all the pieces. Various teachers and staff member also made squares for the quilt. The art teacher then added borders to all the squares using a cheerful pink, yellow, and purple flannel fabric and she used a soothing blue butterfly flannel as backing—this created what is called a "rag time" quilt. As a quilter, I was totally overwhelmed by the amount of work that I know went into this. When you look at each square and see the thoughtfulness and care that went into creating it—you can't help but feel that each and every person that contributed to it—especially the 3rd graders—have an amazing spirit. This spirit totally emanates from the quilt when you look at it.

The quilt was presented to Julianna by her teachers and class on field day. When speaking with the art teacher, her feelings came across clear to me that this quilt was done "by the kids," but I am telling you she also put hours and hours and hours of her own time in to make this amazing gift. (She also made mention of her Mom helping out.) The kids were so sweet in expressing to me how much they *loved* working on their squares.

I have posted a photo, but I hope that all of you get to actually see this quilt at some point so you can really "experience" it. Even though the temperatures are heating up, Julianna has cuddled under it quite a few times already. It is not only physically warming to use this quilt, but absolutely emotionally warming as well. (Remember that Grinch feeling of our hearts growing 10 times their size—this totally happens to you when you see this quilt.)

"Labor of Love" quilt made by 3rd graders for Julianna.

CarePage Messages

Spirituality

Marie June 08, 2007, at 10:40 a.m. EDT

Jo,

How ironic that my current class is in "Spirituality in Healthcare." And everyday when I receive an update from you it speaks in volumes of all the spiritual care that has taken place for you and your family. It's totally rewarding to see that the true essence of spirit exists. My hat's off to all of you for your love, courage, and faith.

Marie
(family)

What A Gift

Linda June 08, 2007, at 11:02 a.m. EDT

Thank you so much for sharing that story and the photo of the quilt of love. I've said it before—it is a wonderful gift for others to be able to do something—anything that might help to bring a smile or let you know how much they (we) care. The kids and their art teacher knew that this would make Jules smile and it is a little snippit of time—to cherish for ever & ever!

Thanks again,
Love Linda
(school friend)

Quilt

Sue June 08, 2007, at 01:47 p.m. EDT

What a beautiful quilt Jules!

Love,
Mrs G
(school friend)

What A Lovely Quilt!

Debra June 08, 2007, at 05:05 p.m. EDT

Julianna, you are so blessed to have such wonderful class-mates and teachers. The quilt is beautiful. I hope you enjoy it, and think of all the people who love you when you cuddle with it.

Hope to see you soon, Debbie
(church family)

Thanks for Sharing!

Jeannie June 09, 2007, at 12:00 p.m. EDT

Hello to the Smith's,

What a wonderful story about the quilt. Thanks for the warning about the tissues, I certainly did need them. The quilt was such a thoughtful gift. It looks so special, and I would love to see it in person. I'm sure it was made with lots of love. I also, loved all the pictures. They are certainly something to be treasured. Hope to talk to you soon.

Love, Jeannie & Bruce
(family friend)

Hi from A Quilt Lover

Mary June 11, 2007, at 11:36 p.m. EDT

Hi Julianna, JoAnn, Brian & Jeffrey…

Just want to say those quilts are *awesome*! Thanks for sharing. The pictures blog is great too. You are looking well and our family continues to pray for you all.

Blessings,
Mary

12

Happy Ninth Birthday

CarePage Post June 12, 2007, at 02:59 p.m. EDT

I just wanted to write a quick update so I don't get in trouble for going too many days without updating. Julianna did get to celebrate her birthday with her classmates on Friday, and she had a very small, low-key party on Saturday with her 3 good buddies— I have posted a picture.

We are thankful she got through those 2 events, and unfortunately it's been a bit downhill from there. She is having some trouble swallowing her pills lately. There have been tears and gagging and choking. She has swallowed these before, but she had 3 weeks off from them so I guess she is out of practice—or her tolerance for being able to deal with all of this is just breaking down. (I posted a picture of her with her pills because she is actually quite funny. These pills have a bad taste so she takes M&M's after each pill. She lines them all up—with color coded M&M's for each pill.) Anyway, we were trying various techniques to get through her swallowing problems and one day—I had a bad headache and needed some Advil anyway—so I offered to swallow with Julianna. We were counting down together 5-4-3-2-1- swallow. Jules thought this was great and, of course, then wanted me to swallow with her all the time. I remembered one of the nurses telling us that some kids learn to swallow pills by practicing with Skittles. I figured if it is safe to do that with Skittles, it must be safe with M&M's too, and since we have plenty of M&M's… each time she had to swallow there I was counting down and swallowing mini M&M's. I was begging her to please just let me bite it a little and not waste that good chocolate flavor, but she was not budging—I was to swallow them whole. Thankfully, she is done with these particular pills for now.

On Sunday, she woke up with some bad back pain, and last night she started with some nerve pain in her neck. I had a bit of a panic with the back pain because flashes of kidney stones ran through my head, but I called CHOP right away and confirmed that kidney stone pain would be just on one side, and she had pain at the sight of the spinal and on both sides of that—*phew*!!

So we have been taking it easy. I am not allowed to stray too far from Julianna so I am getting a bit cranky. Brian is really being sensitive to my crankiness and has been so good in helping me to get through these last few days. Hopefully, all this will pass soon and we will have some better days, so I won't plan to write unless there is something to report.

Keep those prayers and positive thoughts coming. Julianna's actual birthday is on Fathers Day and we are hoping to spend the weekend celebrating with lots of family.

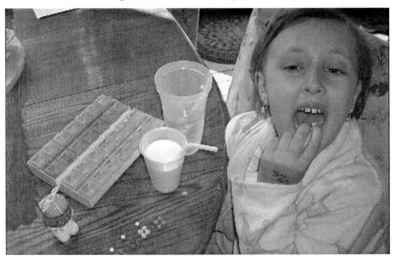

Julianna and her Pill Taking Set-up.

Julianna Celebrates her 9th Birthday!!

CarePage Messages

Happy Birthday

Denise June 12, 2007, at 03:45 p.m. EDT

Julianna,

Glad you got to celebrate with your buddies on Saturday! We hope you have a lovely birthday on Sunday—as well as nice Father's Day! What a double treat day!!

    Take care and our thoughts, prayers are always with all of you!!

Love,

Neil, Denise, Isabella, Victoria and David

(school friend)

P.S. a special hi to Jeffrey from David!!

Tuesday

Linda June 12, 2007, at 04:14 p.m. EDT

Hey there friends:-)

I knew that Jules wasn't in school because Cailyn updates me daily! I'm so sorry that there's pain around that spinal site. I will keep good thoughts and prayers headed your way as always. I hope that it clears up enough for Jules to get into school for the end of school. It's always more fun at school when work is not the focus!!

I'm so glad that Jules got to have some birthday fun. Hopefully Sunday will be pain-free and there will be lots of cake to celebrate!

If you need an adult to keep you company for a few hours—give me a call!

Take care, Love as always,
Linda & Cailyn (school friend)

Happy Birthday Jules!

Jeannie June 12, 2007, at 09:13 p.m. EDT

Hello to the Smith's,

The celebration picture was great, loved the happy face antennae. As far as the M & M's go I definitely would have wanted to taste that chocolate. JoAnn you are certainly a good sport! Let's hope a little rest will go a long way. Thanks for the update, hope to see you real soon.

Love Jeannie & Bruce
(family friend)

Happy Birthday Sunshine!!!!:)

Diane June 12, 2007, at 10:45 p.m. EDT

Well, Well, Well, 9yrs old and finishing up third grade. My all of you girls are getting so big! Your birthday looked like a bash! It's a bummer that you ended up not feeling well but at least you waited till after the party:) JoAnn my heart goes out to you! Hopefully, the typical lazy summer days will apply to you and your family! Also, I think for every M&M you swallow for Jules you should also get to chew one for Jeffery! Now, I want to stress this diet plan has not worked for me but I can't speak for everyone! Take Care! As always positive thoughts and prayers are coming from us to you!

Diane and Family
(school family)

What Beautiful Pictures!

Amy June 13, 2007, at 09:07 p.m. EDT

We loved your pictures!! Jules you are so beautiful! Wow, almost 9, it seems like it was only yesterday that you and Ally were in Miss H's kindergarten class. I hope that your birthday weekend will come with pain free days! We love you all and are sending you all of our prayers and positive thoughts. Stay strong!! Call if you need anything!!

Lots of love, Amy and Family
(school friend)

Happy Birthday!

Donna June 19, 2007, at 10:18 p.m. EDT

Dear Julianna,

Happy! Happy! Happy! Birthday! Your pictures are beautiful and you are too!

Love, Donna
(school friend)

Hi there

Linda June 24, 2007, at 11:05 a.m. EDT

Hello Smiths...just a little note to say 'Hi' and check in. Praying that all is well and you are enjoying some peaceful relaxation. We are looking forward to your next update.

Love,
Aunt Lynne, Aunt Carolyn, Cara & Mia too

CarePage Post June 26, 2007, at 10:47 a.m. EDT

We've been in such a good mode I haven't had to write any updates. We got through the end of the school year, and Julianna's birthday with her feeling great!! We spent our first week of summer vacation last week swimming somewhere—4 out of the 5 weekdays. I kept saying that after school was over we would be having a low-key summer, but last week was anything but low-key. This week we are going to be more low-key—or as I have been telling Jules and Jeffrey "my head is going to explode." When I say this, Jeffrey, of course, giggles hysterically—I am sure he has some Star Wars-like scene playing in his mind of my head really exploding.

Today I am starting to count down our last week of what has been an easy "maintenance" phase for Julianna. On Tuesday, July 3rd, we start the next phase which is officially called "delayed intensification." To me, I find it a bit cruel, but what they are really doing is giving her a chance to get strong these last 56 days, so then they can "bring out the big guns" as her doc says, and basically knock her down these next 56 days. We knew this was coming so we have been gearing up for it. We don't actually have the detailed "roadmap" yet, we will get it on Tuesday. All I know is that we will be back to weekly trips to K of P and there will be a variety of new medicines. We go on Monday July 2nd for an EKG and Echocardiogram because one of the new medicines is apparently rough on your heart so they have to be sure her heart is strong going into to it. Also, her "counts" will be very jeopardized, so I will have to be vigilant about any fevers—and if she gets one we have to get to the hospital immediately. Her doctor, in the beginning, teased me about not chasing Julianna around with a thermometer in my hand—but don't be surprised if you catch me doing that the next 56 days. The good thing is that this is a more germ-free time of year, so the chance of her "catching" something is less than other times of the year.

When we were at clinic 3 weeks ago, the one nurse had the idea that Jules should bring friends with her to clinic over the summer—a lot of the kids do it. She also said she would arrange with the child life specialist to get nail polishes and we will do manicures. We also talked about milkshakes—so I think I am going to bring some ice cream and a blender and make a party out of it. It sounded to me like they really try to make the summer visits extra fun for the kids—and I am all for it!!

So, for next week, we have the EKG and Echo on Monday, and on Tuesday she is having a spinal and getting her IV Push of chemo—these are the procedures/medicines that sometimes cause the back pain and nerve pain. So, you all know what we need those 2 days—all the prayers and positive thoughts we can get.

We are actually going to head to north Jersey to visit my family this week, because after next week we are not straying too far from CHOP. I am trying my best to just enjoy this last week of our maintenance phase... so I will probably not write again until after Tuesday. Thank you to all of you for your continued support of us—we would not be faring as well without it.

CarePage Messages

Thinking Of You

Marchell June 26, 2007, at 11:26 a.m. EDT

Hello Julianna and the Smith family:

Even though "school is out," we think and pray for you all every day. We look forward to reading the posts, and certainly understand when you are too busy or tired to write.
    We will keep praying during the upcoming phase. Emma says hello.

Marchell
(school friend)

Hello to the Smith's!

Jeannie June 26, 2007, at 11:29 a.m. EDT

We are real happy to hear that things have been positive. Swimming sounds like a lot of fun. And we know you can all use some of that! Prayers are always coming your way, whether you ask for them or not. Looking forward to hearing from you soon and helping out over the summer.

All our Love, Jeannie & Bruce
(family friend)

Thanks For The Update!

Linda June 26, 2007, at 01:16 p.m. EDT

We are so glad to hear the there has be a break in the pain-filled days. and Jules, you can do anything for 56 days—look what you have done so far! You can beat this and you will. Just keep that positive attitude and that wonderful heart of yours will get you past this part of the adventure. And before you know it, this will be a part of your history. We love you, and pray for continued good news. We are here if you need anything!

Enjoy the week!!!

Love,
Aunt Lynne & Aunt Carolyn, Cara & Mia

Sending love to Julianna from Mrs. D your Pre-School Teacher

Josephine June 26, 2007, at 05:51 p.m. EDT

Hi Julianna,

Just want you to know that we are thinking and praying for you at the Pre-School. Your website is great, it's wonderful to be able to keep in touch with you! We love your pictures. Stay strong and be positive Julianna, we love you!

Love and Hugs,
Mrs. D (preschool teacher)

Hello to the Smiths

Beth June 26, 2007, at 06:17 p.m. EDT

Hello Everyone!

Thanks for the update. We will certainly keep you in our thoughts next week. We hope that all goes well for you. We are so glad to hear that you are able to go swimming. Swimming is one of the most favorite summer activities for Hayley and Jenna. We are at the Univ. of DE pool as much as we can be. We are headed up to Connecticut this weekend to visit with John's Aunt. She lives right on a lake and their are lots of fun activities to do. Enjoy the visit with your family and we are thinking of you.

Love, Beth, John,
Jenna, and Hayley (cousin)

Hi JoAnn & Jules

Karen June 26, 2007, at 08:29 p.m. EDT

Glad you're all able to enjoy swimming on these steamy days. My mum has just left after her visit and we have no commitments now until the 28th July, so if I can drive you to CHOP, please *do not hesitate* to phone me.

All our love, Karen, Mike, Aimee and Emily
(school friend)

Hi from Pauline!

Pauline June 27, 2007, at 02:57 a.m. EDT

Dear Julianna, Happy to hear that you have been doing some swimming. It has been so warm and muggy the past two days. I will be away with my family over the 4th but we will all keep you in our prayers. I have some students who don't know you but who visit your care page and ask about you all the time. Keep strong. Lots of hugs!!

Pauline and Tiffy
(piano teacher)

Hi to All

Amy June 28, 2007, at 02:08 p.m. EDT

We just got back and were so glad to hear that you have been swimming and relaxing. Ally misses you Jules and she can't wait to see you! We will give you a call soon!!!

Love, Amy and Allison
(school friend)

Hello There...

Linda June 28, 2007, at 03:28 p.m. EDT

Just a short note to say Hi and let you know extra prayers were with you yesterday. Also, I love the pictures from your birthday and your pill-taking setup! I hope you are saving that little M&M dispenser, because *someone i know* collects *everything*!

Love to all,
Aunt Lynne & Aunt Carolyn
Cara & Mia too

CarePage Post July 04, 2007, at 02:04 p.m. EDT

Here we are again at another "Day 1" of a treatment phase. Julianna is feeling fine so far today—I could tell from the minute she walked down the steps this morning with a smile on her face that she was OK. It wouldn't be Julianna's care page without a few stories to share of our adventure recently…it's going to take 2 posts, so, here goes…

CHOP recently went to a new appointment scheduling system, and while I know this sounds mean—I hope the people in charge of it have been fired—because it is a *disaster*. I spent hours upon hours trying to get through the system to make appointments for the the EKG and Echo Julianna needed to have before her procedures yesterday. Finally, after 2 days of trying to get through I was switched around to 4 different people and the last person made me an appointment, then put me on hold, and told me to call back the next week. I called the Chalfont office the next Monday—this is where I wanted to have the tests done— and I actually got through. I made an appointment for this past Monday. We get to the Chalfont office for the appointment on Monday at 10:00am. We go to check-in and they tell me I do not have an appointment. I stand there with my mouth open for a minute. Now, with my voice quivering I start to tell them all I have been through trying to make this appointment. They check the computer and tell me I am scheduled downtown. I said "I called this office 215-997-etc to make an appointment and you are telling me that I was scheduled downtown and no one told me that is where they were scheduling me." They ask me if I can go downtown. I say no. Now the tears are welling and here I go "My daughter is an oncology patient here and needs to have these tests so that she can start her next round of chemo tomorrow. Why would someone schedule me downtown if I called this office?" Now I have their attention. Jeffrey, who has been busy trying to find Star Wars stickers in their basket looks up at me and says, "Mom, your eyes are all watery."

The problem is that there is not even a technician there to perform the Echo. There is a nurse there who looks at me and says she will at least get the EKG done for me. They take another 20 minutes to register us—3 people trying on this new computer system and it takes forever to get it figured out. Once that is done the nurse takes us right back. She does the EKG and she says to me, "Off the record, everything looks fine. I thought maybe you could use one less stress for today." It was nice of her and I thank her, but I am still upset over the whole situation.

The 30 minute drive home was enough for me to gather myself together and move on. I called K of P to see if we could get the Echo done there before the procedures on Tuesday. They couldn't tell me, they said they would call me back—they never did and unfortunately I lost track of it until it was too late. This was what I had been trying to avoid. I wanted these tests out of the way, so that we could just worry about the spinal and chemo on Tuesday. "Oh well," I tell myself. I tell myself that a lot lately...

13

No Coincidences

Carepage Post July 04, 2007, at 02:28 p.m. EDT

Tuesday, we leave for K of P around 8:45am. Our friends pick us up. (Just to add to the complications—I realized my van was due for inspection this past March—oopps!! how did I miss that?? so our friend/mechanic has my van to fix a few things and get it inspected.) Julianna is very excited to be bringing a friend to clinic. I had called Burger King the night before and ordered 30 chocolate milkshakes. My friend and I thought we would bring the ingredients and make them at clinic, but we decided that was too ambitious and we should buy them. We get to Burger King, and I say I am here for the milkshakes I ordered last night. The person looks at me like I have 2 heads. I am now wondering if I am living in the "twilight zone" because I can't seem to get things right. Is it me?? Don't really answer that.

While we are waiting for them to make the milkshakes, a woman comes in. She sees us and says, "oh girls day out?" We all smile at her. Then she asks something about are we going shopping. I don't exactly remember. I just remember looking at her and I am not sure what to say, so I said the truth that we were actually on our way to the hospital for chemo. She looked at me and said, "for you?" I said, "no actually, for her," and I pointed to Julianna. The woman got her stuff and wished us luck. At the same time, my friend had gone out to the car. When my friend came back in, she said the woman asked her Julianna's name. This woman said she has a sister who lives in Hawaii and is very involved in a prayer chain and she would have them pray for Julianna. As the woman was leaving, she said to my friend, "there really are no coincidences in life."

We get to the clinic. I tell one of the nurses about my problems with the echo. She is going to try and get us scheduled next door. We tell them about the milkshakes—the staff there is very excited. While Julianna is getting examined a nurse comes in to say they can take us now for the Echo. We rush over. Julianna is starting to be hungry since she is fasting for the spinal. They take forever to call us in. Finally they call us. I think it's about 12:30. We get back to the oncology building. Everyone is asking what happened to us. They had even called over to check on us. We make our way to the procedure room. Some of us take just a few sips of milkshake because we have to. They sedate Julianna and she does great through the spinal. *Now*, she can eat!! I start her with a chocolate milkshake, but then I have to take it away because she is not taking nice, easy sips like I want her to. We also have her favorite snack of flavor blasted goldfish.

The nurse starts her IV for the new drug (DOXO) she is getting—the one that could potentially cause the heart problems. First they give her a dose of anti-nausea medicine, then the DOXO. The actual medicine is very orange in color. Hopefully, with the anti-nausea medicine, we can avoid all nausea. She also gets a dose of the medicine that sometimes causes the nerve pain (VCR).

The staff continually thanks us for the milkshakes when we come out of the procedure room. We also had them offer them to the patients while we were in the procedure and they said the families—kids and parents—were very happy to have them.

I got our roadmap for the next 56 days. I am still digesting it. It is less medicine, but tougher ones. We are going to have to go to clinic this Friday at 11:30 for Julianna's most dreaded treatment. She has to get a drug that is given by needle—one in each thigh. It is very painful, and caused many tears last time. We are hoping this will be the last time she has to get this drug. We need mega prayers and positive thoughts about this.

For today, Julianna is feeling good. She had a little back pain last night, but it is gone. She is busy making a pillow for her Webkinz animals. You know the drill—prayers and positive thoughts. Happy 4th!!

CarePage Messages

Happy 4th of July

Mary July 04, 2007, at 03:01 p.m. EDT

JoAnn, Julianna & Family...

On this special holiday, a thought occurred to me this morning about Julianna's care-taking and our freedom... that *you* can choose your own doctors, type of care, medicines (to a certain degree) all because they are considered our "rights" as free citizens. I can also pray freely and openly for each of you—such a gift.

To that end, please know that we do and will continue to pray especially during this next phase.

May the peace that passes all understanding guard your hearts & minds in Christ Jesus our Lord.

Lovingly,
Mary (family friend)

For All the Smiths...

Nancy July 04, 2007, at 09:21 p.m. EDT

Just want you to know we are thinking about all of you and praying for you Julianna!!!

Love, Nancy & Tom
(family friend)

Tennessee Greetings!

Stephanie July 04, 2007, at 11:39 p.m. EDT

Just so you know—there's a bunch of us praying for you here in Tennessee too! Our God is a *Great God*—and I pray you will feel his peace and comfort. Don't forget to breathe!:-)

Love You All!
Steph

Oh Well!

Jeannie July 05, 2007, at 09:37 a.m. EDT

Hello to the Smith's,

It sounds like everything worked out in the end. So your Oh well, attitude didn't seem to hurt things any. We hope Julianna is feeling good today. Hope you had a restful 4th. You guys have come a long way, keep doing what you are doing and keep your chins up! We are certainly sending lots of prayers your way.

Lots of Love to you all,
Jeannie & Bruce
(family friend)

Happy Late 4th Of July!

Amy July 05, 2007, at 12:33 p.m. EDT

We were happy to read your update! Wow 30 milkshakes!!! That sounds like fun. We will be praying that things go well on Friday! Love from Amy and Family

Hugs from Allison
(school friend)

It was great…

John July 05, 2007, at 02:35 p.m. EDT

…It was great to see you and your family yesterday at the picnic. Weren't the fireworks wonderful? I wish that there had been even more of them! Happy Independence Day to you and yours!
     God bless you.

(neighbor)

Happy Belated Fourth!

Linda July 05, 2007, at 04:32 p.m. EDT

Many prayers for tomorrow, and for no nausea!
     I hope to see you all soon, and yes, there are no coincidences.
     MAHALO to the woman with the Hawaiin prayer group!

Love, Aunt Lynne & Aunt Carolyn, Cara
& Mia say woof woof

CarePage Post July 06, 2007, at 04:38 p.m. EDT

We just wanted to let everyone know that we are home from K of P and everything went well today—easy for me to say of course—I was not the one that had very painful needles shot into my thighs.
     We went prepared with our iPod and iDog so that we could play music nice and loud as a distraction. Julianna decided on a Hannah Montana song that we could sing. My sister was there— Julianna's "Auntie A" so that was a comfort for her also. One of the nurses knew the song also, so we were all singing. I could see the two nurses prepping out of the corner of my eye. I heard

them quietly count down 3-2-1, and within seconds Julianna was crying. I have been told these are very painful shots. It took only a few seconds more and I saw them pull the needles out. I told Jules it was all over. She was still crying. They had her sit up right away and one of the nurses gave her a hug. Then they told us to walk some laps around the inside of the building. Apparently walking around really helps the medicine to get flowing. We walked around for a while still playing her music.

After that we had to sit for 2 hours while they monitored her for any side effects. This used to only be 30 minutes, but the nurse told us that kids were having reactions in the parking lot, so they have extended the time. So, we sat and relaxed for 2 hours, and now we are home and very, very, very happy to have this behind us.

Oh yeah, I did buy Julianna yet another Webkinz on the way home. In anticipation of these needles today, I promised her I would buy her something and that is what she wanted… oh well

CarePage Messages

Brave girl!

Clare July 06, 2007, at 05:31 p.m. EDT

Dear Julianna-those muscle shots are the worst but it sounds like you came through with a badge of courage! What a brave girl!

(church family)

Thanks For The Update!

Linda July 06, 2007, at 10:05 p.m. EDT

Phew! Another day over, and on to more healing! *You did it julianna*! You are such a brave warrior. We are very proud of you, and we are praying for you every day and even at night, too. It must be working, huh?

God Is Good!

Love,
Aunt Lynne & Aunt Carolyn Cara
& Mia too

Welcome Home Webkinz!

Jeannie July 06, 2007, at 11:44 p.m. EDT

Hello to the Smith's,

Well, just another critter to enter the Buckingham Zoo! We were real glad to hear things went well today. Jules you and your Mom are doing a great job through all of this, keep up the good work. We hope to see you guys again soon.

Love to all, Jeannie & Bruce
(family friend)

Friday PM

Linda July 06, 2007, at 11:58 p.m. EDT

Hey there Jules & JoAnn,

I'm so happy that today went well. You were on my mind all morning and I said prayers that those nasty shots would be quick and done. I'm so happy that they are behind you now.

If we ever cross your mind—it must be because we're thinking of you too! I'm praying for few side effects and comfortable days and nights.

See you soon:-)

Love,
Linda and Family (school friend)

You Are So So Special

Jane July 07, 2007, at 08:18 a.m. EDT

Our prayers have been with you all day and we are so thankful all went well and you are home. You are such a brave wonderful girl. We love you and keep praying.

Aunt Jane

So Happy To Get The Update!

Amy July 07, 2007, at 01:32 p.m. EDT

Hi Smith Family,

We were so glad to hear that the shots were over and done with! As always, you were in our thoughts and prayers! Jules, Allison can't wait to meet your new webkins! Rest up this weekend. Stay strong! So many friends are sending prayers your way!

Much Love, Amy and Ally
(school friend)

Still Thinking Of You!

Pauline July 07, 2007, at 07:46 p.m. EDT

Dear Julianna and JoAnn, I think of you both so often. I miss you and I am remembering you in my prayers. I like to get the updates because I feel more in touch with what you are going through. You are both so brave. Hang in there and please let me know if I can be of any help. Love to you.

Pauline and Tiffy
(piano teacher)

Glad That Is Over

Donna July 08, 2007, at 02:17 p.m. EDT

Thanks for the update I am sure it is a relief to have Friday's treatments past you...You have been and will continue to be in our prayers during this phase of your treatment!

And really a girl can never have too many webkinz... or shoes?!! Annie will give you a call before our trip-she will miss you!!!

Hugs and love from Annie and Donna
(school friend)

I Don't Blame You For Crying!!!

John July 08, 2007, at 05:25 p.m. EDT

Julianna, I don't blame you for crying when they stuck that nasty needle in your leg. I would have been bawling too. Keep up the good fight!!!

Hugs all around,
John, your down the street neighbor.

Thinking of You

Laurie July 09, 2007, at 08:56 a.m. EDT

We think about you often...stay strong and try to keep a smile on your face!

Laurie & Ken
(family friend)

What A Relief!

Donna July 10, 2007, at 09:12 p.m. EDT

So glad those awful shots are over. I hate giving them in the muscle to cats and dogs too and never do it if I can give stuff some other way. Those milkshakes sounded great! I must be an old lady, because I have no idea what a webkinz is. I like the sound of it though. I carry you up to God in prayer every night and think of you all and pray here and there during the day. I'll continue to pray that God would widen the path and keep you from stumbling through the quagmire of scheduling. This stuff is tough enough without that nonsense to go through. Keep slogging, this is a marathon with a lot of hurdles. We are running with you in spirit.

Love from Donna and Dan
(church family)

CarePage Post July 13, 2007, at 11:25 a.m. EDT

We are back to our weekly trips to K of P on Wednesdays. We went this past Wednesday and it was pretty uneventful, although the doctor could not believe Julianna is not having mouth pain. Apparently, it looks like some serious mouth sores starting to happen, but even today Julianna has been fine. I have her brushing and rinsing like crazy, so hopefully we might be able to avoid them. Julianna got her two medicines—VCR and DOXO—through her port with no complications. We both brought a friend which always helps to make the trip less stressful. Just having someone to talk to for the 2 hours in the car is a great distraction for us both. The same medicines will be given to her next Wednesday, so hopefully that will also be uneventful. Julianna is back on the steroids for the first 21 days of this phase, so she was eating some salami at 9:00 in the morning yesterday- *yuck*!! With the steroids she also takes Zantac to avoid any reflux. She was having trouble swallowing the Zantac last month. I asked if there was an alternative and it turns out that there is a prescription version—of course it costs more—but it melts in her mouth. We are going with that option and it has been worth every penny!!

I spoke to the doctor a little more about this phase of treatment. It is very unfortunate in that the worst of it all is going to fall during our planned vacation time. Way back when, we planned a three week vacation at the Jersey shore—spending ½ the time with Brian's family and ½ with mine. Julianna may actually be OK for the first week of it, but the rest of the time is very uncertain. She will be getting 2 new medicines during that time—one of which I have to give her by needle—yes I will be learning yet another new skill. The medicines will potentially make her feel like she has the flu. They may cause fevers which would require a trip to the hospital—just to be sure it's not a fever from something else. The doctor did say that some kids do just "skate through" this phase. That was just the little hope I needed to hear. I am praying constantly that she will be one of those kids.

Julianna and I decided that instead of counting the days of this phase starting at "day 1" and going *up*, we are going to count *down* starting at day 56. So, today as I am writing this we are already down to day 47. I think it will help us both to count down the days this way.

One last thing, early on I wrote about how Brian said that the next person that asked if Julianna needed anything, he was going to answer a plasma TV. Well, today "Julianna" (you know I really mean Brian) got that plasma TV. Last week one of the lightning storms took out a few of our electronics—including our TV. So, of course, we had to buy a new one because she is spending a lot of time resting on the couch watching TV and movies, and of course, we have to keep up with technology. I think Brian and Julianna were both happy that our old TV got zapped—what's that saying—how convenient... It was very funny when they delivered it today, Jeffrey was reading the outside of the box out loud—plasma TV, etc., etc., the delivery guys were hysterical. Oh well, at least I have one very happy family today.

CarePage Post July 19, 2007, at 10:07 p.m. EDT

Please everyone keep doing what you are doing—prayers, positive thoughts, etc. because it is totally working. We went to K of P this past Wednesday and Julianna's counts were really good. Most kids need blood transfusions during the first part of this phase and it looks like we may get through it without needing that. They don't even want us to come in next week for blood counts—unless of course Julianna has any issues with bruising, or extreme tiredness, or paleness, etc. This was very exciting for us. We are going to keep doing what we've been doing too—praying, eating healthy (most of the time), taking vitamins and other supplements, constant hand washing, resting, and nightly massages. When Julianna's "Auntie A" was here she brought us some articles on foot massages and detailing some key pressure points for relaxation, and Julianna just *loves* getting these massages. She almost gets delirious when I do these for her and I think this complete relaxation is important for her right now.

In general, Julianna is doing good. She is more tired than usual and we are really taking it easy, and by dinner time she is practically falling asleep at the table. She is also being needy with me—a friend was here today and she said it best, "I see she is clinging to you like a barnacle." For right now, I am OK with clingy.

We go back to the clinic on July 30th. Please just keep those prayers and positive thoughts coming for Julianna to stay strong and for her counts to stay up!!

CarePage Messages

Lots of Prayers.

Pauline July 19, 2007, at 10:45 p.m. EDT

Dear JoAnn and Julianna, We can all certainly lift our voices in prayer for both of you and your family. I am only one but i know that there is not one prayer which goes unheard. I am so glad to hear that you have so many still praying. And God seems to be listening. Hang in there and I will pray that you have more strength. You are all going through a lot and we can hardly comprehend. You are in my thoughts and in my prayers.

Lots of Hugs!! Love, Pauline
(piano teacher)

Positive Thoughts!

Jeannie July 20, 2007, at 12:26 p.m. EDT

Hello to the Smith's,

We are very happy to hear things are moving in a positive direction. Prayers will definitely keep coming. As for your barnacle tell her to keep hanging on. We all need someone to hang on to sometime. Hopefully you will be able to scrape her off soon.(lol) Take care of yourselves and don't forget I'm always around.

Love to all, Jeannie and Bruce
(family friend)

What Great News!

Linda July 20, 2007, at 01:46 p.m. EDT

We are so excited to hear that you are doing so well, Julianna! Hang in there! and keep smiling!
    we love you and are praying everyday!

Love,
Aunt Lynne & Aunt Carolyn Cara & Mia too

Good For You, Julianna

Joan July 20, 2007, at 07:22 p.m. EDT

I am always inspired by the messages received on your blog and am happy that everything is going well. We have all of you in our prayers and hope that a miracle is in the making. How is Brian feeling? Missed him at the reunion.

In the meantime, keep up the good work, cutie, and I am sure everything is going to be A OK for you soon.

Love, Aunt Joan

Hello to the Smith Family

Beth July 22, 2007, at 08:10 p.m. EDT

Dear Joann, Brian, Julianna, and Jeffrey,

We are thrilled to hear that Julianna is doing well. Please know that we are thinking of you all. It must be such a relief for you all when Julianna can bypass just a little bit of the scheduled blood work. We hope that things continue to go smoothly. The girls and I spent several days in Dingmans Ferry last week. Our big event was we went rafting on the Delaware. We had a great time even though it rained a bit. We got stuck on some rocks a few times but some of us got out of the raft and were able to get it free.

This week the girls are at their school's Day Camp while I work. Thanks for keeping us updated and we continue our good thoughts.

Love,
Beth, John, Hayley, and Jenna
(cousin)

So Pleased Things Are Going Well

Donna July 23, 2007, at 10:43 a.m. EDT

Thanks for the updates! We are so happy to hear everyone`s prayers are working…for our part they will keep coming! Annie is thinking of Jules a lot during our current travels and hopefully Jules will "coast" through the rest of treatment so you can enjoy your vacation as planned!

Plasma TVs can be medicinal you know…not to mention a good foot massage! Lots of hugs and prayers from Annie and Donna…

(school friend)

Hi Julianna

Kate July 29, 2007, at 09:16 p.m. EDT

Hello Julianna,

I often think about you! Tomorrow (the 30th) I will really be thinking about you since you have another visit. I am enjoying my time off with Tim and Thomas, but I really miss seeing you and the other Buckingham students. I hope you continue to have a nice summer filled with many relaxing foot massages and great shows on your new TV. I will see you soon in September.

Love, Mrs. H
(third-grade teacher)

Emma K

Alison K July 29, 2007, at 11:15 p.m. EDT

Dear Julianna,

My mom is a good friend of Clare from your church. I would like to be your pen pal. Hope you are doing better and all goes well tommorow. I am praying for you. Please write me back when you feel up to it. Do you like webkinz? Are you one webkinz world? I will write again soon.

Sincerely,
Emma Newtown PA 12 years old

14

Songs of Love

CarePage Post July 31, 2007, at 08:24 p.m. EDT

Well, it's been a while since I have written. Today we are at day 29 and counting—½ way through "delayed intensification."

If Julianna's counts are good—and my feeling is that they will be—she will be sedated tomorrow—Wednesday—for a spinal. She will get a new slow-dripping medicine through her port, and she will get the 1st of 8 shots—she gets 4 shots this week and 4 shots next week. (These are the shots I have to give her.) And she will start on a new medicine in pill form. If her counts are not good—she gets another week or so "off" and we will go back to K of P either next Wednesday or next Friday from the beach. Yes—we leave this Saturday for hopefully 3 weeks of vacation. While I am losing my mind a bit trying to pack for the various possibilities—like needing to get to CHOP fast—we are all so looking forward to a change of scenery.

The medicines for the next 2 weeks have all the usual scary "possible" side effects, but there is a more likely chance of fever and flu-like symptoms that would require a trip to the hospital. So… Julianna is really requesting prayers that she does not experience *any* side effects—we will be praying for that also.

Julianna has lost almost all of her hair these last few weeks. She is mostly OK about it. I am more emotional about it. It's exactly what a Mom told me in the hospital back in March. She said it was very hard for her because it is just such a visible sign of what's going on. Sometimes I just have to turn my head away and get a grip. I am in need of a good cry—my Mom offered to slap me the other day—Julianna laughed in hysterics over that. The social worker also offered to let me get it out of my system in her office tomorrow—we'll see.

A few weeks ago, Julianna received a song written just for her by an organization called "Songs of Love Foundation." Their tag line is "The Medicine of Music." I had filled out a form for this via the social worker at CHOP. Anyway, it is a really cute song and Julianna just loves listening to it. It is just another amazing organization dedicated to bringing joy to kids who are going through serious illness. If you have any interest—their web site is www.songsoflove.org. Please don't feel obligated to do this, but the foundation has made the song available "to enable everyone to support our mission of music." There is a fee of 99 cents. Once on the web site type "Smith" in child's last name and 12420 in child's record number. Their web site is interesting, and we ended up listening to songs written for other kids—it was very cool. Again, please don't feel obligated—but I just wanted to share about this.

Jeffrey also received another gift from SuperSibs I wanted to tell you about. They sent him a mini Carabiner. Here is what the card said that came with it. "Did you know that the full-size carabiners are used by mountain (and tower) climbers to keep them safe in challenging situations? They also connect climbers to one another, as they get through long journeys and face the ups and downs together. We wanted to make *you* this mini-carabiner keychain as a reminder that you're linked to thousand of other SuperSibs! Kids who are on a journey like yours, just trying to be the best you can be in spite of the challenges you face each day. As you meet your ups and downs each day, just click this mini-carabiner… and as you do so, we hope you feel supported and comforted by the link we all share together." How great is that message!!! I really love this organization too. I think I am going to carry around this carabiner for right now.

That's all for now. I am not sure if I will be "connected" while on vacation, so it may be late August before you hear from me again. Thanks to all of you for hanging in there with us, and being there for us during our ups and downs these past few months.

CarePage Messages

Praying Hard For A Happy (Hospital Visit Free) Vacation

Clare July 31, 2007, at 09:07 p.m. EDT

Hi Julianna and JoAnn,

I heard from Brian that you are hoping for an uninterrupted vacation in the next 3 weeks. So I am praying hard for Him to grant you rest and relaxation by the sea, without any worrying trips back to CHOP. In the old days everyone went to the seaside for "taking in the sea air". I pray that it is truly restorative for the whole family while you: Julianna and the drugs, are fighting this nasty disease. Have lots of cotton candy and icecream too and sink those toes into the sand! Come back feeling strong!

Love Clare and Family xx
(church family)

Hi Julianna,

It is Jared. I'm up listening to the Phillies game in my parents' bedroom. My mom just shared your Photo Gallery with me. Cool pictures! I hope you are having a good summer. I'm looking forward to 4th grade and hope you are too! See you in September.

From,
Jared :-)
(school friend)

P.S. Have a great vacation!

Hello From Syracuse

Ann July 31, 2007, at 09:46 p.m. EDT

Hi JoAnn and Julianna! Even though we are not living in PA anymore, we think of you daily and continue to pray for you every night. We love the updates and always open the CarePage right away, hoping that it is good news. Thanks for taking the time to write the updates that mean so much. Your 3 week vacation to the beach sounds wonderful and is so well deserved. We miss you!!

Love, Ann and Family
(school friend)

To All of You!!!

Pauline July 31, 2007, at 10:11 p.m. EDT

A really wonderful vacation free of any complications. Great family time together and hopefully, a chance to rest and put aside the difficulties of life. This is what I am going to be praying for you. Love to you all.

Pauline
(piano teacher)

Have A Great Time At The Beach

Mary Pat July 31, 2007, at 11:29 p.m. EDT

We'll keep you in our thoughts and prayers and hope that you all enjoy the beautiful shore. good luck with everything and thanks for the updates.

MaryPat and Family
(family friend)

Sunny Shores Ahead

Wendy August 01, 2007, at 09:42 a.m. EDT

Julianna, JoAnn, Brian & Jeffery—

Lots of prayers your way for a safe journey through this treatment phase and lots of fun in the sun at the beach.

Hugs and Kisses—
Wendy (church family)

Once Again, Thanks For The Update!

Linda August 01, 2007, at 11:53 a.m. EDT

Here's to a side-effect free vacation! That is my mantra for now—no side-effects, no side-effects...just keep on smiling and knowing that this is all to make you better!!!!! Keep your eyes on the prize.

We love you and pray every day,
Love, Aunt Lynne, Aunt Carolyn, Cara
& Mia too

Well Deserved Vacation!

Jeannie August 01, 2007, at 12:39 p.m. EDT

Hello everyone,

You are always in our prayers and our hearts! We will keep positive thoughts for a completely uneventful vacation. Jules every time I see you, you always have a smile for me, make sure you keep sharing it with everyone around you. Enjoy your vacation, you all deserve it.

Love to all of you, Jeannie & Bruce
(family friend)

Thanks For The Update…Julianna Is A Trooper.

John August 01, 2007, at 05:45 p.m. EDT

Joann: I don't know how you do it lady. I guess that is why women have the babies…because they are a lot tougher than men. By the way, a carabiner can also used in a scuba diving rescue situations where you hook the other diver to you so the two of you can share one air supply.

Julianna: Hang in their young lady. Half way is a long way done and a lot less way left.

(neighbor)

Love to All

Amy August 06, 2007, at 10:01 a.m. EDT

We pray that this message finds you enjoying your vacation! Our prayers are working overtime for that.

Love from Amy and Family
(school friend)

15

Vacation?

Carepage Post August 14, 2007,
at 07:41 p.m. EDT

3S14—yes that is our room number at CHOP where Jules and I have been hanging out since yesterday—Monday. It's a long story...We went to K of P yesterday for a scheduled blood transfusion. We had been there on Friday and they said come back on Monday because they anticipated her counts to keep going down—and they did. So, we left the beach at 7am on Monday to get to K of P for 9am. I told them that she was really complaining because she had stubbed her toe and it was causing her lots of pain. They took a quick x-ray, but because her bones are so thin from the chemo they were not able to determine anything. As the day went on, her toe become more and more red, and they started to draw on her with pen to mark the redness so they could see if it was "growing." They even let Julianna draw some of the lines— she smiled quite a bit while doing this.

They got the blood transfusion all set up and then they waited a minute to take her temperature. She had spiked a very high fever. From there it became a whirlwind of antibiotics, they pulled the blood transfusion, and we waited, and waited, and waited for an ambulance to bring us here. By the time we got here and the doc came in around 8pm and looked at Julianna's toe—it looked like a full blown infection. The doctor could not say for sure if that was causing the fever, so they had to cover all the bases. It is risky because as one of the nurses commented, "her counts are in the toilet," so her body has no ability to fight anything. So here we are getting lots of antibiotics and under careful watch. The truth is, I really like being here. It's a nice break from being the one watching her every move and making sure she is OK. There are lots of great nurses and equipment here to do that.

Last night, Jules and I talked about the nurses that we knew, and she said her favorite was Amy. Wouldn't you know at 8am today, Amy walked in the room and was her nurse *all day*!!

She has had no fever today, and the redness is getting better, but there is something suspicious under her toenail. We discovered it after we removed the pretty blue nail polish. Her counts were back up enough today to let her home, but they have to keep their eye on her toe—hopefully only one more day. They did get her that transfusion around 11pm last night. She slept through all of it.

Julianna did pretty good with those shots I wrote about earlier. Our neighbor, who has experience with needles, gave her the 1st three and did an excellent job. I only ended up having to give her 2 because my sister-in-law (a nurse) happened to be over at the beach house so she gave her one, and the nurse at clinic did the other. I totally did not enjoy doing this, and pray that I never have to do it again.

As for the beach house—it is great and we are anxious to get back to it. We are on the end of a lagoon, so our water views are just beautiful. There is a table in the kitchen we call the cruise ship table, because when you sit at it you only see water—very cool. Every nurse and doctor that has walked into this room knows we were on vacation and they are very compassionate and want to get us back there as quickly as possible. Please send prayers and positive thoughts our way so that we can leave here and get back to vacation. Julianna really believes in the power of these CarePage requests, so she was anxious for me to write today—we had trouble getting connected earlier today.

I just gave Julianna her medicine that she takes with chocolate ice cream. She said to me, "what is this? It doesn't look like chocolate ice cream, it looks like a latte." Add that to the fact that today I got her hooked on HGTV. Oh boy, she is really spending too much time with me. Please pray for her to keep getting stronger and stronger and more independent.

That's all for now. I will write and let you know if we get "released" on Wednesday.

CarePage Messages

Praying That Your Vacation Is Wonderful

Linda August 14, 2007, at 02:24 p.m. EDT

Just wanted to let you know we miss you all and are thinking of you, and praying for a relaxing, rejuvenating time for all of you.

Talk to you soon!

Love
Aunt Lynne and Aunt Carolyn

Are You Finished With The Book Yet?

Marie August 15, 2007, at 07:07 a.m. EDT

Jules,

Let's see, its been 6 days since I saw you—so you should have a lot of pages done by now! And don't forget I get the first signed copy! Get to work.

Aunt Marie

Happy Vacation?

Linda August 15, 2007, at 08:36 a.m. EDT

OK...that darned toe!

It must have been a huge relief to turn over "the watch" to the doctors and nurses (for a short time). Hopefully that toe is looking good today, the suspicious something has been taken care of and that morning is bringing the beginning stages of the check out process at the hospital.

As always you are in our thoughts. Cailyn wanted to talk to Jules yesterday so I left a message. I was hoping that your phone was off because you were sitting on a boat in the bay...I'm so sorry that it was not that scenario.

I was with some friends last night and your ears must have been burning. I was updating them with information and I know that they all keep you in their prayers. I'll relay this latest update as well. More is better in this case—prayers, that is.:-)

I look forward to hearing more news from the beach soon. I love to think of you all lazing around the beach on these hot August days!

Take care and "Thank You" so very much for updating us on this latest hiccup. Prayers are coming your way—storming Heaven once again!

Love as always,
Linda and Family
(school friend)

Keep Smiling!

Linda August 15, 2007, at 09:07 a.m. EDT

A stubbed toe, huh? Well, we are praying you are back to the beach pretty darn quick...

Ship Ahoy

Wendy August 15, 2007, at 09:16 a.m. EDT

Julianna—

Praying for strength and healing so you can get back to the "cruise ship table" and enjoy all those wonderful beach sights and sounds. Looking forward to hearing all about your beach adventures.

Love, prayers and kisses—
Wendy (church family)

Prayers Being "Shipped" To You Every Minute!!

Denise August 15, 2007, at 09:40 a.m. EDT

Hi Everybody,

We wanted you to know you have our prayers. Hopefully by the time you read this you will be back on vacation! Take care and tell Jeffrey hi from David.

Denise and Family
(school friend)

Prayers Are Floating Your Way

Clare August 15, 2007, at 09:56 a.m. EDT

Glad to hear the hospital visit was short and that you are back to your lovely view of the sea. Take care of the toe Julianna (I said just rub those toes in the sand not stub them!!!) and think rest, relaxation and rejuvenation JoAnn. We will renew those prayers with vigor. Unfortunately I have not been able to do my late night prayer walks with Merlin this past week because of knee surgery. I hope to resume them soon. We look forward to those updates JoAnn too.

All our love: Clare and Family
(church family)

Beach Thoughts Coming Your Way!

Amy August 15, 2007, at 11:31 a.m. EDT

I hope that when you get this you will be heading back to the beach! We are sending prayers and positive thoughts your way! Ally wants Jules to know that she is sending "air hugs" to Jules as I write this!

Love to All,
Amy and Family
(school friend)

Thinking Of You

David August 15, 2007, at 01:55 p.m. EDT

I hope you feel better, we are always thinking of you,

Dave,Cathy and Dylan
(cousin)

Always In Our Thoughts

Ann August 15, 2007, at 04:03 p.m. EDT

JoAnn, Thanks so much for taking time again to update the webpage. I can't imagine having to leave vacation as you did, but we are hoping/praying that you can get back to your vacation spot as soon as possible. You are sure going through a lot. You always remain in our thoughts and prayers. Hugs to Julianna from Melissa.

Fondly, Ann and family
(school friend)

CarePage Post August 16, 2007, at 09:52 a.m. EDT

We just wanted to let you know that we are back at the beach house having a nice relaxing morning sitting around the cruise ship table. We did get back on Wednesday around 6:30 in the evening.

So, at the end of this latest episode, we have added an ambulance ride and the definition of pus—*Yuck*!! to our adventure. It turned out that the suspicious stuff under Julianna's toe was a "collection of pus." They numbed her toe just with some cream and tried to suction it out. The numbing part did not work so well and she cried quite a bit in pain—which of course meant she got to get a few goodies from the gift shop. The good news was that the blood culture showed it was just a local infection, and that is why we were able to come back to the beach. If we can find a local doctor down here willing to look at her toe early next week and talk with the oncologist back at CHOP, we will not have to make any more trips to CHOP during this vacation.

So, I have carefully placed Julianna inside a bubble and that is where she will be staying the rest of this vacation. Thanks for all your great encouraging messages—they really do a lot to lift our spirits and make us smile.

We are scheduled for K of P on Wednesday August 29th for a spinal and another chemo medicine. Let' pray that you don't hear from me until after that visit...

CarePage Messages

Doctor In Area

Marie August 16, 2007, at 10:05 a.m. EDT

Jo,

Dr. Glenn is someone that I trust in the area should you need someone to take a look at Jules' toe. Let me know what you decide and if you need help with that. I'll be glad to make a few calls for you.

Marie
(family)

Have a Great Holiday!

Pauline August 16, 2007, at 11:02 a.m. EDT

JoAnn, Thank you for the updates. Hearing every so often about Juliana's' progress is so encouraging. I hope you will ALL have a very relaxing and fun vacation. My Love to you all. Pauline

(piano teacher)

Cure for Pus

Karen August 16, 2007, at 02:32 p.m. EDT

Hi JoAnn & Julianna, Glad your back at your vacation home and hopefully getting back into relaxation mode. Julianna—I hear cotton candy, ice-cream and lots of chocolate is great for getting rid of pus!!! Good luck with your toe. Looking forward to seeing you again soon.

Love from Karen and Family
(school friend)

Back to the Beach!

Amy August 16, 2007, at 06:44 p.m. EDT

So glad to hear that you are back to relaxing at the beach! Enjoy the rest of your vacation! We are sending prayers and love your way!

Jules, Ally is so excited about the both of you being in class together again. 4th grade—It seems like only yesterday that the two of you were in Kindergarten together!

We are here if you need anything! Enjoy, Enjoy!

Amy and Ally
(school friend)

Good News!!

Joan August 16, 2007, at 07:04 p.m. EDT

We are glad to hear that you were able to get back and resume your vacation. Hopefully you will all get some rest now and stop running for a few weeks or so. Enjoy the remainder of your vacation and relax. Our heartfelt prayers are with all of you, we know that all will be well and this whole episode will be something to look back on and you will be able to give a sigh of relief. Our love to all of you,

Aunt Joan and Uncle George

Stinky Toe?

Steve August 17, 2007, at 07:50 a.m. EDT

Hi Julianna, Keep that pus to yourself..No sharing with Jeffrey.

We Miss you guys love you guys always thinking of you guys!!!!

You know what? I just figured out how to post a message to you.

Boy.. I am a dope when it comes to computers!

I am so Happy you are back to the beach House!!!!!!!!!

Have Fun. Be good to Mom & Dad!

Mr W.
(church family)

Back At The Beach Is Great News!

Linda August 17, 2007, at 04:01 p.m. EDT

So we need to get Jules some steel-toed beach shoes, and a 'no stubbing allowed!' sign for her feet! How silly would that look? I know, too silly. Have fun!

We love you!
Aunt Lynne

Happy Beach House Time!

Susan August 19, 2007, at 06:37 p.m. EDT

I've been checking the care pages and keeping posted. Just got back from LBI myself, but prior to going I checked in on you guys… so glad to hear you are back at the shore!! Praying you stay there until vacation time is up. Think of all of you often.

Sue
(church family)

Enjoy the Beach!

Jeannie August 19, 2007, at 08:04 p.m. EDT

Hello to the Smith's,

Sorry we haven't posted a message. We just got back from vacation today. Never a dull moment for you guys. Just keep hanging in there and hopefully the rest of your beach days will be uneventful. Take care and talk to you soon.

Love to all, Jeannie and Bruce
(family friend)

Miss You

Donna August 20, 2007, at 08:36 a.m. EDT

We just got the last two updates...I don't have computer access very often! We have been praying so hard that the vacation would not be interrupted..but alas...well we will continue to pray very hard for an infection free remainder. Enjoy the house it sounds like a great place for you all to *rest*!

Lots of love, prayers and kisses from the UK!!!

Annie sooo misses you Jules...Feel good...no more pussie toes!!!

Donna and Annie (school friend)

Hi Julianna

Kate August 21, 2007, at 09:35 p.m. EDT

Hi Julianna! I really hope you are relaxing on vacation and staying dry after all of the rain. I think about you and your family often. Your mom is an amazing writer. I have some good news—Brigid Anne was born on Thursday at 2:02 pm. She weighed 7 lb 13 oz. Can you believe Mrs. F had a girl? I can't wait to see pictures. I hope your toe is better soon and that the sun comes out tomorrow!

Mrs. H
(third-grade teacher)

16

Chemo Cut

Carepage Post August 30, 2007, at 12:41 p.m. EDT

Hello everyone. It feels like a long time since I have written—which is good. We spent the day at clinic yesterday—Julianna had a spinal tap and her VCR medicine. Her counts are low, but they were high enough to start this "Maintenance" phase of treatment which was good. This is, hopefully, our last phase of treatment. It is based on 12 week "courses." I forgot to ask how many courses we have to do—but I think it is going to be until May 2009—which seems forever to me. The key is that Julianna stays in remission and does not relapse. When I speak to the doctor about relapse, they very matter-of-fact just say that we will change the course of medicines, but Julianna and I pray every night that she stays in remission.

We have actually done this phase before—it was called "Interim Maintenance." It is a lot of medicine, but it is "easier" medicines than the other phases. It does involve swallowing pills for 5 days of each month, and 10 pills every Wednesday—it used to be 9, but she has grown so the dose has changed. Last night there were some tears before the swallowing because she didn't realize she would have to be doing this again, but she did it perfectly without gagging, so that is encouraging.

She will only have a spinal tap every 3 months, and we will go to the clinic monthly for her VCR medicine. This will be much nicer than the weekly trips we have done in the past. Her strength is returning slowly. Our insurance will no longer cover physical therapy—which she still needs—so we are trying to work out something, and I am exploring having it at school at least once per week—which is sometimes an option. The other concern her doctor said is that many kids experience "fuzzy brain" after all of this intense chemotherapy. It's hard to say right now if that will be an issue for Julianna—I guess we will see. Also, from the toe incident, they saw her bones were very thin. This is a common side effect, so we need to be mindful of her calcium intake—luckily, she loves, loves, loves cheese.

Her hair is starting to grow back, and yesterday the doctor said she expects that by Christmas Julianna will have a full head of hair again. This made Julianna very, very happy!!! The doctor also said that all the kids say that everyone always gives them millions of compliments on their great short hair cuts. The doctor said tell them it is a "chemo cut."

Today, the Martha Stewart Show was going to be at the clinic filming the "Con-Kerr Cancer" group that makes the colorful pillowcases for the kids. These are pillowcases that are always at the hospital. They are nice and bright and cheerful, and they really help to "hide" all the hair falling out. This group also goes to the clinic and the kids can make their own pillowcases. I wrote about Julianna making one quite a while ago. Anyway, we were invited to go, but Julianna didn't want to. I will let you know when it is going to air. It is really a great group and such a nice idea, so I am happy for them to get some press about their efforts.

Jeffrey got a SuperSibs T-shirt the other day, so you will be seeing him wearing that. The founder of that organization recently received an award from the "Energizer Battery" company, so that was great press for that organization also. We celebrated his 7th birthday while at the beach—his Webkinz collection has expanded to almost match his sisters.

School starts all day on Tuesday the 4th. Jules is really looking forward to it. I don't think she will make 5 full days yet, but we will be working towards that.

I am out of room because I have written so much again. Here are some things you could be thinking about for us and praying for. First, that Julianna stays in remission. Second, for no side effects from all of this medicine that she has received and continues to receive. Third, for easy swallowing of all these pills. Lastly, for continued strength and healing of her body.

CarePage Messages

Missing You!

Linda August 30, 2007, at 10:11 a.m. EDT

Just a little note to say I miss you all and look forward to hearing the latest progress report, and I am praying for good news!!! I hope Jeffrey's birthday was a fun one. Talk to you soon.

Love and hugs,
Aunt Lynne & Aunt Carolyn Cara
& Mia too

School Days

Wendy August 30, 2007, at 01:07 p.m. EDT

Hi Julianna & Jeffery—

Wishing you wonderful blessings as you start this new school year. Glad to hear you're all doing well and had a great vacation.

Best wishes—Wendy
(church family)

Thanks For The Update

Linda August 30, 2007, at 03:37 p.m. EDT

JoAnn,

You always seem to write at the perfect time, just when I can't bear to wait another minute!

Julianna,

You know we are praying for you all the time, for you to have all the strength to keep you strong through this 'adventure' so you can enjoy all of life's future, happier adventures!

We Love You All!!
Aunt Lynne and Aunt Carolyn

Hello to the Smith's!

Jeannie August 30, 2007, at 03:44 p.m. EDT

We were real happy to get an update. It sounds like things are headed in the right direction. We hope everyone enjoyed their beach vacation. We also hope you have a great start back to school. Hope to see you soon.

All our Love, Jeannie & Bruce
(family friend)

Hi Julianna

Monica August 30, 2007, at 03:56 p.m. EDT

Hi Julianna

Just want to wish you a happy first day of school next week and hoping that you have a great school year...we are very happy you are feeling good and we are praying hard that you stay that way!

Love from Samantha, Dylan and everybody!!
(cousin)

Looking Forward To Seeing You At Buckingham!

Mary August 30, 2007, at 05:23 p.m. EDT

Hi Julianna and Mrs. Smith,

My computer at school is up running and our new e-mail system is installed.

I must tell you Julianna that you are a great patient to swallow down 10 pills…most kids have trouble swallowing one. I would gag too if I had to down 10 pills.

All of us at Buckingham are looking forward to your return. Please call me with any questions or concerns. I will give you my home number when we talk.

I will be at Bridge Valley on Tuesday and Wednesday.

Enjoy your labor day weekend and we will see you in September.

Love and prayers,
Mrs. H School Nurse

Hey

Jessica August 30, 2007, at 07:48 p.m. EDT

Hey guys!

As always I am praying. I hope you guys had a nice vacation at the beach. I am really sorry I didn't get to say goodbye before going back to school, but I should be home soon so I will definitely stop by for a visit! Miss you tons and good luck with the beginning of the school year!!

Love,
Jess (babysitter)

Hi Smiths

Joan August 30, 2007, at 09:33 p.m. EDT

God bless all of you, we are praying like crazy that all of this will soon be over. We hope that Julianna will be able to continue her life soon, at the point where it was interrupted. We want to say good luck in school, we know you will be one of the top students, Julianna. Best wishes for a successful school year. Feel well.

Our love to all of you, Aunt Joan
and Uncle George

Dear Julianna., Joann, Brian & Jeffrey

Kelly August 31, 2007, at 12:59 a.m. EDT

For many months I have read and prayed for your trials and health. Today I was so inspired because I too *Love Cheese*! As a non-milk drinker I swear it is the only way my bones stay strong.

It is truly this comment that has inspired me to write a note to you all. I knew that my silent prayers would be enough! For so many months I have found myself at a loss of words, but have continued to pray for your family's health and strength.

Please know that in spite of my silence I continue to pray and think of you.

I can do all things through him who gives me strength (Philippians 4:13)

Kelly
(church family)

Summer!!!

Christine September 05, 2007, at 10:41 a.m. EDT

Hi Julianna,

It has been a *long* time since I've written you a note. The summer was *crazy*. Please tell your mom and dad that the Seese's have finally completely lost their minds, we got a St. Bernard puppy. He's 27 weeks now and bigger than Jack!!!!! Jack and I now have to contend with Toby Mac on our prayer walk each morning. He's comical—all puppy. I'm so glad that you are doing *much* better... and we will continue to pray for your remission. It will be fun to have your hair grow back in... be sure to gel it up and make it funky while it is short—won't that be fun!

Ta ta for now and squeeze everyone for us... maybe next summer you guys will come to Michigan again... that would be *awesome*.

Love ya—Chrissy, Kevin, Abby, Nathan, Jack, Toby Mac, Marie, Oliver and Twist—did we tell you we got a new outside cat too???? We are nuts.

(family friend)

CarePage Post September 15, 2007, at 03:15 p.m. EDT

I wanted to give everyone an update since I have recently been reminded that I haven't written since August 30th. Julianna is really doing *great*!! She did end up with a stuffy nose and a cough last week, but luckily, it didn't turn into anything serious. She is getting to school around 3 full days a week—which is what we had hoped for. (I did post a picture of her 1st day of school, and I also included a picture of her floating in our lagoon on vacation with her cousin Morgan.) She has the same tutor as last year on the days she stays home—which is also great! And

best of all—her hair is totally coming in. She looks just so adorable and is very happy about her hair. She is just hoping it really
doesn't come back thicker than it was—which is what we have
been told—because it was already *so, so* thick. She actually liked
it when it was in its "thinned out" stage. I have explained to her
about "women and hair"—how we always want what we don't
have—she is just experiencing that at a much younger age.

Her pill swallowing has not been going that smoothly. She
actually does well with the 10 pills on Wednesdays, but the pills
she has to take 5 days a month she just has trouble with. It actually seems to be more of an emotional thing than physically,
because she swallowed pretty easily, but we had to get through
the tears of having to do it. We will have to do them again starting September 26th twice a day for 5 days. Please keep her in
your thoughts and prayers during this time.

We have not gotten anywhere yet with our insurance company regarding physical therapy. I am trying one last letter-writ-
ing effort. In the meanwhile, I just want to say it has worked
itself out, and we have been astounded by the generosity of people willing to help us out with this, but it won't be necessary. I
have shed many tears over the last few days, because every time
I think about how wonderful people are to us, the tears just start
forming—and I was doing so good with keeping my emotions in
check lately—oh well. So, we are back at physical therapy twice
a week, and I am confident that it will go a long way in helping
Julianna regain her strength.

I feel like we are definitely going in an upward direction right
now, and I think I am actually having moments of feeling real
happiness in my heart again. There is a part of me that still feels
like I can't let my guard down just yet, and I am sure a therapist
would have a field day with me right now. I clearly realize that
the *only* way we have coped so far is because we *all* truly believe
that this is God's plan for our lives, and we may have questions,
and we certainly have wished this wasn't His plan for us, but we
haven't felt anger and as a friend commented recently, we are able

to appreciate the good that has come out of this so far. Our perspective has certainly changed about what is important, and we definitely consider that a good thing—I just hope we can maintain that perspective. Julianna has an unbelievable spirit, and I am confident that this will shape who she becomes in an amazing way.

I will keep you posted on Julianna's progress. Please remember that for the most part no news is good news with this CarePage, but I will most likely be writing from time to time to share our experiences. As a matter of fact, I am updating 2 posts today because I did have 2 other stories to share. Thanks for reading, and thanks for your continued support of our family.

Julianna—1st day of School!

17

Lives Forever Changed
in a Good Way

CarePage Post September 15, 2007, at 03:13 p.m. EDT

We had two cool experiences this week that I wanted to share. Since school started we have been seeing a young woman walking on our road. We always smile and say hello to her as we are waiting for the bus. The other day she walked over to Julianna and said I just wanted to give you a hug. She said she noticed her wearing the bandana and she has worn bandanas just like that and wondered about Julianna. Then she looked at me and whispered "is it cancer." I said yes. She then told Julianna she had cancer and finished treatment last May. She told Julianna that she thought Julianna looked great, she asked how she was feeling, she commented about Julianna having eyebrows and eyelashes because she said she lost hers. She then took off her baseball cap to show Julianna how long her hair has grown in the last year. She also told us that she has good friends who have a 16 year old son with leukemia, so she is pretty familiar with it. She then told us that she has been walking because she is training for a 60 mile walk for breast cancer. Her name is Sandra and as she left she said she will be praying for Julianna. Julianna and I prayed for Sandra that night and we discussed that when we see her again we are going to ask if we can be a sponsor for her walk.

Thursday of this week there was no school, so we ended up going to a park for the afternoon to get Julianna some exercise. We met a family there that also had a daughter Julianna. The Mom, Kathryn, and I started talking and it turned out that Julianna's school principal used to be neighbors with Kathryn. There is also a family in that neighborhood who have a 3 ½ year old daughter just diagnosed this past July with leukemia. When Kathryn last talked to Julianna's principal about this little girl, the principal told her all about Julianna and how good she was doing, etc., and here we were in the same park that day. When Kathryn left the park, she gave me a hug and said she would be praying for us.

As I was thinking about meeting these people this week I am reminded of when we first adopted Jeffrey. So many times I would be out with him and people would come up to me and ask questions and almost always tell me a heartwarming adoption story. I remember thinking and telling people that our world has really expanded through this adoption: I was meeting people I would not have met otherwise, and people were sharing with me some really great adoption stories. Lately, I am thinking that this experience is turning into the same kind of thing. Although, as I have said before, the honest truth is that I wish this wasn't happening, and I wish we weren't part of this world, and I don't necessarily want to meet other people that are part of this world, but I am holding on to my faith and the words that my friend, who's daughter had cancer 20 years ago, wrote to me when this all began, "…to walk this road and come out on the other side stronger in your faith, closer in your relationship and amazed at what He gives you the strength to endure. Your lives will be forever changed, in a good way, by this."

CarePage Messages

Thanks For The Updates!

Linda September 15, 2007, at 03:46 p.m. EDT

Yes, it is hard to feel lucky, but we all are blessed that this journey is going well. And while none of us wants to travel this particular road, here we all are, supporting each other through it, and praying harder than we ever may have, and appreciating each day more than we ever might have, which is what we are supposed to be doing right now. I think M&M's will help with the pills, and promised Jules I would put in a plug for them. We also have a friend walking in the 3-day in honor of her mother, and have been supporting her as a sponsor in Julianna's name. If anyone gets the opportunity to go to the opening ceremony of that walk, it will move you beyond words. Last year it was at the Willow Grove Mall, and I was lucky enough to find my friend in the crowd, in the rain. It was amazing.

Here's to more great days and amazing memories and miracles.

Love,
Aunt Lynne, Aunt Carolyn, Cara & Mia

I Have Been Thinking About You Julianna

Mary September 15, 2007, at 09:37 p.m. EDT

Hello to Everyone, I was so glad to hear from you today—I just had to write a note. You are in my thoughts and prayers. I miss seeing you guys at Uncle Stevens. But I do get to see him at least once a month. He is doing well and looks great too. He tells me about you and I hope you are feeling better soon.

Love, Mary, Louis, Anthony and Michele
(family friend)

Great To Hear From You!

Jeannie September 15, 2007, at 09:54 p.m. EDT

Hello to the Smith's,

Thanks for the update, we have been thinking of you a
lot lately. We were so happy to hear that Jules is going to
school 3 days a week and that things are going so well. We
will keep you in our thoughts and we hope to see you soon.

All our Love, Jeannie & Bruce
(family friend)

Great To Receive An Update!

Donna September 16, 2007, at 02:42 p.m. EDT

Thanks JoAnn for the update. You really are a beautiful
writer! Annie has loved seeing Jules at school and we are
thrilled to hear things are mostly on an upswing…but not
to worry the prayers are continuing from here! Yuk, swallowing that many pills has got to be a major drag!!! We are
praying for you but also…Jules have you asked your Mom
to bury some of the pills in a big ice cream sundae?! *Tee
Hee* just a thought!

We are also thrilled for Jules that her hair is growing
back…no hair, thick hair or thin hair you are gorgeous
Jules…inside and out. Now the only issue is -I don't think
Annie will stop wearing the scarves-she seems to have
adopted them as her new look!

Lots of hugs and prayers from our family!

Donna and Annie
(school friend)

Back To School...

Pauline September 16, 2007, at 08:27 p.m. EDT

Dear Julianna, I am so happy to hear that you are doing three days of school. That's Great!! I will start teaching on Tuesday and I am looking foreard to it as well. It's been a long summer for me, but many wonderful friends have come and helped me get through it. I will keep you in my prayers and I know that you will get stronger and be the old Julianna again. Maybe I'll be able to visit you one day. Take care and know that I think about you all the time.

Love, Pauline }
(piano teacher)

Blessed With The Mess...

Marie September 16, 2007, at 09:54 p.m. EDT

Jules,

I'm laughing while reading your Mom's post about you not wanting "thicker hair." Just think it could be worse, you toooo could have been blessed with the mess. hahahahaha

I'm so happy to hear you're back in school and doing well. We're still thinking about ya everyday. Keep the good news coming.

Aunt Marie

Hi Julianna from Holy Nativity Pre-School

Josephine September 16, 2007, at 11:29 p.m. EDT

Hello Julianna,

Hope you are feeling better! Just want you to know that we are thinking of you and keeping you in our prayers. Your website is beautiful just as you are. We love you Darling.

Love,
Mrs. D and Staff
(preschool teacher)

Carepage Post September 21, 2007, at 10:34 a.m. EDT

A Letter of Thanks...

"If I Accept the Sunshine and Warmth, I Must Also Accept the Thunder and Lightning." (Kahlil Gibran)

I came across this saying in high school and for some reason it has always stuck with me, and I have thought about it from time to time over the *many* years that have passed since my high school days.

The task of writing "Thank You" cards for all the wonderful things that have come our way since March has been hanging over my head lately. I have been convinced by enough family and friends that this is not something that is expected of me, and I should wipe it off my "to do" list. My struggle is that I really want you all to know how much your thoughtfulness and generosity has meant to us, how we have truly appreciated every thing you have said, written, done, or sent to us, so I am going to try to convey it through this CarePage...so, here goes...

Thank you for each and every card, note, email, joke, balloon, snack food, chocolate bar, flower arrangement, edible arrangement, plant, journal, quilt, stuffed animal, WebKinz, Vermont Teddy Bear, Build-A-Bear, art kit, craft kit, game, book, pair of pajamas (which always get rave reviews by all the nurses and doctors in the hospital), set of stickers, homemade meal, piece of jewelry, fundana, angel, bath & body product (did you know they make a hot cocoa product with the most delicious smell that is a shampoo, body wash, and bubble bath? I highly recommend it), "Pooh" item, "Princess" item, treasure from Japan, toy truck/motorcycle, activity CD, activity book, DVD, magazine subscription, coffee/tea mug, set of note cards, gift card, bank card, and $$$.

There were also a few things that people have done for Julianna that we are also very thankful for. I think many of you know our church held an Easter Breakfast Benefit for Julianna, and they set up the "famous" prayer clock for 24 hour prayers for Julianna. Her cousin Beth made a donation to the American Cancer Society for a fundraiser being held at Wilmington's Riverfront. Julianna's name was put on a luminary bag and a candle was lit in her honor. A local family from school recently opened a children's clothing shop in Doylestown called Monkey Business. They had a "Fashion Show for Julianna" which benefited our family. The teachers at Julianna's school selected her as the recipient for their fundraiser for one of their "Denim Days." Our insurance agent and his family rode bicycles in a fundraiser with Julianna named as their inspiration. A group of Mom's from Julianna's school filled our freezer with "Dream Dinners." The "Heart to Heart" organization at Julianna's school chose her as one of their recipients.

Whenever something would arrive in the mail either home or at the hospital, Julianna's face would totally light up, and we could for that time forget about everything else that was going on. The other most amazing thing is that everything that was given to her (and Jeffrey, and Brian, and me) always was just so perfect. Somehow, everyone knew just what to say, and just what to send. Many of the things that you sent also provided a distraction at times when distraction was something we truly needed. Each gesture that you made truly touched our hearts in a wonderful way, and meant so much to us at the time, and will always be remembered in a special way.

I think in the end, what I am really trying to say is... *Thank You* for providing the sunshine and warmth in the midst of all our thunder and lightning.

With Heartfelt Thanks,
Brian, JoAnn, Jeffrey, and especially Julianna

CarePage Messages

This Race Is For You...

Marie September 21, 2007, at 11:55 a.m. EDT

Jules,

Uncle Eddie and Cousin Anthony are racing in Cambridge, Maryland this weekend and they asked me to post for them a special message.

"They said this race is dedicated to Jules with all the thunder and lightning"..."and should they win they will announce on stage that it was because Jules was riding with them in the back seat the whole time".

I'll let you know how they make out.

Aunt Marie

Bravo!

Marna September 21, 2007, at 02:11 p.m. EDT

Bravo JoAnn! That was truly a symphony of words!

(neighbor)

Wonderful Thought!

Jeannie September 21, 2007, at 03:59 p.m. EDT

Hello to the Smith's,

The saying you shared was perfect. It is one that will definitely be passed on to family and friends. Hope all is well, and we hope to see you soon.

All our Love, Jeannie & Bruce
(family friend)

Thank You!

Amy September 21, 2007, at 04:12 p.m. EDT

Your message of thank you was so beautifully said. I think that so many of us probably would also like to thank you! We thank you trusting us to help, for inviting us into your lives, for allowing us to be there for you and for letting us get to know and be a part of your wonderful family!! So thank you!!

Love to all, Amy and Family
(school friend)

Beautifully Stated!!

Dawn September 22, 2007, at 02:08 p.m. EDT

JoAnn, It was great to see you guys the other day at the picnic!!! Julianna looks happy and strong…it is obvious she gets a lot of that from her wonderfully supportive and courageous Mom and Dad!!! As for your "thank you" message, like everyone told you…thank you notes ARE unnecessary and take it off your mind and to do list!!! However, I want to tell you that the message was eloquently stated!!! Your strength is inspirational and amazing!!! Julianna is a very lucky girl to have such a strong and beautiful mother!!! I loved your quote about the sunshine and thunder…it is so true!!!! I would like to share some motherhood quotes with you…the courageous and angelic mother that you are…

"A mother is not a person to lean on but a person to make leaning unnecessary." -Dorothy Canfield Fisher Mother…

"love is the fuel that enables a normal human being to do the impossible." -Marion C. Garretty…

"I cannot forget my mother. She is my bridge. When I needed to get across, she steadied herself long enough for me to run across safely." -Renita Weems…

"A mother is the truest friend we have, when trials heavy and sudden, fall upon us; when adversity takes the place of prosperity; when friends who rejoice with us in our sunshine desert us; when trouble thickens around us, still will she cling to us, and endeavor by her kind precepts and counsels to dissipate the clouds of darkness, and cause peace to return to our hearts." -Washington Irving…

"A mother's love is patient and forgiving when all others are forsaking, it never fails or falters, even though the heart is breaking" -Helen Rice

(cousin)

Thinking Of You All

Marlene September 24, 2007, at 11:26 a.m. EDT

Dear Julianna, JoAnn, Brian and Jeffrey,

So glad to read up on how Julianna is doing and that things are going well. Since Sean sees Brian almost every day/week, we get updates via Brian. Of course, women write or say much more than our guys do…so we are grateful to you

JoAnn for keeping up with this website and keeping us all updated. I actually print this out so everyone in our family can read it. We will keep the prayers and good thoughts and wishes coming your way. Keep the faith and know that you have MANY, MANY friends out here that are praying for miracles and 100% perfect health for Julianna.

Love to all, Sean, Marlene, Carrie and Kate

(family friend)

Some Jokes I Have Saved For You

Clare September 27, 2007, at 09:56 p.m. EDT

Hi Julianna,

I have been saving up some funny jokes for you (well i think they are!) for you to tell your teachers, Drs. and nuses and keep them laughing.they come from Justin's Scouting magazine.

Here goes;

Chris:Great news! The teacher said we have a test today rain or shine.

Mary; What is so great about that?

Chris: It's snowing!!!!

Patient: Doctor, Doctor! I think I have turned into a pack of cards!

Dr. I'll deal with you later!

Patient:

Doctor, I'm shrinking! You have to do something about it quickly!

Dr: Take it easy. You just have to be a little patient.

Aiden; Why are boys only born Mondays through Saturdays/

Avery: Why?

Aiden; Because ther is no male delivery on Sundays!

Patient;Dr. Dr. I keep thinking I'm a bridge.

Doctor; What's come over you?

Patient:Two trucks, 4 cars and 1 motorcycle so far!

Teacher;Billy why are you late for school?

Bily:well, I was walking to school and I saw the sign:School-go slow!

Hope they bring a smile to your face. We keep you and all your family in our prayers. Love to hear that you are doing well and can go to school.

Love Mrs F and the rest of the family
(church family)

CarePage Post September 28, 2007, at 12:28 p.m. EDT

We were at the Kof P clinic this past Wednesday, and I thought I would give you an update on Julianna. The first nice thing that worked out was that my Mom got to come with us this time. She is usually the one at home watching Jeffrey, but we were able to make other arrangements, so she got to come see the clinic and meet the nurses and doctor, and watch what an amazing patient Julianna is.

It had been a month since we were at clinic—which seemed like forever to us. It turned out it seemed like forever to the staff too, because there were hugs from everyone to Julianna and everyone saying how much they missed her, and they could not stop saying *how great she looks*!! and how happy that makes them.

Her counts were relatively good; however, we learned that if they get too high, they are going to increase the medicine. They told us that it is important for her counts to stay suppressed, so they actually won't let them get too high. This is not good news for Julianna because she it really losing her patience with all this medicine as it is. So I guess now we need to pray for low counts—go figure!

While we were at the clinic, we went to show my Mom the procedure room that is painted with the beach scene. When the nurse took us to the room, there was another patient in there. The nurse said she was glad the other patient was in there because she is a 10 year old girl, and the staff there all feels that this girl and Julianna are very similar, and they were hopeful that they would meet. We only stayed a few seconds because we didn't want to disturb them. As we walked away, the nurse said I am so glad that happened, because they are a family that also lives in your area. When we went back to the day hospital, I pulled out my notebook that is supposed to keep me organized, and I found a note I had from a Mom at school. She had given me the name of a friend of hers who's daughter had been diagnosed with leukemia in July of 2006. At the time, she said her friend would be fine if I wanted to contact her—I have never contacted her—although I have thought about it from time to time. The name of the girl in my notebook was the same name of the girl we had just met. When they came back to the day hospital, I went over and showed my note to the Mom and asked if that was her. She said yes. We ended up talking quite a bit, and it was very encouraging for both Julianna and I to see this girl with a full head of hair, and finished with physical therapy, etc. We will both be there again in 4 weeks on Wednesday, and we are looking forward to seeing each other.

I have spent a lot of this week trying to dig my way out of the paperwork that has accumulated over the last 6 months. It is kind of interesting that I would come across various things dated in March—which is just a reminder of when everything else stopped. Anyway, I did come across a mailing from The Leukemia & Lymphoma Society. I remember getting it and starting to read it, and being overcome with emotion and having to put it at the bottom of the pile. When I came across it yesterday I was able to read it through. This Saturday, they are having their 2007 Annual Light the Night Walk. It is a 2-3 mile, non-endurance walk featuring illuminated balloons. Friends and family can "carry red balloons to signify their personal commitment to finding a cure for blood cancers." Survivors can "carry white balloons as a glowing symbol of hope for all." This year they are introducing "gold balloons to memorialize loved ones whose lives have been lost to blood cancers." Julianna and I talked about it this morning. We might try and go to the local walk here in Bucks County tomorrow, but we decided that we are definitely going to participate next year if Julianna is able—and we will definitely be inviting all of you to join us.

Unless a need arises for me to write, don't be surprised if you do not hear from us for another 4 weeks.

CarePage Messages

Your Surprise Meeting At Kop...

John September 28, 2007, at 01:54 p.m. EDT

What a wonderful read! Your meeting up with the local mother and 10 year old daughter (finally!). I guess that things do happen when they are supposed to...and I am sure that there is a logical (if not mystical) explanation how & why it happened. My guess is that your mother's (and Julianna's grandmother) presence had something to do with it. The best of good luck to everyone!!!

(neighbor)

Thanks for the Update!

Jeannie September 28, 2007, at 10:07 p.m. EDT

Hi to the Smith's,

Thanks for the update. We always love to hear your newest happenings. It seems your meeting was meant to be. We were glad to hear your Mom (grandmom) made it with you to King of Prussia. Well take care of yourselves and hope to see you soon.

All our Love, Jeannie & Bruce
(family friend)

Happy To Read Your Update

Amy September 29, 2007, at 10:52 a.m. EDT

We would love to walk with you guys next year. Caitlin is dancing in Newtown tonight for "Light the Night." We will be thinking about Jules tonight!!

Love Amy and Family
(school friend)

Thank You For The Updates!!

Denise October 01, 2007, at 09:59 a.m. EDT

Hi Smith Family,

I have been without e-mail for 2 months, but I was thrilled to get back on to your last two messages. Your "thank you" touched my heart and brought back so many wonderful memories. Being in this position is God's way of showing us how He created His children and when they act according to His will, they are truly beautiful. I was also glad to hear how well Jules is doing. The once a month stuff is a breeze after the past six months. I'm glad you met another family to bond with. The girls will warm up and what a gift they can be to one another. Just a reminder—I am now a "lady of leisure" and available to help with anything, even a day out for mom!!!! Keep the good reports coming.

Much love and prayers.
Denise and Family
(church family)

Thanks For The Update

Linda October 01, 2007, at 12:06 p.m. EDT

We are praying for 'just right' counts, because this high and low stuff is so confusing! JoAnn, that Thank you post was just beautiful—I cry whenver I think about it. We are so blessed to have you and Brian, Julianna and Jeffrey, and the rest of your families in our lives. Julianna, did you get any M&M's? Jeffrey, we got tired of waiting and picked out presents for you for your birthday—we hope to get to see you soon.

All our love,
Aunt Lynne & Aunt Carolyn, Mia & Cara too.

Thinking Of You

Diane October 03, 2007, at 11:30 a.m. EDT

I am so glad that the roller coaster has slowed up a bit! My hopes and prayers are with you every day! I look forward to seeing you at school!

Peace, Diane W
(school friend)

18

One Thousand Cranes

Carepage Post October 16, 2007, at 03:53 p.m. EDT

As unbelievable as this adventure has been, I never imagined in my wildest dreams that I would be sharing a story as incredible as this one. It's a story of an amazing gift to Julianna, and I just hope I am able to tell it as well as it deserves to be told. Once again, this is going to take 2 posts.

Last Saturday, one of our neighbors called to say their son, Blake, was at their house and he had a gift for Julianna. My neighbor said Blake had been working on this gift, and she had been hearing about its progress, and now it was finished, and could they bring it over. I said yes, and my curious brain was making a mental list of some things it could possibly be. I guess because of Brian and his woodworking abilities—I was thinking the gift would be along these lines...boy was I wrong!

They walked in carrying the gift, and at first I could not quite figure out what it was. Blake started to explain to Julianna about a Japanese legend that he learned about. It refers to 1,000 origami paper cranes. He explained that the legend is that if you give 1,000 paper cranes to a person who is sick, they will become well. He went on to tell us that his Mom had died from cancer. He learned about this legend after her death, and he decided that the next time he learned of someone who was ill, he was going to make them 1,000 paper cranes. Here is part of what he wrote in the card he gave Julianna, "I wanted to make this project for you. In Japanese it is called 'Senzaburu' meaning 1,000 cranes. Legend has it that if you fold 1,000 origami cranes for someone who is sick that it will make them well. They are also folded for couples getting married and as a wish for peace. I began folding these shortly after Easter after I heard that you were sick, and even though they probably won't make you well, I hope they will at least make you feel a little better. As I folded each one of these I made a wish for your recovery & happiness..."

He had the idea to string the cranes and anchor them to a base so that it forms the shape of a tree. He actually got the idea from a paper towel holder they have where he works, and a friend at work gave him some fishing line to string the cranes together with. He presented the cranes to Julianna along with a hand made book. The book has cranes on the front and back cover, and was made by a woman he works with. It provides details about the crane and its legend. Here are a few things from the book, "Japanese cranes are possibly one of the oldest birds on earth. Legend holds that cranes live for 1,000 years. In Japanese, Chinese, and Korean tradition, cranes stand for peace and long life." He also talked about a Japanese girl with leukemia and I found the story in an origami book we happened to have. (I have written more about this in the second post.)

As you can imagine, I was somewhat numb during this visit and I want to tell you it actually took days to absorb the extent of this gesture. The 1,000 cranes sit in our main living area, and I can only tell you that they truly emit something powerful into our house that is impossible to describe. I think part of it is just the overwhelming sense of a gift so completely from the heart, and also the pure and genuine wish for Julianna to be well. The beauty of this just flows out from the cranes. As you might imagine, Julianna is also in awe of this gift. Blake, thankfully, also made her a single crane that she could touch and hold, and he made her an origami box to keep it in. She can't seem to keep her hands off of that single crane. We have had to Google "how to fold paper cranes" so that we could make the original crane again, and again, and again. Then there is Jeffrey—he loves to tell everyone that comes here and sees the cranes that I can't even look at them without crying. Then he will turn to me and say, "don't look Mom."

Read on to the next post...

CarePage Post October 16, 2007, at 03:50 p.m. EDT

After Blake left that day, we found our origami book that we have called "Math in Motion." In the back of the book I found the following story. (I believe this is the story that Blake was referring to during his visit.)

There is an old belief in Japan that a crane can live a thousand years; and that if you fold 1,000 paper cranes you will live a long life and they will keep you well.

Twelve year old Sadako Sasaki made 644 paper cranes before she died of leukemia, ten years after the atomic bomb fell on Hiroshima.

Her friends and classmates collected 7,000,000 yen ($20,000) to build a monument to Sadako and other child victims of the bomb.

Over the years, Sadako's life and death have become well known. The paper crane has become an international symbol of peace. Read "Sadako and the Thousand Paper Cranes" by Eleanor Coerr.

Today, children from all over the world send paper cranes to decorate Sadako's monument, a statue of a young girl, standing atop of mountain, holding a golden crane in her outstretched hands. At the base of the statue, it reads: "This is our cry, this is our prayer: peace in the world."

A few days after Blake's visit, I called my friend whose daughter, Jessica, had cancer 20 years ago. I was telling her about the cranes. When Jessica was 6 and battling cancer, she asked my friend if she could be baptized—she wanted to be "a child of God." The day before the baptism was to take place Jessica ended up in the hospital. The morning of the baptism, the resident doctor, who was Asian, walked in with a bag and gave it to them. Inside the bag were folded paper cranes. He knew Jessica was going to be baptized that day and he stayed up and made her as many cranes as he could. They were completely down to the wire getting to the church on time, but they made it, and the cranes were thrown up into the air during Jessica's baptism. I couldn't believe my ears as I was hearing this story. How awesome that we could share in this similar experience. Needless to say, Julianna got one of those smiles that lights up her whole face when I told her that Jessica's doctor had made her paper cranes when she was sick. Julianna didn't say much, but I could just tell how special she thought this was.

So… that's my amazing story. Part of me would love to blindly believe that these 1,000 cranes could really make Julianna well, and while I know I don't believe that, what I certainly believe is that all this love and goodness and thoughtfulness generates a very positive energy—and that definitely goes a very long way in Julianna's overall well-being.

I have posted 2 pictures—one of just the cranes, and one with the cranes and Julianna and Blake.

1,000 Paper Cranes folded for Julianna.

Blake holding 1,000 folded paper cranes he made for
Julianna with the wish "to get well."

CarePage Messages

Another "Wow" moment

Linda October 16, 2007, at 04:08 p.m. EDT

Hey there friends,

I so love to hear these wonderful stories of love and healing. What a kind and thoughtful man to take such time

and care to make all those healing cranes. Every prayer is heard and every wish is considered. It is indeed another story of "storming heaven!"

We are so happy to know that Jules is in school almost all the time. Cailyn loves to spend time with her friend!

Take care & love as always,
Linda
(school friend)

Amazing!!

Denise October 16, 2007, at 04:19 p.m. EDT

Wow how wonderful. It is great to hear someone took such time, care and thoughtfulness in something. just think Smith Family all that you are and all that you give—has been coming to you through all these wonderful people who love you and care about. Energy & love can do lot for people and I am so glad you are truly surrounded by both!

Denise
(school family)

Wow! 1,000 Cranes!!!

John October 16, 2007, at 04:22 p.m. EDT

What an interesting and from-the-heart gift that Blake gave Julianna. We can hope and pray that the legend is true and they pass their power for health and long life on to the whole family.

(neighbor)

Amazing Gift!

Jeannie October 16, 2007, at 08:37 p.m. EDT

Hello to the Smith's,

What a wonderful and thoughtful gift. This past year at the school where I work, Bucks County Community College brought their Art Mobile for our students to tour. Inside was oragami from many different places. In one of the glass cases they had 1,000 cranes and they told of the story of the young girl from Japan. I am so glad your friend was able to share this story with you and what a special gift you will have forever. You are very lucky to have a someone so special in your lives. Enjoy your crane tree it looks beautiful.

All our love, Jeannie & Bruce
(family friend)

Amazing.

Jessica October 16, 2007, at 09:29 p.m. EDT

Reading that story I was in awe of the 1,000 cranes. I actually remember hearing that story a while ago. That's an amazing and wonderful story.
I hope to see you guys soon! I miss you so much. always in my thoughts.

Jess
(babysitter)

Thank You For The Updates!!

Denise October 16, 2007, at 10:17 p.m. EDT

Great job JoAnn! You shared this very loving gesture in a way that touches all of our hearts who love and pray for all of the Smith's. I really enjoyed this morning. I'm on my second ball of yarn!!!! You looked wonderful and I thank God for His mercy on Jules and giving you back some semblance of normalcy. This experience will shape your life in a way you will be eternally grateful for. Thank you for helping me remember my many blessings after 20 years. I'll keep you informed about the "baby."

Much love and prayers to all, Denise W.
(church family)

The Cranes

Donna October 17, 2007, at 09:15 a.m. EDT

Thanks so much for sharing this amazing gift with us. The cranes are so beautiful and you can see that each one has a piece of your friend's heart and soul in it..I am sure this gift is capable of a miracle or two.

Donna and Annie
(school friend)

Wow!!!!!!

Diane October 17, 2007, at 12:40 p.m. EDT

I am at work and I am trying to control the tears that are running down my face. The cranes are stunning but the thought and the story behind it are so beautiful! You are so loved by so many! Good thoughts and prayers from us to you always.

Love, Diane W. and Family
(school friend)

Amazing!!!

Amy October 17, 2007, at 12:58 p.m. EDT

Thanks for sharing that amazing story! I felt like crying and smiling at the same time!

Love, Amy and Family
(school friend)

CarePage Post October 23, 2007, at 10:26 a.m. EDT

I wanted to write and give an update on Julianna, and I actually have another story to share.

Julianna has been doing very well, but I wanted to ask for some specific prayers and thoughts. This maintenance phase is based on 28 day cycles of medicine, and the first 5 days of each cycle are filled with lots of medicine. We start a new cycle tomorrow—Wednesday. What happened last month—after I wrote that everything was fine, was that she had 5 days filled with bouts of extreme tiredness. She was at a point where she was so tired she couldn't even speak. She would point to her water glass if she needed water, or to the TV remote, etc. If this was... say Jeffrey or Brian, I would say it was drama, but Julianna is really not a drama queen—a princess yes, but not a drama queen. During the tiredness, she would get sad and shed some tears simply because she didn't like feeling this way and she really wanted to go to school. She also struggled with all the extra medicine these first 5 days. As you might imagine—she has moments of just not wanting to take all of this medicine. All I can tell her is that we don't have a choice. I also try to convince her that being tired is *definitely* better than being in pain, right?? She looks at me and shakes her head up and down to indicate yes, but it is not very convincing. Anyway, after these initial 5 days, she was really so much better.

She has had lots of energy. She has been getting to school 4–5 full days per week!! And really being herself—silly and all.

After clinic tomorrow, I am suspicious that this tiredness will happen again for the next 5 days, and while I don't want to complain about tiredness, I would ask for prayers and positive thoughts that Julianna would be able to handle the tiredness. Please also keep praying for no other serious side effects as she continues to ingest all this medicine.

On to happier topics… last week was "Education Week" at the kids' school and it was also the "Scholastic Book Fair" all week. They had been collecting money as part of a fundraiser related to the book fair. All I knew was that Julianna took $5 of her own money to contribute to the book fundraiser, and Jeffrey asked me to give him a $1 of my money. (OK, so that's a glimpse into the difference between my 2 kids.) Later in the week, the kids got off the bus, and Julianna was just beaming. She said she had something really good to tell me. She wouldn't tell me until we got all the way up our long driveway. Then she started to tell me that the librarian pulled her aside today and told her they would like to take the fundraiser money and buy books to donate to CHOP in Julianna's name. The librarian asked Julianna if she would like this. Julianna of course said yes, and she was thrilled. They told her they were going to let her shop and choose all the books. She was so excited, and so happy as she was telling me this. Of course my eyes started to water, and then she and Jeffrey get real close to my face and wait for the tears to stream down my face. You would think me crying at this point would not be such a novelty anymore.

On Friday, Julianna and I went to the book fair and they told us she had $253 dollars to spend on books. It took us a very long time to choose all the books. While we were choosing Julianna reminded me of a little girl we had seen reading some of the books at the clinic. This was the day they ambulanced Julianna down to the hospital, and this little girl's brother ended up in the hospital that night also. We decided that it would be a good idea to split up the books between the clinic at Kof P and the oncology floor at the hospital. This book donation turned into one of those situations where Julianna was able to experience complete joy, and she definitely has a heart for "giving to others." We can't wait to bring all the books to clinic tomorrow.

Thanks for reading, and for your continued support of our family.

CarePage Messages

Prayers Going *Up Up Up*!!!!

Suzy October 23, 2007, at 11:36 a.m. EDT

Hey Julianna! I am going to be praying for you extra lots these next few days. Count on it! I really want to see you at the Zone next Sunday! If you can't make it, I will understand, but I am going to pray that you feel *great*!!! Please Julianna, let me know if there is anything special I can pray for for you too. I will get Maggie to pray with me, since God's word says (and we know it's *true*) that "when two or more are gathered together He will be with them1" (I think that is so cool! He is *with* us when we are together!) Also, tell me how many pills you have to take because I am going to pray about each one of those pills for you. I am so glad you're in my group at the zone because I really like you, and together you girls are all the best!

Lots of love and hugs from your Zone
"shepherd", Mrs. M:)
(family friend)

When I Saw You Last Saturday At Tyler State Park...

John October 23, 2007, at 11:52 a.m. EDT

...and you told me this wonderful story, I thought the *best* part of it all is the fact that there will be a sticker of some kind in each of the donated books that tells the reader that Jules is the donor.

Jules certainly lights up a lot of lives!!!

(neighbor)

God Bless

Joan October 23, 2007, at 03:54 p.m. EDT

All that I can say is God Bless all of you. I know through all of the prayers offered for Julianna, a good ending is definitely in sight. I pray that the medicines etc., will all be more gentle on her this time around and she will be returning to good health soon.

Take care and keep happy thoughts.
Love you all, Aunt Joan

Prayers and Smiles

Linda October 23, 2007, at 04:11 p.m. EDT

Hey there friends,

Prayers are being sent your way for the medicine this month. I pray that each month gets easier with reactions and that the pill swallowing wil not be as traumatic.

It is so great that these the donations are being put to such a wonderful cause—what a wonderful gift to be able to take to CHOP. It must make your hearts so very happy to be able to give back in Jules' name. I know that every person who donated a dollar will feel that spirit of giving as well. That in itself is huge:-)

Thank you so much for keeping these updates going.

Love you,
Linda and Family (school friend)

Hello to the Smith Family

Beth October 23, 2007, at 04:59 p.m. EDT

Dear JoAnn, Brian, Julianna, and Jeffrey,

We will be thinking of you during the next five days and hoping that Julianna will not be as tired as she was before. Thanks for the updates and especially for the pictures of the thousand cranes. The birds look just beautiful! We are also glad to hear that Julianna has been able to get to school so much. Good luck this week!

Love,
Beth, John, Hayley, and Jenna
(cousin)

Prayers Coming Your Way!

Jeannie October 23, 2007, at 08:03 p.m. EDT

Hi Jules, JoAnn, Brian, and Jeffery,

We were real glad to hear things are going well. As for prayers, you are always in ours. Lets hope this time around goes more smoothly. We were real happy to hear about the books, what a great idea. Sharing with others is a great feeling. Hope to see you soon.

All our Love, Jeannie & Bruce
(family friend)

How Wonderful!

Linda October 24, 2007, at 10:11 a.m. EDT

Jules, you know I think of you as my hero, and this is just one reason why—no matter what you are going through, you still see that giving to others is a good thing. We are so proud of you!

We are praying that the medicine does its job, and if you do get tired, just remember how much better you felt afterwards. The tiredness will not last forever—you know that from last week. Keep your smile going and keep your thoughts happy. And take the tired time to rest and give yourself that time to heal. I know you feel yucky when you can't do stuff, but what works for me is I keep saying to myself, "This too shall pass" and before you know it, it gets better!

We love you!!!!

Aunt Lynne & Aunt Carolyn, Cara and Mia too

Happy Thoughts From Our Family

Amy October 25, 2007, at 04:32 p.m. EDT

Hi Everyone,

We are sending special prayers for the effects of the medicine to be gentler on Jules. So glad to hear that everything else is going well.

Being able to pick out and bring those books to CHOPS sounds wonderful. What a great idea! I am sure that Jules brightened the day of so many children!!!!

(school friend)

Its Been a While

Pauline November 07, 2007, at 09:15 p.m. EST

Dear Julianna, I know it's been a while since I wrote. I have been keeping up with the care pages. I want you to know that you are always in my thoughts and in my prayers. I miss you at piano.

Lots of love. Pauline
(piano teacher)

CarePage Post November 14, 2007, at 09:57 p.m. EST

I wanted to give you all an update on Julianna. The weeks are just flying by around here. We are at the end of Julianna's first 12 week cycle of this maintenance phase. If her counts are where they need to be next week, she will get a spinal and we will repeat what we just did. We *all* continue to be very tired and cranky of this medicine protocol. "*This* is soooooo unfair," those were the words Julianna uttered to me a few times during the last few weeks. I can only look at her and say, "I know. Nobody wants this to *not* be happening more than me." We are getting through it, mostly because Julianna's actual pill-taking schedule is circulating among some friends who have offered to pray for each and every pill. I remind Julianna of this with each swallow and it does seem to help. Plus, one of the days that she had to swallow 15 pills, my Mom was here and offered her a $1 for each pill that she swallowed in under 10 seconds. Not surprisingly, that worked really well. She also did have tiredness, but not as severe as last month. I think it's because we really had her take it easy this time around and that was better. Once that 1st week was over, she really got much happier and had good energy. She looks great right now, with good color in her cheeks that everyone comments about.

At our last clinic visit we did see the other family we met from our area. The 10 year old girl was not doing well and was awaiting a blood transfusion. The Mom and I emailed a bit about how hard this is on our girls and how frightening it can be at times. On the one hand, I am feeling very thankful lately for how good Julianna is doing, and on the other hand, while I am trying not to do the "what ifs," I am reminded of the uncertainty in all of this.

As far as the timing of this protocol, it worked out that once Julianna got through her tough week, she was able to enjoy Halloween. We took advantage of her short hair and she dressed as Elvis—this was her idea as her cousin has turned Julianna into a big Elvis fan. In the local town where we trick or treat, people were all saying to Jules, "Elvis lives!! I knew it." She thought that was pretty cool and pretty fun. Of course, I have included some photos. Jeffrey was a "Shadow Ninja" and could not have been happier to be swinging a sword around. Luckily, he didn't actually cut off anyone's limbs.

We also just got back from 2 days with Brian's Family at The Great Wolf Lodge—this is a big indoor waterpark in the Poconos. Julianna and Jeffrey had a wonderful time being with their cousins and it was a really nice time for our family.

This coming Tuesday we head to clinic and Julianna will be getting a spinal. I would ask for prayers and good thoughts for that day. As I have said before, Julianna doesn't mind getting these, but I just suffer through them. Just the thought of this is already sending the tears streaming down my face—luckily the kids are sleeping so they can't make jokes about my tears. So, Tuesday is the spinal, and then Wednesday starts Day 1 of this 28 day cycle that we just keep doing, and doing, and doing. Assuming the pattern continues, the 1st 5 days or so will be rough, and then we should have another good 3 weeks.

One last thing, Julianna was re-evaluated this week at physical therapy. She continues to have muscle weakness in her legs, so it is recommended that we continue p.t. twice per week as we have been. The good news was that she could actually lift her toes up off the floor. They were all so excited about this. It was a big moment, and I couldn't help but get a bit emotional. Anyway, prayers for her strength would be appreciated.

If all stays quiet, I won't write again for a few weeks. I would like to wish you all a very Happy Thanksgiving, and don't forget to count your blessings—I know we will be counting ours!!!

Julianna as Elvis—Halloween 2007

Watch out it's the "Shadow Ninja!"

CarePage Messages

Hello

Erica November 14, 2007, at 10:24 p.m. EST

Hi Julianna and Family,

We are so happy to hear you are continuing to do so well! Your mom's updates really touch my heart. You are such a sweet girl and I hope to see you around school sometime soon!

Mrs. C (and Jared too!)
(school friend)

Love From Syracuse

Ann November 14, 2007, at 10:36 p.m. EST

Julianna and family, We continue to pray for you every night. We hope that you are enjoying 4th grade. The updates are so appreciated as well as the photos. It is so good to see you, even if it is in a picture.

Love from Syracuse! ~Melissa and Ann
(school friend)

Miss You Guys!

Jessica November 15, 2007, at 12:11 a.m. EST

It has been way too long, luckily I keep up on my CarePage reading to make sure things are going well. I miss you all tons. I will be home Tuesday evening for Thanksgiving, but hopefully I will be able to stop by.
 Always praying for you guys!

Love you,
Jess(babysitter)

PS. I loved the Halloween costumes. Julianna being Elvis reminded me of the time she sang teddy bear to me. And Jeffrey makes the best Ninja!

What a Pill!

Suzy November 15, 2007, at 06:44 a.m. EST

Juliana, I was just thinking about when I was younger (back when dinosaurs roamed the earth, as Maggie says) my mom would call me a "pill" when I was being difficult. I have four brothers and sisters, and that was her favorite word to use when someone was bad! Reading your update this morning reminded me of that. Picture this: (me) "But Mom, I don't want to wear that ugly dress!" (my mom) "Oh Suzy, You are *such a pill*!!!!" Here's another one: (my brother) "Mom! Tell suzy to stop! Her singing is terrible and she's bothering me!!!!" (my mom) "Oh Suzy, You are *such a pill*!!!!"

anyway, you get the picture. I don't think anyone really likes pills. Pill are such *pills*!!!!! I am glad to know that we missed you at the Zone because you were at Great Wolf Lodge. That is a much better reason to miss Zone. I was hoping that you didn't feel too bad to come. Now I am jealous instead—I have heard that Great Wolf Lodge is a total BLAST! I hope to see you this Sunday! and if I don't, have a *wonderful* thanksgiving!!!!!

Oh by the way, my cold is all gone, so I can give you a big hug next time I see you. Until then, give your little brother a hug and tell him he's substituting for me.:) *that* oughta be fun!

Love and *hugs*, Mrs. M
(family friend)

God Is Faithful

Carla November 15, 2007, at 08:02 a.m. EST

This is a note of encouragement to you all. We too have a daughter who was diagnosed with ALL. We remember the tough 3 years of chemo,the countless spinal taps and the fear. We just celebrated 15 years of remission!!!! Our daughter is now 19 and a freshman in college. She is sweet, loving and (we think) gorgeous! We hope this is a comfort to you. We will continue to pray for Julianna and your entire family.

Carla J. G
(friend of a friend)

Thinking Of You!

Jeannie November 15, 2007, at 08:15 a.m. EST

Hello Jules, JoAnn, Jeffrey, Brian,

It sounds like things are going in the right direction. Jules we totally enjoyed your Elvis costume. Not everyone could pull that off, but you did it. We can't wait to see you so we can hear you sing like Elvis. It was great to hear you guys had a fun time on your mini vacation. Remember if you need anything at all you know where to find us. Have a great holiday and hope to see you soon.

All our Love, Jeannie & Bruce
(family friend)

Hello From Monica

Monica November 15, 2007, at 09:32 a.m. EST

Hi guys

Thanks for the update—I was waiting for one!! Julianna—you are the best looking Elvis—I loved that outfit... Jeffrey—what a handsome Shadow Ninja. I don't know who that is, but you sure looked great!! I am glad you are all OK. Have a wonderful Thanksgiving—will keep praying for good news and an easy time with those pills...love you all...

(cousin)

Happy Thanksgiving!!!

Pauline November 15, 2007, at 10:04 a.m. EST

I wish you all a Happy Thanksgiving. Yes, we should count our blessings in spite of so many sad happenings around us. I know there is a purpose in all of this and I hope that

I will see my purpose one of these days. I think of Julianna everyday and pray that she will be strengthened and that God will perform one of His Miracles.She is such a brave little girl and I know that you are each Thankful that you have one another.

> Take Care and stay strong. Pauline
> (piano teacher)

Thanks Again For The Updates!

Linda November 15, 2007, at 10:58 a.m. EST

Jeffrey—you look so scary! and Julianna—ELVIS LIVES is right! What fun!

Yes, we are continuing to pray that the treatments do what they are supposed to do, and that they are as easy to get through as they can be. Thanksgiving will never be the same for us—just a day to enjoy family and friends and prepare to shop for bargains. Blessings will never again be taken for granted; pain will never be as easily complained about as before; personal problems are put into perspective and anxiety, well some things never change. We are soo thankful for having your family in our lives.

> Aunt Lynne

Hello to the Smiths

Beth November 15, 2007, at 08:03 p.m. EST

Hello Everyone,

We will be thinking of you on Tuesday and hoping all goes well at the clinic. Have a peaceful Thanksgiving and Hayley and Jenna send a special hello.

> Love,
> Beth, John, Hayley,and Jenna
> (cousin)

Prayers on Tuesday

Denise November 17, 2007, at 07:50 p.m. EST

Hi Julianna and Family, Glad to hear that Halloween was fun!! You will be in our prayers all day on Tuesday (extra prayers for mom). Looking forward to seeing you all on the 30th. Wishing you all a blessed Thanksgiving. We do have so much to be thankful for every day. I hope you have heard that Jess will be adopting an adorable 8 mo. little boy. His name is Chase Alexander. He will be joining their family on 12/1.Be Well.

Denise W.
(church family)

Hi Julianna from Mrs. D your Pre-School Teacher

Josephine November 25, 2007, at 11:08 a.m. EST

Hi Julianna,

Just want you to know that I am thinking of you often and praying for you. I hope you are feeling better! Know that you are a true blessing to your family and friends. I love you!

Love, Mrs. D
(preschool teacher)

19

When Will This Craziness End

CarePage Post December 19, 2007,
at 10:31 p.m. EST

It's hard to believe another month has gone by since I last wrote. Today, we had our monthly clinic visit, so I thought it was a good chance to write.

I do have a few things to share. First of all, at our last clinic visit, I did ask Julianna's doctor how many of these 72 day courses we would be doing as part of this last phase of treatment. She said to me, "you mean you would like to know when all this craziness is going to end." I said yes, and she said, "it is nice to have that goal." She said she needed to go look over the paperwork to figure it out. When she came back she said the end date of treatment—*assuming* Julianna stays in remission—is May 9th, 2009!! The date came as a shock—even though we knew this was a 2-3 year treatment. I decided what it is, is that it seems like we've already been doing this so, so long. The reality is that it actually hasn't even been a year since her diagnosis. When we got home, Julianna said to me, "you mean, Mommy, that I will have to take this medicine all through 5th grade too?" I simply said, "yes." Today, while Julianna was swallowing her 11 pills, she was talking about the big party she wants to have on May 9th, 2009.

At Julianna's last month visit, some of her pill dosages changed because she has grown, and her counts were a little bit high. At first, we thought this we really bad news because it would mean more pills. It turned out that for this one particular medicine that she really dislikes, the prescription went from taking 3 pills to only 1 because of the dosage change. The pill is still small in size, and just a different color, Instead of swallowing 2 pink pills and 1 yellow pill 10 times per month, now she just has to swallow 1 blue pill. It sounds silly, but it has really made a difference. Keep in mind that there are tons of other pills that she takes that have gone up by ½ pill or so, but they are a little more bearable for her.

While I am on the topic of pills, I decided last month that it would be "fun" to know at the end of all this, how many needles Julianna has gotten, how many pills she has swallowed, how many pills I have crushed, etc. I put together a spreadsheet, and am recording all the medicine she has taken to date. I don't have it quite complete yet, but I think at the end of the day, if we look back at this, she can really be proud of what she has done—or maybe we will have fun burning the spreadsheet at the end of all this– either way I am going to keep tracking it. So, stay tuned for some crazy pill statistics in future postings.

Something amazing that has been happening is that more and more 4th grade girls have cut their hair for "Locks of Love." It is almost starting to feel like an epidemic at school. It has been so cool. Everytime I have seen one of the Moms, and have commented about it, they all give me the same answer, "their daughter was inspired by Julianna." Interestingly enough, two of Julianna's very good friends had cut their hair for "Locks of Love" right before Julianna got sick. Then Julianna got sick, and lost her hair, and now more and more friends are donating their hair. We learned this week that one of her preschool friends, along with a younger sister, donated their hair very recently. What more can I write about that. Wow!

For the last few weeks, Julianna has been doing fantastic. She looks great and is full of energy. Today at clinic, her doctor was even talking about her really getting back to doing activities that she was doing before she got sick. We are going to wait and see what they say at her next physical therapy appointment, because doing p.t. for an hour twice a week is already a lot. He doctor is hoping she can replace 1 of the p.t. visits with something else. We will see. We will not be *rushing* into anything.

I must not wait this long to write again as I am already out of space.

Wishing you all the joys only this season can bring…

CarePage Messages

Holiday Greetings To The Smith Family

Phyllis December 20, 2007, at 09:52 a.m. EST

Hi everyone,

We wish all of you a Very Merry Christmas and Happy New Year. Juliana, you are in our prayers every night and we know God is watching over you. We look forward to May, 2009 and your special celebration. Be strong and it will be here before you know it.

Love and Kisses,
Phyllis & Lou (grandma's friend)

Love to All

Amy December 20, 2007, at 03:20 p.m. EST

Count us in for that party on May 9th 2009!!!!

Merry Christmas to all of you and a Very Happy New Year!!

Love from Amy and Family
(school friend)

Time Flies!

Linda December 20, 2007, at 04:31 p.m. EST

Dear Jules,

You know how you turn around an summer is over, then you turn around and it is Christmas already? Well, soon you will turn around and it will be May of 2008, and then you will turn around and it will be Christmas, and you will turn around and summer of 2009 will be over. May of 2009 may seem like it is far away, but time flies. Keep your spirits high, and the smile in your heart. Prayers are with you every day, and now the biggest prayer will be—*Keep Our Jules Strong*! We are so proud of you.

JoAnn, you are a statistician at heart! It will be quite the accomplishment (another of many) when the spreadsheet is up to date. Is it me, or do you have too much time on your hands?:)

All our love, Aunt Lynne and
Aunt Carolyn, Mia and Cara too

Lovely Locks!

Jeannie December 20, 2007, at 08:41 p.m. EST

Hi, Jules and all the Smith's,

So happy to hear you are doing well. It was great seeing you. I was amazed at how great you looked and I love your soft lovely locks. We hope you all have a wonderful holiday. Hope to see you when I get back.

All our love,
Aunt Jeannie & Uncle Bruce
(family friend)

Party? Did Someone Say, "Party"?

John December 21, 2007, at 01:15 p.m. EST

Count us in on the party in May 2009!!!

I have to admit that I got a little bit teary reading about the 4th grade girls participating in the Locks of Love program. What a fantastic & selfless thing for these young girls to do!

I am sympathetic to Jule's "pill count" ordeal. My wife has me taking about twenty nutritional supplements daily. I absolutely hate to have to swallow pills. It is no fun at all.

Merry Christmas and Happy New Year to the whole Smith clan but most especially Julianna!!!

(neighbor)

20

It's a Mom Thing

CarePage Post January 17, 2008, at 11:54 a.m. EST

Even though I said last time I wouldn't wait another month to write, somehow we all got lost in that black hole that follows the holidays, and so here it is another month later. We had our monthly clinic visit yesterday, and all went very well.

To catch up a little bit—Julianna had a really great Christmas. Luckily, her heavier medicine cycle started enough days before Christmas, so that by Christmas she was past the worst of it. We really had a very nice and quiet (most of the time), low-key Christmas—which is how we like it anyway. We did, of course, have the complication of Jeffrey having walking pneumonia all throughout the holidays—which does seem a bit unfair if you ask me—but apparently no one is asking me. I have to say, even though Julianna is doing so well, it is still sometimes hard to deal with all the other regular things that are part of life, and would under normal circumstances just be the normal everyday things. Even her oncologist said, when I told her about Jeffrey, "you mean you had to spend even more time going to doctors." I said, "I know!" I have this newspaper clipping on my refrigerator that reads "Caregiver: Sharing a loved one's suffering," and a quote from a mother who's child is undergoing chemo that reads, "You have this incredibly abnormal situation and you still have to live normally. It's very, very isolating." I was telling this quote to the kids' teachers in November as I was trying to have conferences with them, all the while thinking about Julianna's spinal tap that was going to be happening the next day. It really is a bit crazy.

On the topic of school, Julianna is absolutely thriving. She continues to maintain straight A's—which the doctors are quite surprised about. I guess many kids really get fuzzy brained from this treatment, but it obviously hasn't affected Julianna—although I think maybe I am having a bit of this side effect. I emailed Julianna's teacher this week regarding Julianna's schedule, and I thanked her for all that she does to keep the kids interested and excited about school. She wrote to me that Julianna is an inspiration to her and she just hopes she is returning the favor.

Last week, Jeffrey was due for his annual checkup, and I scheduled Julianna too, just to not lose touch with her pediatrician's office. We were seeing a nurse practitioner that we have never seen before. As she began to examine Julianna, I start to say the words, "March of last year, she was diagnosed with leukemia" the water starts to fill my eyes. I apologize and swallow the tears. She says, please don't apologize, she understands. We told her about the kidney stone. She went on to tell us that her 5 year old has a chronic illness that causes his body to continually make kidney stones. Julianna and I looked at each other and shrieked. Further along in the exam the nurse turned to me and said, "I want to tell you something. You are going to reach a point, where time will pass and you will find that your daughter's illness was not the only thought that was in your head." She started to get a bit emotional and she went on to say that someone had told her this, and so she was keenly aware when after a few hours one morning she realized that it had happened to her. She had actually spent the morning going along and thinking about other things beside the illness. She said, "I just wanted you to know that." Now we are both wiping away the tears, and we look at my kids and she says, "It's a Mom thing." I am thinking, yeah! another Mom who cries as easily as me!!! Driving home, I was thinking about what she said, and I realized that this moment had already happened to me. I don't know exactly when, but I am already passed that point, and it felt good to realize that. I just continue to be amazed at the people I meet, and the conversations I am having through this journey, and I am thankful for all of you who are taking this journey with us.

CarePage Messages

January

Linda January 17, 2008, at 01:25 p.m. EST

I love getting the update message in my e-mail! I expect good news now and lift up Thankful Prayers when I read these good news posts:-). I thought of you guys yesterday and sent good thoughts your way for a good treatment day. I'm happy to know that it wasn't bad.

What a blessing to realize that you've moved a bit forward in this journey. To have your head share space for other thoughts is a huge step. I'm so happy that you're there and looking back instead of sitting in the beginning and looking forward. There is still plenty of forward to deal with but I expect and pray and am continually grateful for good news.

Love you guys:-)
Linda and Family
(school friend)

Thanks For The Updates!

Donna January 17, 2008, at 01:33 p.m. EST

Thanks for the update JoAnn and for all the wonderful, sad, scary, inspiring stories and insights you have been sharing with us.

As always our prayers are focused on Jules and your family!!!

Annie and Donna
(school friend)

Thanks JoAnn

Linda January 17, 2008, at 01:45 p.m. EST

JoAnn, it isn't just a 'mom' thing. I read these at work, and I am a blubbering fool by the time I get to the end. I am so amazed at the strength you all have shown through this *journey*—it is really inspiring. The prayers are working as we prayed they would.
We are looking forward to our next visit!

Love Aunt Lynne and Aunt Carolyn
Mia & Cara say arf!

Love to the Smiths

Amy January 17, 2008, at 04:18 p.m. EST

Thanks for sharing your ups and downs, highs and lows! We are amazed everyday by your strength and are blessed to have all of you in our lives! Keep Smiling!!

Love Amy and Family
(school friend)

Yes It Is A Mom Thing-And A Great Thing Too!

Clare January 17, 2008, at 05:19 p.m. EST

JoAnn,

So lovely to hear the good news about Julianna: that even on this extra-ordinary journey everything has settled into more of a routine for you i.e. General pediatrician visits rather than emergency room visits! School tests rather than hospital tests! So glad that Christmas was a quiet and reflective time for your family and that you can now think about other things instead of the Big C word. We keep sending those prayers up to God and He obviously is sending down those blessings to you. Keep dwelling in His Spirit JoAnn. From one Mom to another-it IS a great Mom thing!!!.

Clare and family
(church family)

Tears of Joy!

Jeannie January 17, 2008, at 08:32 p.m. EST

JoAnn,

Thanks so much for sharing all your personal and inspiring stories. I would like to think that I have become a better person for being on this journey with you and your family. And of course by the end of this update I too was brought to tears. Tears of joy, knowing that you are able to move forward. I am glad things are going so well for Julianna. Hope to see you soon.

Love Jeannie
(family friend)

See You Soon ~

Pauline January 18, 2008, at 03:36 a.m. EST

Dear Julianna, When your Mom called to tell me that you want to continue playing the piano and would like to come for lessons soon, I was thrilled. I miss working with you, you were such a good student. There will always be a spot for you in my studio. I also miss seeing Jeffrey. I'll have to stock up on the skittles. Look forward to seeing you soon. I just viewed your video. I loved it!!!

Pauline
(piano teacher)

Thanks For The Update…

John January 19, 2008, at 03:15 p.m. EST

I was so nice to read what Jules's teacher said about hoping that she was returning some of Jules's great inspiration. That says a lot about Jules and about her inspirational family.

(neighbor)

CarePage Post February 04, 2008, at 03:28 p.m. EST

I wanted to give you all an update on Julianna. She actually has been having a hard time—just with tiredness—since her last treatment. After our last visit to clinic, she ended up in school all day the next 2 days and then got together with some friends. That night, she pretty much collapsed and did not recover until a week later. It was the case again where she could only whisper to speak, she did not smile, she was just *exhausted*. It was Martin Luther King weekend, and we had planned to visit my brother for the weekend. We still did that—she made the trip in her pj's and luckily my brother has this very cool, large, round pillow-type chair. That chair was her spot *all* weekend. I think she overdid it those 2 days after treatment, and it seems if that happens, she just can't seem to recover from it. We had this happen a few months back, and I thought we had learned our lesson, but she had so many things going on at school—5 tests that week, an assembly she wanted to see, etc., etc. I don't care what is going on from this point on, we are not going to overdue things again.

It is Monday and she is home from school again today because she just doesn't have the energy to get there. She also seems to be fighting some congestion—so my inclination is to keep her here resting. There is apparently all kinds of sickness going around, so extra prayers for her to stay healthy would be appreciated. There is another family from school with a niece who is currently "inpatient" at CHOP, and we have been told that the entire oncology floor is full right now, so their niece is having to stay on the surgical floor. This saddens me to think of all these sick kids, and it makes me really want to keep Julianna healthy, and not have to go to the hospital right now. As I have told you before, just a cold and fever could send her to the hospital.

I also wanted to tell you about another amazing gesture by a friend of mine. As you all know, the pill-taking regiment Julianna has to endure is pretty intense. During this last month of Julianna's tiredness it has been almost unbearable. She has this especially yucky medicine morning and night every Monday and Tuesday. It was taking her an hour and a half to get the medicine down each time, and I was having to sit with her through it. One week, by Tuesday night I was pretty much at the end of my rope with this. I start yelling at her to just take the medicine, she starts crying, I start crying, and then we both apologize. (This is probably good practice for me for when her teen years come.) Anyway, my friend told me she had been working on a project to help Julianna with her pill taking, and she came over with it on Saturday after our "episode." She presented Julianna with one of those old-fashioned glass candy jars with the round metal cap on the front. Inside, my friend had made up 200 of what she calls "Julianna's blurbs." They are small folded sheets of paper that have all kinds of sayings and graphics on them. Some of them are inspirational, some are just funny, some have things that Julianna likes to do, or things she just likes, etc. They are all really fun to read and to look at because all the fonts and graphics are so cheerful, and it is always a surprise as you unfold it.

Well, clearly my friends timing could not have been better. The rules my friend wrote state that Julianna has to swallow a pill before she is allowed to pick a blurb. Well Julianna *loves* to put her hand in the jar and pick through to choose a blurb. It is amazing how this has motivated her to get her pills down. I am so thankful. It has added a fun element to this pill taking that we truly needed. I have told Julianna if she really works on her "speed" with taking these pills I may even add a few surprises to her blurb jar for surprise gifts.

Wed. Feb 13th is our next clinic day and Jules will be getting a spinal. Prayers and positive thoughts are welcome.

CarePage Messages

Great Big Virtual Hug!

Wendy February 04, 2008, at 03:49 p.m. EST

Hi Julianna—

I'm sending you a great big virtual hug (((((Julianna)))))! Keeping you in my thoughts and prayers.

Fondly—
Wendy (church family)

Hi!!!!!!!!!!!

Suzy February 04, 2008, at 04:32 p.m. EST

Jule Lee Ann Uh!!!!!! Wake up! it's Morning! Just kidding LOL! You better take it easy because the world just isn't the same without your smile! I miss seeing you at the Zone, and so do all the other girls. We *need* you! Really and Truly, please rest up so we can see you again. Tell your mom to give you a big hug from me.

Love, Mrs. M
(family friend)

P.S.

Suzy February 04, 2008, at 04:33 p.m. EST

Jules, give your mom a big hug from me too! Thx!:)

Love You!!

Pauline February 04, 2008, at 04:43 p.m. EST

Gear Julianna. please rest up and get better soon. I miss seeing you and I so look forward to when you will have piano again. I have a lot of sick students, so waiting until this changes is probably better. You are so brave with the pills. I have a difficult time taking mine, but I know they help me to get through the day, so that makes it easier. You are in,my prayers.

Lots of love to you and Jeffrey. Pauline
(piano teacher)

Thinking Of You

Beth February 04, 2008, at 08:20 p.m. EST

Dear Julianna, Jeffrey, JoAnn, and Brian,

Thanks for keeping us updated. We wish you weren't so tired Julianna, and that you were able to go to school more. Your Mom is right though, try to stay healthy during these winter months so that you can stay at home and not have to go to the hospital. Our thoughts are with you and we wish we could bottle up some energy and send it you way.

Love,
Beth, John, Jenna, and Hayley
(cousin)

Bump in the Road!

Jeannie February 04, 2008, at 10:00 p.m. EST

Hello to the Smith's,

Sorry to hear Julianna is so tired. I guess it is a good idea for Jules to get some much needed rest. Sometimes things have a way of sneaking up on you. We will keep you in our prayers and hope to hear you are back on your feet in no time.

All our Love, Jeannie and Bruce
(family friend)

Thinking Of You!!

Melissa February 05, 2008, at 09:52 a.m. EST

Hi Julianna and Family,

We just wanted you to know that we are always thinking of you and pray for you every day. At dinner we pray for you together and before bed Leanna always ends her prayers with "And dear God, don't forget to take good care of Julianna." It's a good thing your mom is so smart and makes you rest. I hope she is resting right along side of you!! We hope to see you soon!

Love, Melissa, Matt, Jessica and Leann
(family friend)

Hi

Amy February 05, 2008, at 02:34 p.m. EST

Sounds like a great way to take pills! What a wonderful idea! We are thinking about all of you all of the time. We will pray for easy pill taking, increase of energy and to keep those germs far away from Jules!

Love from Amy and Family
(school friend)

Thanks For The Update!

Linda February 05, 2008, at 04:31 p.m. EST

Hi everyone,

I sure do appreciate the updates, and especially with all that is going on, that you take the time to let us know how things are going really means a lot. Julianna, everyone at our new church prays for you now too, and you are also enrolled online at the Mary Queen of the Universe Shrine prayer request. That is a shrine that we visited one Sunday while on vacation in Orlando. It is beautiful and lots of people go there. We are praying you get the strength to continue to get healthy. We know you will!

We love you and will see you when you are feeling better. Happy Mardi Gras! Love, Aunt Lynne and Aunt Carolyn, Cara and Mia too. We can't wait for our movie night sleepover.

What A Great Idea...

John February 06, 2008, at 01:08 p.m. EST

...that your friend had to overcome the pill taking problem!!!

And yes, you just wait for the "after-thirteen years old" days, weeks, months, years…!!!!

(neighbor)

CarePage Post February 17, 2008, at 11:25 a.m. EST

Hello all. Julianna needs some encouragement here at the Smith house, so I told her I would write a CarePage and ask for all those prayers and positive vibes that I know you are willing to send her way. She has not had an easy time since her treatment this past Wednesday. The treatment actually went fine. She had a spinal tap. They sedate her, and then have her curl up in the fetal position. A nurse wraps her arms around Julianna so that her head and all stay totally tucked in. I sit by her head and stroke her hair. The doctors love her because they say she just lets the medicine work to relax her and the procedure is actually over in about 2 minutes. It is quite a big needle, but Julianna only feels a pinch when they first put the numbing medicine into her back. After they are done, they always compliment her in a big way. This time they said "Julianna, you are a dream." Apparently, there a some kids who get so worked up over this that the sedation medicine has the opposite effect, and the doctor has told us that they are literally chasing the kid on the table to get this done. I *can't even imagine*!!

Anyway, what has been going on is that Julianna is extremely tired again. On top of that she has gotten some mouth sores—which is not really expected at this time. She was quite miserable the last few days, but it seems she is actually better today as far as the mouth sores are concerned. The other thing that keeps happening each month after her treatment is that she gets itchy all over. It only lasts a few days, but it just adds to her misery. If we can't get it under control with cream, I give her Benadryl—

which makes her feel more tired and yucky. Last month, I had her put some cream on her face because that was itchy too, and the cream actually made it so much worse. She started freaking out—I had to run to the bathroom and get a warm wet rag and that seemed to make it stop. The itchiness only lasts a few days, so I think I have forgotten to write about it. Last night she was so itchy we had to resort to Benadryl—but she got a good night sleep out of it, so that wasn't so bad. Now she just told me that back of her throat feels all yucky. Of course, I always have the thermometer very close by, so as soon as I finish writing I will go take her temperature.

When Julianna feels like this, she gets very, very needy. These last few days she has had a new thing where I have to sit next to her and hold her hand. It has become a bit of a joke because now she will look at me—if I happen to be across the room—with these sad puppy-dog eyes and put her hand out. She doesn't say a word—we just both know what she wants. Most of the time, I am more than willing to accommodate her—but there are other times—well, you know.

So, if you could pray for these things for Julianna, she (and the rest of us here) would really appreciate it.

By the way, March 1st will be one year since Julianna's diagnosis. I am sure we (OK mostly me) will have some reflections on the year that we will want to share.

CarePage Messages

Sunday

Linda February 17, 2008, at 12:12 p.m. EST

You've been on our minds since Wednesday. Adding extra symptoms to the already existing ones doesn't seem quite fair does it??

We will say some extra prayers for Jules (and You!!) this week. Jules—you are such a trooper to take your meds and be the continued light in our lives. JoAnn—you are amazing. It is a lot to shoulder. I know that you and Brian have a lot of support—but it is mostly on you guys. Our prayers go out to you for this as well.

Stay strong.

Love you guys,
Linda and Family
(school friend)

Hugs and Prayers!

Donna February 17, 2008, at 12:25 p.m. EST

We are sorry to hear Jules is dealing with more discomfort!!! I think sometimes the "little" (not so little when you are dealing with it!) pains and discomforts can get you down more than when you are dealing with the huge challenges!

Well lots of cyber hugs and prayers are coming your way from us! We really hope that you are pain and discomfort free very very very soon.

All our Love…Annie and Donna
(school friend)

Love You, Julianna

Monica February 17, 2008, at 12:29 p.m. EST

Hi Jule

Sorry about the sores…I hope by the time you read this they are all gone!!! We'll all keep praying that you feel better and not so tired or itchy…

Keep sending us the emails—we need to know how you are doing, OK???

love you—Monica and everybody!!
(cousin)

We're Thinking About You Jules!!!

Nancy February 17, 2008, at 12:32 p.m. EST

and all of you. You're in our thoughts and prayers. Every time I'm going through something hard, a friend of mine always says, "this too shall pass." I'm passing these words on to you. It gives a little hope to better things to come!

Love, Nancy (Nini) & Tom
(family friend)

You Are Good Patients!

Suzy February 17, 2008, at 01:36 p.m. EST

Julianna isn't the only good patient here! JoAnn, thanks for letting us know how we can pray for you! Today our pastor taught about the object of our faith. Some people believe that if they just have enough faith, their need will be met. But what is the object of that faith? You can have tons of faith in the tree branch that you're hanging on to, but if the branch is weak, you're still going to fall… On the other hand, when the object of your faith is strong—like a nice solid tree branch—then even your small, tired, weak (and itchy!) faith will be enough. Jesus is our nice strong tree branch! Yea! I will pray that you will feel the strength of Jesus in a fresh new way today and in the coming days.

Love to you all! Suzy
(family friend)

His Mercies are New Every Morning!

Stephanie February 17, 2008, at 03:37 p.m. EST

Dearest Smith Family ~

You are all in our prayers—even far away here in the pan-handle of Florida! May tomorrow dawn with no itchies and no sores!

God Bless you all—Steph and Gary
(family friend)

You're So Brave!

Clare February 17, 2008, at 05:30 p.m. EST

I am taking that old Carly Simon song and changing the words-because it sounds like you are a really brave girl and a brave Mom! When I think how hard it is to stay still just for having a regular shot, I am amazed how you can stay so still for the spinal. We will add prayers for those horrible itchies and mouth sores to go away. Keep your chins up, girls.

You're so brave!
(church family)

So Brave!!!!!!

Pauline February 17, 2008, at 06:10 p.m. EST

Dear Julianna, You are so very brave. God has certainly given you the strength to face all of these challenges and I know He has His arms around you.. I will pray for you a lot...I promise you that!

I love you and when you are ready, I am here for piano lessons. I will come to your house if you prefer. You just keep being Brave and know that so many many people Love you and are praying for you.

Pauline
(piano teacher)

Hi Julianna from Holy Nativity Pre-School

Josephine February 17, 2008, at 07:02 p.m. EST

Hi Julianna, Hope you are feeling better soon. You are such a brave little girl with all your treatments. I am keeping you in my thoughts and prayers. Give Mommy and hug for me and Jeffrey too and an extra big one for you! God Bless!

Love and Hugs,
Mrs. D
(preschool teacher)

I Wanna Hold Your Hand!

Linda February 17, 2008, at 07:47 p.m. EST

Dear JoAnn, Julianna, Brian and Jeffrey,

Dust off those Beatles records (remember vinyl?) and sing I wanna hold your hand! As for the itches—you know what my hands and feet are like? Well, I take Benadryl every night about a half hour before I go to bed, and I don't scratch all night long. During the day, there is a spray I use that is clear and doesn't smell—it is made by Benadryl and I get the extra strenth one. Maybe that will help a bit. We are holding our hands out and wishing and praying for your itches to stop being itchy and those yucky sores to go away. Julianna you are our hero, in so many ways, you inspire us to not complain and to smile through the rain. It will get better, just know that, and remember—we are always praying for you and we love you all very much! Try to keep smiling.

All our love,
Aunt Lynne and Aunt Carolyn, Cara and Mia too

In The Garden…

Kim February 17, 2008, at 09:06 p.m. EST

Hello Smith family. We talk about you and pray for you often. A few things have happened in the past week that have brought you to mind even more. Nate had to go to the doctor again today, and I insisted that he get a throat culture, and a monospot (which means a simple needle stick for a drop of blood from his finger). Well, he was just devastated that he had to endure those two things. As we waited for the nurse to come in, I said, you know, Nate, you have never really experienced a serious illness. Just think of what your cousin Julianna endures each day since her diagnosis. Maybe this puts things into perspective, and we can thank God that He allows us so many healthy, happy days. Nate is still learning to think past himself, but I think it may have impacted him a little bit after I described the things you have experienced this past year.

I was reminded myself, of the need to put my life in the proper perspective when our pastor preached about Jesus' prayer in the Garden of Gethsemane. Jesus asked God, His Father, to "take this cup from me if possible." Of course Jesus knew that His death and resurrection was the only hope for mankind's sin. Thankfully he ended his prayer "not my will, but thine be done." So when I begin to feel sorry for myself about any situation, I need to remember what Jesus faced for me. I was really convicted about how I get upset over inconveniences (in comparison to your past year). God's grace was sufficient then, and now. Thank you for always being so open about the trials that you are facing. I can only imagine how long your days may seem, but then you always seem to have a blessing that encourages you to keep going! We are praying for you, and will specifically pray for the fatigue and mouth sores that are weighing you down now.

Praise God for bringing you all through this year!

Love, Ray, Kim, Nate, Peter, and Olivia
(cousin)

Hello to the Smith's!

Jeannie February 17, 2008, at 11:44 p.m. EST

Hi Jules,

We are sorry to hear you are having a tough go of it. We hope things only get better from here. It sounds like you are a star patient to those doctors and nurses, you should be proud of that. We will continue to pray for you and keep you in our thoughts every day.

All our love, Jeannie & Bruce
(family friend)

I'm Holding Your Hands Too

Ravenna February 18, 2008, at 02:37 a.m. EST

Dear Julianna and JoAnn and Jeffrey and Brian,

I'm so sorry that you've hit a bump in your road. Julianna, I hope your mouth and throat will feel better when you wake up tomorrow! As for itching, have you tried an oatmeal bath? You can get colloidal oatmeal at the drug store, and put it in the bath, it has helped me with burning or itching skin.

Julianna, please when you feel very tired of all the discomfort you are enduring, try to see the light on the horizon in that painting I gave you; look at the blue and think about water, the way it looks like it is always there, always the same—but really it is always moving and changing.

You will be better!
Love, Ravenna (family friend)

Thinking of All of You

Susan February 18, 2008, at 07:15 a.m. EST

JoAnn,

Missed you yesterday! Both Trisha and Brian had updated me on Julianna. Keep holding her hand!! You will all be in my thoughts and prayers.

Love, Sue
(church family)

It Seems So Much Longer Than Just A Year...

John February 18, 2008, at 10:21 a.m. EST

...I'll bet it seems more like TEN years for you-all. Our thoughts and prayers are with all of the Smiths but most especially Jules.

Your Lower Mountain Road neighbors...
John & Jeanne

Love from the Fells

Amy February 18, 2008, at 02:52 p.m. EST

Wow, one year! I hope that this message finds all of you a bit more rested and feeling better! As always are prayers are with you! Jules, you are in our thoughts and prayers every day. Remember that you are an amazingly strong person! Allison is sending you a big hug right now. We are here if you need us!

> Amy and Ally
> (school friend)

Prayers And Thoughts Sending Your Way!

Denise February 18, 2008, at 04:39 p.m. EST

Hello to all of you!!

Aveeno makes a oatmeal bath—it is great for itchy skin, maybe that will help. Your on our minds, in our hearts and very much so in our prayers.

> Take care!!
> Denise S and Family
> (school friend)

Sending Our Love

Melissa February 19, 2008, at 08:45 a.m. EST

Julianna,we are praying and praying for you. I know a year seems like such a long time but just think, it is one year closer to being all better! Pretty soon it will be spring and you will be able to get out in the sunshine and that will be the best medicine ever! We keep you in our thoughts and prayers everyday. Keep smiling!!!!

> Love, Matt, Melissa, Jessica and Leanna
> (family friend)

21

Ronald McDonald House

CarePage Post February 20, 2008, at 09:15 p.m. EST

It's me again. I wanted to let you know that your prayers and encouragement have worked—as usual. Julianna has been much better. The mouth sores and itchiness have subsided. She has come down with a head cold—but no fever—so she is just staying home and working on getting better. I am hoping that maybe she can get to school for at least ½ day tomorrow. We will see...

I did want to write about her medicine. I forgot to mention that her counts were a bit too high again this past clinic visit, and she has grown a bit, so they did increase some of her medicine. She is now having to swallow 14!!! yes that is correct—14 pills every Wednesday. She is in the process of doing it right now. Luckily, she prefers Brian to sit with her for these particular pills. These are the better pills of all of them since they do not have a bad taste, and they are small, but she still will only swallow 1 at a time, so it can be a bit of a long and painful process to sit through—depending on your patience level. Again, luckily she always chooses Brian for this particular pill session.

Also, I wrote about an episode we had with one of the yuckier medicines, and the tears, etc., etc. I spoke to the doctor about it, because I know they really are concerned about issues like this and will try to work with you as much as possible. Julianna's doctor suggested we try a liquid version of that particular pill. We hadn't pursued this before, because the nurses always tell us that the other kids say that the liquids are *horrible*. The doctor said we should ask the pharmacist to flavor it, and try it. It turned out it already was grape flavored and Julianna gulps it down like nothing. What a great relief this was. First of all, these pills are very hard for me to crush. If I am not careful, pieces go flying all over and I am trying to retrieve them, and then for the past few weeks, Jules has been taking *forever* to get this medicine down. I am just so glad we decided to try this liquid.

One more thing…last year, our church had an Easter Egg Hunt and Breakfast and it was a benefit for our family. This year, our church so very kindly asked us if we would like to be the beneficiary of this year's event. I am thrilled to say that we turned down the offer; however, they asked for an alternate suggestion, and Julianna chose "The Ronald McDonald House." They have an amazing "Family Room" on the oncology floor with a full kitchen and lounge area. There is always coffee and snacks available there. They also provide all kinds of great services for families with children being treated at CHOP—such as gift cards for fuel, birthday presents, holiday presents, etc. They have the Ronald McDonald House in Philly, where out-of-town families can stay, and they really take care of them very well. We are fortunate to live so close to CHOP, but I always thought about the families that don't, and the extra complication that adds to the mix. They also have Ronald McDonald Camp, where for 1 week each summer, oncology patients and their siblings can go and just have tons of *fun*!! Many of the doctors and nurses volunteer for the week, and we have been told it is just *fabulous*! Julianna and Jeffrey will be going this year. So, we are all hoping to attend this year's breakfast, and we hope many of you can come again this year. The date is the Saturday before Easter, March 22nd. I will send more details soon.

Now Jules is tired, and just wants me to say "good night", so good night and thanks for all of your encouragement this past week—it was just what we needed.

CarePage Messages

Praise God!

Wendy February 21, 2008, at 09:31 a.m. EST

Hi Julianna, JoAnn, Brian & Jeffery—

Praise God for His provision and answer to prayers providing you with comfort and protection through this trial. I am so glad to hear that Julianna is feeling better. You are all such wonderful examples of perseverance in faith to all of us…thank you. Blessings to you all.

Hugs—
Wendy (church family)

Thanks Again For The Update!

Linda February 21, 2008, at 11:32 a.m. EST

Thank You!!! JoAnn, you are such an excellent writer, really, you make it seem like we are right there at the table watching Jules take one at pill at a time. These updates have really brought us closer to the every-day life of our little Jules, and your whole family, and opened our eyes to what so many, too many, other families are going through while we go about our merry little way. Your sharing absolutely is a blessing and we do look forward to all the news.
    Love to all!

Aunt Lynne, Aunt Carolyn, Mia & Cara

Hello to the Smith's

Jeannie February 25, 2008, at 03:01 p.m. EST

Hi to all,

We were glad to hear that Jules is doing well for now. That is great that there are some alternative ways of taking some of the meds. Let's hope things will only get easier from now on. Of course you know your whole family is always in our prayers. Keep doing what you are doing because it seems to be working. Hope to see you soon.

All our Love, Jeannie & Bruce
(family friend)

Hi Jules!!!

Dawn February 26, 2008, at 06:27 p.m. EST

Hi Julianna…and everyone!!!! Just wanted to say Hi! and wish everyone well.

Much Love,
Cousin Dawn and family…

PS: JoAnn, have you tried a pill scorer that you can purchase from any pharmacy (Walgreens, CVS, etc). It not only scores evenly and perfectly, but it contains any fly-aways…

22

One Year

Carepage Post February 28, 2008, at 10:43 p.m. EST

One year ago today, we were told by Julianna's pediatrician that we needed to take her to CHOP—they would be waiting for us. This was after fevers and fatigue and blood work that showed her various counts were extremely low. It was during this car ride that I tried to tell Jules that we should look at this as an adventure. When we got to CHOP, the attendant told us to follow the ramp down to enter the parking garage. At the bottom of the ramp there was a metal bar hanging with clearance numbers on it. Brian's truck was not going to clear this bar. We backed up, and the attendant said we were OK and that a lot of trucks hit that bar. We went back down, and that pole totally clunked the top of Brian's truck as we went under it. I remember looking at Julianna and saying, "See, I told you this was going to be an adventure."

I remember later that night standing outside the glass door of her ER "room" speaking to a doctor, and being told that this was serious, and being told what the possibilities were. The next day we were asked to attend a "family meeting." When the docs came to get us there was a social worker with them. Walking to the meeting room it was clear this was not going to be good. I remember hearing the word "leukemia."

It's been an amazing year in so many ways. Because of this CarePage, many people have asked me if I have written before. I have not. It has never been an interest of mine, nor have I ever kept a journal. In the last year, I have filled 3 personal journals and continue to love writing the CarePage. I decided last week that these CarePage entries come from my head, get filtered through my heart, and are released via my fingers. I guess that is why it is so therapeutic for me.

The social worker from CHOP has told me that the diagnosis date is a date that everyone always knows. Julianna's official diagnosis came on March 1st. Julianna is calling it "her day" and we will actually be celebrating. She has been through a lot this past year, and she has handled it with such strength, and with such a good attitude. It just seems right that we should celebrate her life and all that she has handled this year. I also think that this year has shown us how blessed we truly are. We are surrounded by the most loving family and friends that you could ever hope for. We are all strong in our faith that this is God's plan for our lives and are accepting of that. We are a very united family in so many great ways now. We can't deny all the good that has come in the past year.

All this week, various thoughts and memories have been buzzing around in my head, and so for the rest of this posting I have decided to just go with that. When I asked Julianna what she thought about the last year she had 2 words: *Kidney Stone.*

Here are some other thoughts and memories:

Not caring about sleeping on a vinyl couch for 2 weeks—all that mattered was Jules.

Brian fainting and ripping down the shower curtain on day 2 of our hospital stay.

How can one child have so many stuffed animals. (Check out the photo)

Not liking being the mother of a human pin cushion.

CHOP—Hope truly lives there.

Getting a call back for my routine mammogram this summer. Being told I needed an ultrasound. Wondering how many mother/daughter cancer patients there have been. Having the